Surviving Chinese Communist Detention

Surviving
Chinese
Communist Detention

Steven Schaerer

Liberty Hill Publishing

Liberty Hill Publishing
2301 Lucien Way #415
Maitland, FL 32751
407.339.4217
www.libertyhillpublishing.com

Printed in the United States of America.

Paperback ISBN-13: 978-1-6628-1488-4
Dust Jacket ISBN-13: 978-1-6628-1489-1
Ebook ISBN-13: 978-1-6628-1490-7

Table of Contents

Introduction

You are about to embark on a painfully real, oppressive and ruthless journey into a barbaric world that the Chinese Communist Party (CCP) works tirelessly to conceal from Western audiences. Sadly, the information enclosed here isn't cleverly scripted Hollywood fiction, it's all painfully real; and I was fortunate enough to survive it.

As horrific as my time in Chinese communist detention was, countless Chinese citizens are forced to endure conditions that are far worse. This book was written to give you an unfiltered, first-person account of what it takes to survive the sadistic world of a communist Chinese prison cell. Just as importantly, this book was written to remind you that countless Chinese nationals are suffering in these horrific conditions at this very moment.

Ironically, this brutal and repressive system sits at the core of China's "peaceful" rise. Without systemic torture, human rights violations, brutal violence, rampant executions, re-education camps, forced labor compounds, and human organ harvesting; the modern CCP miracle would collapse. International Human Rights groups are routinely barred from not only accessing these torture sites but also China, as a country, itself.

The prison compound I was detained in operates on a "need-to-know" basis. These detention centers are routinely hidden from the local population and can't be found on international or domestic online map services. In other words, I was detained in a Chinese black-site prison complex.

And once you are detained and kidnapped by Chinese authorities, you disappear instantly.

My biggest hurdle, by far, has been attempting to convey this alien environment to Western audiences as there is simply no point of reference.

How do you describe color to someone who has been blind since birth?

Despite repeated efforts to convey CCP kidnapping to people in the West, I'm well aware that they ultimately fail to grasp what it took to survive these conditions, or that they even exist in the first place. On one hand, that is a blessing, which also underscores the fundamental need for this book. If nothing else, it's a reminder of how fortunate we are in the West to be free of the horrors of communist governance.

This book will challenge everything you thought you knew about China. Decades of carefully crafted Chinese propaganda will be flipped on its head. China is fundamentally different from the relentless CCP propaganda that has infiltrated Western media outlets.

That being said, I want to emphasize that this book is not a critique of Chinese people or Chinese culture.

Quite the opposite in fact, there is a lot that I believe The West could learn from China such as placing a higher value on education, the prominence of strong family-units, and a rock solid work-ethic.

On the other hand, this book *is* meant to be a critique of an incredibly corrupt, authoritarian, violent, communist and Orwellian Chinese government that continues to wreak havoc, murder, and torture its own population on a daily basis. In order to properly understand this book, it is essential to emphasize that the Chinese people and the Chinese government are two vastly separate and unique entities.

After five years of living and working in Beijing, I developed a profound and deep respect for Chinese people, their work-ethic and culture. While I want to emphasize that China's population has great values to impart on the world, the concurrent expanding global influence of the CCP cannot be understated.

For a peaceful China to rise, it's current communist government must fall.

> *"If the Chinese Communist Party survives, then China will surely fall. If China is to survive then the CCP must fall."*
>
> ~ Professor of Economics at a Chinese University

Prologue

Communism is far and away the best political, social, and economic system in human history. This is readily apparent to anyone who is willing to simply research its unparalleled record of global success.

Countries that successfully implemented communist governance are routinely gifted with unprecedented levels of prosperity, wealth, and freedom. A few notable historical examples of successful communist implementation include,

> "*People's Republic of China: Body Count: 73,237,000*
> *Union of Soviet Socialist Republics: Body Count: 58,627,000*
> *Democratic People's Republic of Korea: Body Count: 3,163,000*
> *Cambodia: Body Count: 2,627,000*
> *Democratic Republic of Afghanistan: Body Count: 1,750,000*
> *Vietnam: Body Count: 1,670,000*
> *People's Democratic Republic of Ethiopia: Body Count: 1,343,610*
> *Socialist Federal Republic of Yugoslavia: Body Count: 1,072,000*
> *People's Republic of Mozambique: Body Count: 700,000*
> *Socialist Republic of Romania: Body Count: 435,000*
> *People's Republic of Bulgaria: Body Count: 222,000*"[1]

Who can argue with a track record like that?

Communism, as it's referred to today, is largely the brainchild of the economist's economist Karl Marx. Although variations of communism existed for centuries, Karl managed to refine and repackage it for modern consumption with his 1848 publication, "The Communist Manifesto."

"The Communist Manifesto" is a 12,615 word[2] masterpiece that revealed what could only be described at the time as a revolutionary proposition: *the industrial economy could be better.*

---

[1] Manning, S. December 13, 2018. Communist Body Count. *Scottmanning.com.* Retrieved: February 2, 2019, from https://scottmanning.com/content/communist-body-count/

[2] 2015-2018. The Communist Manifesto. Reading Length. Retrieved: January 27th, 2018, from https://www.readinglength.com/book/isbn-0717802418/

Thank you, Karl, for your fascinating insight.

Unbeknownst to many, Marx didn't really have a problem with capitalism in and of itself as he felt that it was simply a precursor for better systems to arise. Furthermore, he was fascinated by the concept of industrialization. He did, however, take issue with the structural relationships upon which capitalism was built, as he felt that it exploited the working class (proletariat). Therein lied his fundamental critique of capitalism as a functioning economic system, exploitation.

And Karl would most certainly know.

As a university student, Mr. Marx majored in ~~finance business statistics accounting math economics international trade~~ philosophy and literature. In doing so, he dedicated himself to the pursuit of a higher calling, academic excellence,

> *"The word about Marx' drinking skills first got around in his days as a student. In 1835 he had a promising start at the University of Bonn, but soon got slightly distracted from his studies, as he was the co-president of his tavern club. Marx even got imprisoned for a day for "disturbing the peace with drunken noise". His period of "wild rampaging", as his father Heinrich Marx called it, in Bonn lasted only a year..."*[3]

Many believe that Marx's exceptional work ethic and inherently studious nature were the culmination of years of dedicated military service,

> *"Shortly after his eighteenth birthday Marx was excused military service because of his weak chest, though he may well have exaggerated his condition."*[4]

Karl's father ended up transferring young Marx into the University of Berlin where he studied philosophy and law. Karl ended up receiving his doctorate from the university of Jena as his dissertation was seen to be too controversial for conservative Berlin academics. Karl ultimately managed to earn his doctorate and began repairing his unprincipled and debauched reputation:

---

[3] Bumbar, Micky. November 6th, 2014. Karl Marx, the drunkard who laid the foundation for Communism. *Lord of the Drinks*. Retrieved: January 27th, 2018, from https://lordsofthedrinks.com/2014/11/06/karl-marx-the-drunkard-who-laid-the-foundation-for-communism

[4] Bumbar, Micky. November 6th, 2014. Karl Marx, the drunkard who laid the foundation for Communism. *Lord of the Drinks*. Retrieved: January 27th, 2018, from https://lordsofthedrinks.com/2014/11/06/karl-marx-the-drunkard-who-laid-the-foundation-for-communism

"Still this didn't stop him from consuming large amounts of beer and taking drunken donkey rides through the villages nearby."[5]

As a university student, Marx joined radical leftist groups like the Poets' Club and the Young Hegelians. This initial exposure to hardcore leftist thought followed Karl out of university where he went on to pursue odd jobs as a journalist; writing for increasingly radicalized newspapers.

These odd jobs would expose Karl to ideas like socialism, sparking a youthful interest in economics. After landing in Paris in 1843, Karl would go on to mix and mingle with other like-minded socialists, ultimately fueling an obsession with capitalism.

In order to better understand capitalism, Karl proceeded to ~~pursue a degree in economics, build a business, hold a steady job, study capitalism, employ people~~ write manuscripts developing his theories on *alienated labor*. Further entrenching himself in socialist movements and secret organizations, Karl and his friend Friedrich Engels would go on to publish the notable, "Communist Manifesto" in 1848,

"...that the history of these class struggles forms a series of evolutions in which, now-a-days, a stage has been reached where the exploited and oppressed class—the proletariat—cannot attain its emancipation from the sway of the exploiting and ruling class—the bourgeoisie—without, at the same time, and once and for all, emancipating society at large from all exploitation, oppression, class distinctions and class struggles."[6]

Marx, an astute academic, toiled tirelessly to end the exploitation of the proletariat. In doing so, he held himself to a higher moral standard, often choosing to lead by example,

"In all his researches into the iniquities of British capitalism, he came across many instances of low-paid workers but he never succeeded in unearthing one who was paid literally no wages at all. Yet such a worker did exist, in his own household ... This was Helen Demuth [the life-long family maid]. She got her keep but was paid nothing ... She was a ferociously

---

[5] Bumbar, Micky. November 6th, 2014. Karl Marx, the drunkard who laid the foundation for Communism. *Lord of the Drinks.* Retrieved: January 27th, 2018, from https://lordsofthedrinks. com/2014/11/06/karl-marx-the-drunkard-who-laid-the-foundation-for-communism

[6] Marx, K. and Engel, F. (1848). Communist Manifesto. 1st ed. Moscow: Progress Publishers, pp.14-27. Retrieved: January 27th, 201

hard worker, not only cleaning and scrubbing, but managing the family budget ... Marx never paid her a penny ..."[7]

There's a lot more to be said about Karl Marx. For example, his dedication to fatherhood,

"In 1849-50 ... [Helen] became Marx's mistress and conceived a child ... Marx refused to acknowledge his responsibility, then or ever, and flatly denied the rumors that he was the father... [The son] was put out to be fostered by a working-class family called Lewis but allowed to visit the Marx household [to see his mother]. He was, however, forbidden to use the front door and obliged to see his mother only in the kitchen."[5]

Marx's personal hygiene,

"...leads the existence of a Bohemian intellectual. Washing, grooming and changing his linen are things he does rarely, and he is often drunk."[5]

Cleanliness,

"There is not one clean and solid piece of furniture. Everything is broken, tattered and torn, with half an inch of dust over everything and the greatest disorder everywhere ..."[5]

Attitudes towards minorities,

"The Jewish Nig*er Lassalle ... fortunately departs at the end of this week ... It is now absolutely clear to me that, as both the shape of his head and his hair texture shows — he descends from the Negros who joined Moses' flight from Egypt (unless his mother or grandmother on the paternal side hybridized with a ni*ger). Now this combination of Germanness and Jewishness with a primarily Negro substance creates a strange product. The pushiness of the fellow is also ni*ger-like."[5]

And so much more.

Karl Marx was a true visionary. An intellectual who understood what others failed to grasp. Karl led the way for ~~over 100 million people to be slaughtered, rampant starvation, mass political incarceration, widespread civil unrest~~ a brave new world.

---

[7]   Ebeling, R. M. 2017, February 14. Marx the Man | Richard M. Ebeling. *fee.org*. Retrieved January 7th, 2019, from https://fee.org/articles/marx-the-man/

Sadly, Karl Marx died on March 3rd of 1883, 105 years before I would become a part of this world. Fortunately for me, Karl's communist legacy lived on, inspiring governments around the globe to adopt his well-tested economic theories.

As a young American entrepreneur, I was fortunate enough to land in a communist Chinese prison cell over fraudulent visa charges, and able to experience first-hand the ~~sleep deprivation, malnutrition, rampant human rights violations, torture~~ wonders of Karl's communist legacy that made a lasting imprint on China's political landscape.

Chapter 1:

The Chinese Communist Party's Top Threat: You!

"*Communists do not fight for personal military power...but they must fight for military power for the Party, for military power for the people... It is very difficult for the labouring people, who have been deceived and intimidated by the reactionary ruling classes for thousands of years, to awaken to the importance of having guns in their own hands. Every Communist must grasp the truth, "Political power grows out of the barrel of a gun." Our principle is that the Party commands the gun, and the gun must never be allowed to command the Party...Everything in Yenan has been created by having guns.*

All things grow out of the barrel of a gun. According to the Marxist theory of the state, the army is the chief component of state power. Whoever wants to seize and retain state power must have a strong army...Experience in the class struggle in the era of imperialism teaches us that it is only by the power of the gun that the working class and the labouring masses can defeat the armed bourgeoisie and landlords; in this sense we may say that only with guns can the whole world be transformed."[8]

---

[8] Mao, T., 1938. *Problems Of War And Strategy*. [online] Marxists.org. Available at: <https://www.marxists.org/reference/archive/mao/selected-works/volume-2/mswv2_12.htm> [Accessed 16 January 2021].

Problems of War and Strategy - November 6, 1938

Mao Zedong: Chairman of the Communist Party of China, 1943 – 1976

Putting modern China into context for a Western audience is a complex task. Western populations have been inundated by decades of well-orchestrated CCP (China Communist Party) propaganda,

> *"Under the CCP, these same strategies are employed directly in its military strategy. The communist regime's "Three Warfares" concept uses psychological warfare, media warfare (to spread propaganda), and legal warfare (to manipulate legal systems), according to a 2015 report from U.S. Special Operations Command.*
>
> *It notes that under the CCP, "media warfare seeks to influence domestic and international public opinion to build support for military actions and dissuade adversaries from actions contrary to China's interests," while legal warfare "uses international and domestic law to claim the legal high ground or assert Chinese interests...*
>
> *"We haven't even begun to coordinate ourselves to take on this challenge," said Richard Fisher, senior fellow on Asian military affairs with the International Assessment and Strategy Center.*
>
> *The first stage, he said, is to grow the CCP's political and economic power globally, and to "promote the notion and to convince most of the world of the inevitability of China's rise." The communist regime will continue this stage, he said, until it is able to displace the United States as the "central political and strategic authority around the globe."*
>
> *If it can achieve that goal, it will move to the second phase of exporting its authoritarian "China model" of governance. Fisher said at this stage, its operations "would be much closer to the Soviet method of 'active measures,' which would mean going out and defending the China model—attacking and defeating all opposition to China's position."[9]*

China's relentless propaganda machine has leveraged a clever term that attempts to reduce the country's international image into a "poor" and

---

[9] www.theepochtimes.com. 2021. China Uses Political Warfare To Influence US Politics. [online] Available at: <https://www.theepochtimes.com/china-uses-political-warfare-to-influence-us-politics_2264575.html> [Accessed 16 January 2021].

innocent "developing country." The problem with that narrative is that it casually glosses over China's well documented authoritarian rule, widespread torture and mass executions,

> *"Amnesty International recorded at least 657 executions in 20 countries worldwide in 2019. The total — one of the smallest since Amnesty began tracking executions in 1979 — was a 5% decrease from the at least 690 executions recorded in 2018 and was down 60% from the 25-year-high total of 1,634 reported executions in 2015.*
>
> *As in previous years, the execution total does not include the estimated thousands of executions carried out in China, which treats data on the death penalty as a state secret. Excluding China, 86% of all reported executions took place in just four countries — Iran (251), Saudi Arabia (184), Iraq (100+), and Egypt (32+)."[10]*

In order to really understand this book, we have to first discard the propaganda that China's Central Propaganda Department (*that's a real thing*) spends billions of dollars flooding into the United States:

> *"A host of corporate media outlets including CNN, The New York Times, The Washington Post, and MSNBC have participated in private dinners and sponsored trips with the China-United States Exchange Foundation, a Chinese Communist Party-funded group seeking to garner "favorable coverage" and "disseminate positive messages" regarding China, The National Pulse can reveal...*
>
> *The effort, according to the U.S. government report, aims to "to co-opt and neutralize sources of potential opposition to the policies and authority of its ruling Chinese Communist Party."*
>
> *"The United Front strategy uses a range of methods to influence overseas Chinese communities, foreign governments, and other actors to take actions or adopt positions supportive of Beijing's preferred policies," it continues.*

---

[10] www.theepochtimes.com. 2021. *China Uses Political Warfare To Influence US Politics.* [online] Available at: <https://www.theepochtimes.com/china-uses-political-warfare-to-influence-us-politics_2264575.html> [Accessed 16 January 2021].

> *This strategy appears to have been deployed in conjunction with outlets such as CNN, New York Times, and the Washington Post."[11]*

Why? Because most of what the West has heard about China is not much more than cleverly crafted propaganda.

For example?

Well let's start with something basic like the country's name. "Well, that's easy! It's obviously China, right?"

It's not.

Sure, that's what *you and I* learned in school. But that name is essentially derived from ancient Hindu scripture referring to the Qin Dynasty. Not that that is particularly relevant, but hey, now you know!

While "China" might be what we are taught in Western schools it is certainly not what Chinese kids learn in school. In fact, one of the most stunning things I found after moving to China is that Chinese nationals will laugh and giggle when they hear the word *China*. Nope, there isn't some misguided translation or phonetic misinterpretation. What is going on is that the Chinese just use an entirely different name domestically.

So, what do the Chinese call China? Officially, it is referred to as "中华人民共和国" (People's Republic of China) aka: 中国 for short. What does 中国 mean? "*Zhong Guo*" literally translates to "*middle/central* = 中 (*Zhong*), *kingdom/country/state* = 国 (*Guo*)." That's right, the Chinese officially refer to *China* as Earth's Middle Kingdom, not "China."

Ethnocentrism?

Aside from the obvious "why", this raises a number of fascinating questions. What is the psychological impact on children of a country refers to itself as "Earth's Central Kingdom." What might they think of, say, foreign counterparts who are not from the "Earth's Central Kingdom?" How might the notion of a "Central Kingdom" influence CCP officials and their relationships with counterparts from *lesser, non-central* countries? How might that mindset dictate domestic policy? What about foreign policy?

---

[11] The National Pulse. 2021. *All Major Western Media Outlets Take 'Private Dinners', 'Sponsored Trips' From Chinese Communist Propaganda Front.* [online] Available at: <https://thenationalpulse.com/exclusive/media-private-ccp-dinners-trips/> [Accessed 16 January 2021].

Domestic Chinese scholars and Western apologists do mental gymnastics to try and mitigate the rationale and proximity of this to 1940's Nazi Germany. "Oh, it's because China used to be divided into multiple states…it highlights strategically important regions in ancient Asia…stems from the demise of the Zhou dynasty…blah, blah, blah…"

It's all a cleverly funded propaganda.

This is *The Middle Kingdom's* modus operandi. Chinese foreign policy is smoke and mirrors designed to confuse, manipulate and deceive foreign governments and populations. The CCP is as good as they come at waving the proverbial shiny red ball while the magician, *China*, does its political tricks on the world stage to a distracted global population.

China's domestic population understands this all too well as they deal with the full brunt of the Chinese Communist Party dictating every last facet of their life with an iron-fist. China, "The Middle Kingdom", is not a country where dissent is allowed or tolerated, period. Feel like protesting the government?

> *"Prominent Hong Kong activist Joshua Wong and two of his longtime colleagues were handed prison sentences on Dec. 2 for their roles in a mass protest that occurred in front of the city's police headquarters in 2019.*
>
> *Wong, 24, was sentenced to 13 1/2 months after a court session at the West Kowloon Magistrates Court. Fellow pro-democracy activists Agnes Chow, 23, and Ivan Lam, 26, received prison sentences of 10 months and seven months, respectively."[12]*

YOLO and FOMO aren't coming to China any time soon and that's by design; they can't. Why? There simply isn't space for these ideas given China's abysmal human rights record, widespread torture, indefinite detention, arbitrary legal system, rampant execution, black market human organ harvesting, mobile execution vans, reeducation camps, and social credit system.

In China, YOLO and FOMO land you in a concentration camp and then you disappear permanently.

From the time a Chinese citizen is born until they die there is one simple guiding principle, *long live the CCP.* You can find those who try to dissent

---

[12] The National Pulse. 2021. *All Major Western Media Outlets Take 'Private Dinners', 'Sponsored Trips' From Chinese Communist Propaganda Front.* [online] Available at: <https://thenationalpulse.com/exclusive/media-private-ccp-dinners-trips/> [Accessed 16 January 2021].

against the CCP in the same black site prison cells I landed in or having their organs ripped out of their bodies without anesthetics (also a real thing), that are later sold on black markets. These people usually die in the process, if they're lucky.

With this in mind, what does the CCP seek above all else? One thing, control of the global population. There are four key elements that fundamentally define China's strategy in achieving this goal,

1) *Control*
2) *Ambiguity*
3) *Deception*
4) *Violence*

Control is far and away the most crucial objective for the CCP to achieve. Deception, ambiguity and violence are simply the most effective tools that help the CCP achieve and maintain this ever elusive and coveted goal. For the CCP, China must always come first and then there's everyone else, "foreigners", as we're referred to on Chinese soil. For all intents and purposes, in the mind of the CCP, China is the world.

Chinese policy genuinely asserts that they are indeed a globally superior race.

Proof?

Well, have you ever heard of Chi Haotian? He's certainly heard of you! He served as China's Minister of National defense for 10 years. He was also China's military leader in charge of enforcement and quelling unrest during China's 1989 Tiananmen Square Protests in Beijing.

The Tiananmen Square Massacre is worth putting into context as it emphasizes the CCP's relentless obsession with control and violence.

Declassified British files released in 2014 estimate that the real number of people killed by the Chinese military during the Tiananmen Square Protests (government murder of Chinese university students protesting for Democracy and freedom) exceeded 10,000 with another 40,000 injured. On the other end of the spectrum, official CCP statistics estimate that the Chinese military killed between 0 – 300 people.

Subtle CCP differences.

So back to our friend, Chi Haotian, the democide mastermind behind the Tiananmen Square massacre.

In 2003, he delivered an interesting speech that some would label hostile. Although the specific details surrounding the speech have been debated, experts have verified that the context is very much in line with internal and current Chinese Communist Party doctrine.

In other words, Chi speaks for the CCP. If you've spent some time talking to CCP members about Chinese policy, you'll see that nothing here is much of a leap. The wording, the context, and the tone are all notoriously in line with the CCP's ethos. But don't take my word for it.

I find it much more effective and easier to let ranking CCP officials, like Chi, speak for themselves.

Originally published by the Epoch Times, the piece can still be found online today, uncensored, and in Mandarin. So, what did Chi have to say about his good friends (you and I, the "foreigners") in the West, to his captive CCP audience? Here's a rough translation of some of the Chi's key elements,

> "It is indeed brutal to kill one or two hundred million Americans. But that is the only path that will secure a Chinese century, a century in which the CCP leads the world. We, as revolutionary humanitarians, do not want deaths, But if history confronts us with a choice between deaths of Chinese and those of Americans, we'd have to pick the latter, as, for us, it is more important to safeguard the lives of the Chinese people and the life of our Party.
>
> The last problem I want to talk about is of firmly seizing the preparations for military battle. The central committee believes, as long as we resolve the United States problem at one blow, our domestic problems will all be readily solved. Therefore, our military battle preparation appears to aim at Taiwan, but in fact is aimed at the United States, and the preparation is far beyond the scope of attacking aircraft carriers or satellites. Marxism pointed out that violence is the midwife for the birth of the new society. Therefore war is the midwife for the birth of China's century...
>
> We Chinese are brighter than the Germans because, fundamentally speaking, our race is superior to theirs. That is why we have a longer history, more population and more territory. On this basis, our ancestors left us two priceless traditional treasures: atheism and great unity. The founder of our Chinese culture was Confucius.
>
> In the long run, the relationship of China and the United States is one of a life-and-death struggle...Only countries like the United States,

Canada and Australia have the vast land to serve our need for mass colonization... Therefore, solving the "U.S. problem" is the key to solving all other problems.

First, it makes it possible for us to colonize there a great deal and even establish another China under the leadership of the Chinese Communist Party. America was originally discovered by our Yellow people first, but Columbus wrote his credit to the white people. We Chinese have the right to enjoy this land! I heard that the yellow lineage of residents in the United States is very low status. We are going to liberate them. Second, to solve the "U.S. problem," Western European countries will yield to us. Let alone Taiwan, Japan and other small countries. Therefore, solving the "U.S. problems" is the task that history has given to the Chinese communists.

The United States is the most successful country in the world today. Only we can learn from all its useful experiences and we can replace it in the future.

Anyone who has been to Western countries can feel that people's living space far exceeds ours. There was a large forest next to their freeway, and we rarely have trees beside our road. Their skies were blue sky and white clouds. Our skies were covered with a black lid. Our water is too contaminated to drink; there are few people on their streets, two or three of them live in a small building, our people crowded, a few crowded in a small room. Someone wrote a book many years ago under the title *Yellow Disaster*. When China reached a population of 1.3 billion, as we all aimed at the high consumption of American-style lifestyles, the limited land and resources would not be able to bear the weight of social collapse. Now that our population has exceeded this limit, we have to rely on imported resources to maintain it.

Let us also never forget that underlining the issue of "keeping a low profile and keeping a low profile" as emphasized by Comrade Xiaoping, its subtext is in the final analysis that for the United States we must endure and must hide our ultimate goal of hiding our ability and waiting for the opportune moment...

But the term 'living space' (lebensraum) is too closely related to Nazi Germany. The reason we don't want to discuss this too openly is to avoid the West's association of us with Nazi Germany, which could in turn reinforce the view that China is a threat. Therefore ... 'living,' but not 'space' ... Western countries established colonies all around the world, *therefore giving themselves an advantage on the issue of living space. To solve this problem, we must lead the Chinese people outside of China, so that they could develop outside of China.*

Can we liberate China if we insist that the Chinese do not kill the (outside) Chinese? As for the millions of Chinese people in the United States, this is certainly a big problem. Therefore, in recent years, we are studying genetic weapons as the biological weapons that do not kill the yellow ones. However, this study is very difficult."[13]

Let's be very clear here. The goal, if you're American, is to KILL you. The CCP is brutally honest about their intentions. They have no issue **killing** hundreds of millions of Americans if it serves their interests.

There's a lot more, but you're probably slowly starting to get the idea. The CCP is actively racing toward complete and unquestioned global dominance, and they'll literally employ any tactic necessary to achieve this goal.

For decades, the Chinese regime has overseen the most extensive eugenics program in the world, attempting to craft their self-proclaimed master race. One of the most obvious examples is China's long and disturbing history of infanticide. This doesn't only include decades of infanticide for those unlucky enough to be born female, but also discarding babies with mental disabilities.

China's answer to this?

The BGI Cognitive Genomics Project in Shenzhen has been working on a project to sequence the entire genome of 1,000 very-high IQ individuals from around the world. Why? Their aim is to pinpoint which exact sets of alleles are responsible for triggering off-the-charts IQ. Experts believe that this research might be coupled with "genetic engineering" techniques allowing Chinese families to increase their children's IQ every generation.

If BGI's research comes to fruition, China would not only have successfully built its master race but exert complete and utter global domination in a way never seen before on a global stage. Furthermore, Western countries have huge moral hang-ups on this type of research and have largely enacted laws either limiting this type of experimentation or banning it altogether.

The kicker? BGI has been working on this since 2013.

---

[13] Tai, Zhong. 2005-08-01. Midwife of the Chinese Century. *epochtimes.com*. Retrieved: February 24, 2018, from http://www.epochtimes.com/gb/5/8/1/n1003911.htm.

Evolutionary psychologists have estimated that Chinese "preimplantation embryo selection" could result in generational IQ gains of 5 to 15-points for Chinese families. Should these generational IQ gains come to fruition, global militaries, universities and corporations would no longer be competitive with their Chinese counterparts.

The Chinese will often try to downplay this by talking about their admiration for the West and the United States. It's all part of the CCP propaganda narrative.

I've personally lived and worked around the world, but it wasn't until I landed in China that I heard a domestic population lavish the US with endless compliments, "Such a big strong country...developed nation...powerful military..." etc. It didn't come off as genuine but more like an actor reciting a poorly memorized script.

And that's precisely what it is; a script that the Chinese learn in school.

Deception is a fundamental component of Chinese culture, tradition and history. The CCP, by design, works tirelessly to operate in the shadows. Local Chinese citizens commonly refer to their own government as the "black box." Why? "Because no one, aside from government officials, has any idea what actually goes on in government. We just occasionally get new rules that we are forced to follow." The CCP has ripped this strategy from centuries of Chinese culture and warfare,

> "All warfare is based on deception. Hence, when we are able to attack, we must seem unable; when using our forces, we must appear inactive; when we are near, we must make the enemy believe we are far away; when far away, we must make him believe we are near."

> ~ Sun Tzu

And this largely explains China's clever Covid cover up:

> "Government documents leaked to The Epoch Times have since revealed that COVID-19 cases may have surfaced months earlier. Wuhan hospital data shows that patients were hospitalized with symptoms similar to COVID-19 as early as September 2019, while several people died in October 2019 from pneumonia, lung infections, and other COVID-19-like conditions.

> In the early weeks of the epidemic, the Chinese regime continually downplayed the crisis and denied that the disease could be transmitted

among humans. The World Health Organization repeated Beijing's claims, and would wait until Jan. 30 to declare the outbreak a global health emergency.

Chinese authorities didn't implement containment measures until Jan. 23, with a lockdown on Wuhan. However, by then, 5 million people had already left Wuhan, amid a typical peak season for domestic and international travel for the Lunar New Year holiday."[14]

Covid didn't happen by accident and the Chinese were acutely aware of the downstream impact this would have on the US.

Your average Chinese citizen couldn't care less if you're American, South African, German, Mexican, Indonesian, Peruvian, Nigerian, Korean or Russian; in their eyes, you're simply a *foreigner*. That is precisely what you are referred to on the streets of China, *foreigner*.

All Chinese policy essentially stems from that central idea. There are the *Chinese*, and then there are *foreigners*. Remember, China is a country that doesn't allow legal dual-citizenship. You're Chinese, or you're essentially a traitor to the master race.

The recurring joke you'll hear from the Chinese in Beijing is, "What is the hardest citizenship to obtain in the world?" Some well-meaning foreigner generally responds with, "American citizenship? Maybe German? British?"

Your Chinese friends will burst out laughing, "No, of course not. The hardest citizenship to obtain in the world is Chinese Citizenship, because it's impossible haha. You can never become Chinese."

And they're absolutely right. Remember the master race reference from our friend Chi? Your bloodline isn't pure like theirs is.

That harsh dichotomy dictates all CCP policy.

You will never become Chinese, in the way immigrants are allowed to become American, Canadian, British, Australian, etc. There is no path to citizenship, nor will there ever be. The rare exception is that you are a leading expert in a specific industry that China has deemed essential for its own development.

---

[14] The National Pulse. 2021. *All Major Western Media Outlets Take 'Private Dinners', 'Sponsored Trips' From Chinese Communist Propaganda Front.* [online] Available at: <https://thenationalpulse.com/exclusive/media-private-ccp-dinners-trips/> [Accessed 16 January 2021].

That is the only case in which the red carpet will be rolled out for foreigners, but again, it's fleeting and largely ceremonial.

You can spend decades in China, learn to speak mandarin fluently, graduate with a degree in a top ranked Chinese university, marry a Chinese citizen, have a Chinese son or daughter, pay taxes, buy a house, etc. Surprise, you still aren't Chinese. I knew plenty of foreigners that were stuck in this unwelcoming limbo that dedicated years of their life in China.

Remember our good friend Chi Haotian.

Sure, you might get some type of Green Card equivalent for temporary residence. You might get to live in China or maybe even get a marriage visa. But you'll never be allowed to become part of the team in the same way that Western countries allow for foreign immigration and integration.

Westerners that landed in China for school in the 80's, learned to speak fluent Mandarin, spent decades living and working in the country, married a Chinese spouse and had Chinese children ultimately come to that painful realization,

> *"Death and taxes. You know how the saying goes. I'd like to add a third certainty: you'll never become Chinese, no matter how hard you try, or want to, or think you ought to. I wanted to be Chinese, once. I don't mean I wanted to wear a silk jacket and cotton slippers, or a Mao suit and cap and dye my hair black and proclaim that blowing your nose in a handkerchief is disgusting. I wanted China to be the place where I made a career and lived my life. For the past 16 years it has been precisely that. But now I will be leaving."[15]*

This is not just as simple as a feeling of general alienation after moving to a foreign country or struggling to adapt to a new culture. The Chinese Communist Party relies on the hardcore indoctrination of anti-foreign sentiment forced on every new generation in the Chinese education system.

Are you familiar with the Eight-Nation Alliance? The Opium Wars? The Sino-Japanese Wars? The Taiping rebellion? The British invasion of Tibet? The Chinese certainly are, and they ensure that each future Chinese generation learns that foreigners have a history of aggression against the Chinese

---

[15] The National Pulse. 2021. *All Major Western Media Outlets Take 'Private Dinners', 'Sponsored Trips' From Chinese Communist Propaganda Front.* [online] Available at: <https://thenationalpulse.com/exclusive/media-private-ccp-dinners-trips/> [Accessed 16 January 2021].

people and are not to be trusted. In other words, if you're Chinese, you're a victim of every historical instance of international aggression against the Chinese people. The Chinese government even gave it a name, The Chinese Century of Humiliation,

> *"It is a period roughly starting from the Opium War in the 40s of the 19th century to the establishment of the People's Republic of China in 1949. China suffered semi-colonization, multiple foreign aggressions and severe poverty during this century.*
>
> *Chinese civilization was at its lowest point during that time. To some extent, it also shaped China's relations with the world, particularly with the West. After the Ming Dynasty (1368-1644) sent the world's largest fleet then on exploration voyages, as far as to the coast of Africa, China adopted a closed-door policy and shut itself out from the rest of the world. It missed the time capitalism and industrialization were budding in Europe and America. The giant agricultural country was later forced to open the door and involve itself in the global trade by gun and cannon.*
>
> *China learnt its lessons from this period of time."*[16]

As a result, China has adopted an "us versus them" mentality when it comes to, everything. It's painfully common to hear modern Chinese women say that they refuse to marry foreign men on the grounds that, "foreign men can't be trusted." Many Chinese men will outright refuse to consider marrying or even dating a "tainted" Chinese woman that has ever dated or been romantically involved with a foreign man.

What about something more straightforward like citizenship, you might ask? What about applying for something like a Green Card,

> *"Foreigners who want to apply for permanent resident in china should obey the Chinese law, be healthy and have no criminal records. At same time, they should accord with one of the conditions below:*
>
> 1. *The applicants have invested in China directly, have with steady investment condition and good revenue record for more than 3 years.*

---

[16] The National Pulse. 2021. All Major Western Media Outlets Take 'Private Dinners', 'Sponsored Trips' From Chinese Communist Propaganda Front. [online] Available at: <https://thenationalpulse.com/exclusive/media-private-ccp-dinners-trips/> [Accessed 16 January 2021].

2. *The applicants take the job continually as or above assistant general managers or factory directors, have the high title of or above the associate professor or assistant researcher, or have enjoy the equal treatment in China for more than four years, during which the applicants have been living in China continuously for more no less than three years and have good revenue records.*

3. *The applicants have great and outstanding contributions to China or meet special requirements of the Chinese government.*

4. *The spouse of Chinese citizens or the foreigners who have got the qualification of permanent resident in China, with the marriage lasted for more than five years and living in China for more than nine months every year and have steady living guarantee and residence.*

5. *The unmarried children under the age of 18 who come and seek refuge with parents.*

6. *The applicants who have no direct relatives abroad, come and seek refuge with the domestic direct relatives, are over sixty years old, and lived in China for no less than nine months every year and have steady living guarantee and residence."[17]*

Good luck traversing that minefield of ambiguity.

So, how are things for foreigners in modern China? It depends. On one hand, you're not part of the team, so the Chinese will largely try to leave you alone. On the other end of the spectrum, China spends more money than any other country monitoring even its own population.

A genuine disinterest, if not outright disdain, of foreigners is not uncommon in China. It's to be expected if you understand how the CCP orchestrates and utilizes education, governance and communism. China just doesn't trust foreigners, and this has been the standard view of Westerners since as far back as the Qing Dynasty (1644 to 1912)

"In the days of early contact in the Qing dynasty period foreigners were often described as Ocean devils: Yang guizi 洋鬼子 or 番鬼 fān guī 'barbarian devils'. Dutch people with red/orange hair were described as

[17] ebeijing.gov.cn. Friday, February 23, 118. Who Can Apply for a Green Card in China? *china.org.cn.* Retrieved: February 23, 2018, from http://www.china.org.cn/english/LivinginChina/185212.htm.

The National Pulse. 2021. *All Major Western Media Outlets Take 'Private Dinners', 'Sponsored Trips' From Chinese Communist Propaganda Front.* [online] Available at: <https://thenationalpulse.com/exclusive/media-private-ccp-dinners-trips/> [Accessed 16 January 2021].

红毛 *red heads and associated with Buddhist demons who are portrayed with red or blue hair."*[18]

I want to emphasize that this isn't a stab at your average Chinese citizen. Most Chinese simply want to work hard, raise a family and live a happy life. At the same time, it must be emphasized that people, in any country, are largely a product of the environment in which they were raised. The culture you've been instilled with since birth, especially in a communist rule, doesn't magically disappear when you hop across international borders.

So, how does the CCP remedy the foreigner problem? Legal ambiguity. China can make you disappear for as long as they deem your absence necessary. The same is true not only of individuals in China but of any entity engaging in business on Chinese soil. In order to operate "above board" in China you have to willfully submit to CCP interests at any point in time.

Businesses know that if they don't tow the party line, their offices will likely be shut down overnight. You don't operate in China without understanding that you must be capable of complete submission to the will of the CCP at the drop of a hat.

How ambiguous is China's legal system?

Both the U.N. Working Group on Arbitrary Detention and the U.S. Department of State have had to team up to tackle egregious instances of arbitrary detention of U.S. citizens in China.

In 2015 an American businesswoman named Sandy Phan-Gillis was traveling through China with a trade delegation to promote the city of Houston. She was arbitrarily detained in the Southern Chinese city of Zhuhai and held incommunicado for 6-months under 'residential surveillance' (house arrest).

She was later moved to a detention facility in Southern China where she was kept in solitary confinement. She wasn't formally charged until October of 2015 and didn't get to see a lawyer until May of 2016, over a year after her initial arrest. Ultimately, she was arbitrarily accused by Chinese authorities of *stealing state secrets*. The US State Department stepped in urging China to

---

[18] The National Pulse. 2021. *All Major Western Media Outlets Take 'Private Dinners', 'Sponsored Trips' From Chinese Communist Propaganda Front.* [online] Available at: <https://thenationalpulse.com/exclusive/media-private-ccp-dinners-trips/> [Accessed 16 January 2021].

resolve the case expeditiously and the UN warned China that this arbitrary detention was directly violating international law.

How did China react? China threatened the UN Working Group on Arbitrary Detention.

Chinese Foreign Ministry Spokesperson Hong Lei warned the United Nations against questioning China's "judicial independence" and warned that the UN must respect China's "sovereignty, and cease making irresponsible remarks about legal cases..." China does not care for international norms, even if they directly threaten the life of a foreign national.

Their turf, their rules, period.

So why is China's legal system so arbitrary and ambiguous? Some things are good for China while others are not. That simple statement is far and away the best barometer of how the Chinese will enforce the law on any given day.

Why does that ambiguity matter? Because the Chinese government apparatus is constantly monitoring everyone to ensure no one, ever, steps out of line. Enter China's Social Credit System,

> *"In the latest move to implement a social credit system across mainland China, Chinese authorities recently launched a credit rating app targeting China's 460 million adults aged 18 to 45. According to this scheme, those who earn the highest credit scores enjoy greater access to training and employment benefits, while those with low scores encounter restrictions even in day-to-day life.*
>
> *Observers say that the Chinese Communist Party (CCP) is trying to use technology to build a unique form of totalitarianism that has never existed in the past.*
>
> *Unlike the financial credit system in the West, Unictown gathers a large amount of non-financial information about its users, including so-called "anti-social" behavior and participation in "volunteer work."*
>
> *Chinese human rights lawyer and visiting scholar at New York University Teng Biao told the Chinese-language Epoch Times that the new social credit scheme is part of a series of measures taken by the CCP to strengthen its surveillance over the whole of society and re-activate totalitarian rule."[11]*

Why does this matter for you? China has been monitoring foreign nationals as well.

Australia, a country that has been on the receiving end of a large-scale influx of Chinese nationals has become the definitive example. Chinese lecturers at Australian universities are being monitored by the Chinese government and Chinese students to ensure that even in Australia, CCP criticism is not to be tolerated.

Make no mistake that this isn't simply restricted to Chinese nationals or Chinese professors. This is happening to professors from countries around the world who refuse to tow the CCP narrative. Their fears are becoming more and more defensible as Chinese influence continues to spread entirely unchecked.

A recent incident at Sydney University underscores the harsh reality of this modern-day Chinese colonialist mindset. Chinese students used the popular Chinese-based WeChat social-media platform to wage a form of populist cyber-warfare against Khimji Vaghjani (Indian), an IT lecturer at Sydney University. Why? He used a map during a lecture depicting India in control of land along the Chinese-Indian border that also happens to be claimed by the Chinese government.

Outraged Chinese students took to WeChat demanding an apology, while others threatened to quit the class in protest or file complaints against the university with the Chinese embassy in Sydney.

So, what happened? Not only was the Sydney-based Indian professor forced to author an apology, but the university apologized for the map as well. How did China respond?

The CCP-owned newspaper Global Times issued a declaration claiming that a Chinese-Indian border dispute had broken out in Australia, and China Won!

It gets worse. All this happened a week after a Sydney-based Chinese auto group drove their luxury cars draped in Chinese flags through popular landmarks in the city. Their destination? The Indian embassy in Sydney. Why, you might ask? It was the 70th anniversary of Indian Independence and this was their way of displaying Chinese superiority over India regarding ongoing Chinese-Indian territorial disputes. One of the slogans posted on one of the Chinese vehicles read, anyone who offends China will be killed no matter how far the target is.

Unfortunately, China's expansion into foreign countries is rarely about embracing foreign culture and discovering new ways of life or seeing the world. It's about dominating local populations through the forced adoption of CCP propaganda aka colonialism, which Mr. Chi Haotian discussed at length. Sadly, the Chinese education system reinforces this negative ideology about foreigners, particularly Westerners.

Imagine being in America, legally, and having the police randomly show up to your office from time to time simply because you're a foreigner. They then demand you show your papers, interview your bosses about your activity, stop the entire office from working and interrogate you in a separate room without cause or reason.

That's normal for foreigners in China. I lived it for 5 years.

When you step into a restaurant, bank, or coffee shop you aren't referred to as sir or ma'am but *foreigner*, every single day. If that behavior was normalized in America, there would be international and domestic outrage and backlash against the "racist" US.

And yet, much of this behavior is simply seen as normal in China. In 2016, China celebrated its first National Security Education Day. How did China celebrate this new, randomly made up, propaganda-holiday? By plastering residential areas with posters warning Chinese women to be on the lookout for smooth talking Western men that are trying to steal state secrets.

I'm not kidding. What's on the government approved poster?

The poster titled Dangerous Love depicts a fictitious story of Little Li a young Chinese civil servant who winds up meeting the story's red-headed foreign antagonist, David. The two meet at a dinner party and things heat up. David and Little Li end up dating and he courts her with lavish gifts, dinners and compliments. But suddenly, things take a turn for the worse.

Yup, this is real.

Little Li agrees to invite David to her government office and divulge classified Chinese documents! The cartoon ends with Little Li in handcuffs being scolded by two CCP police officers. "You have a shallow understanding of secrecy for a state employee" the CCP officers shout at Little Li!

Welcome to China. Aside from the legal implications, if the US government tried something like this, the poster would be mocked, ridiculed, and torn down. But if you tore this down in China, you would disappear.

In a communist state, in practice, the government exercises complete control over everything. Remember, we are talking about a country where Youtube, Facebook, Twitter, the New York Times, Gmail, Google Maps, Blogspot, Instagram, Pintrest, Dropbox, Vimeo, Soundcloud, Scribd, Bloomberg, the Epoch Times, WikiLeaks, Reporters Without Borders, Flickr, Tumblr and the Wall Street Journal, and many more Western platforms are entirely banned.

China does not tolerate anything that it cannot exert complete control over. If something does become operational or legal in China, it has likely submitted a lot of autonomy and control to the CCP.

My first summer in Beijing was my first experience with China's handling of foreigners. Around May of 2012 a foreign tourist from the UK attempted to drunkenly rape a Chinese woman during a late-night stroll home from a bar. The entire thing was caught on camera by various Chinese citizens and went viral online. As you might expect, this individual act of complete stupidity further fanned mainland China's already notorious anti-foreigner sentiment. The reaction wasn't simply, let's hold this one man accountable for his actions but, *all people from the UK and the West are bad.*

In response the Chinese government implemented, overnight, a nation-wide campaign targeting *illegal foreigners*. Although the Chinese government didn't officially state that the campaign was in response to the incident, the timing is pretty definitive.

The 100-day government led campaign aimed at cleaning out illegal foreigners was popularized online by Beijing's PSB (Public Security Bureau) that handles related domestic issues. The post depicted a strike-hard fist, typically associated with domestic CCP-led campaigns. The PSB even provided a new hotline that Chinese citizens could use to report suspicious foreigners.

Chinese citizens responded by flooding anti-foreign sentiment on WeChat. *Illegal foreigners* became a trending top-10 topic on China's social media giant, Sina Weibo. One commenter posted, "I raise both hands and feet in support of clearing out illegal foreigners: send that foreign trash rolling back to where they belong." Others thanked the police for, "clearing out foreign trash."

This was my first summer in China.

Whether in the country legally or not, foreign expats constantly looked over their shoulders trying not to draw any unnecessary attention that summer. Bar districts known to have large international crowds largely dried up with some foreigners opting not to leave their apartments unless it was absolutely necessary. Furthermore, stories of the Chinese government cranking up the detention and deportation machine made their rounds through expat circles throughout the country.

These stark differences provide the harsh but necessary context to properly understand China, the CCP, and this book moving forward. There's a lot more, and this doesn't even scratch the proverbial CCP surface.

Nonetheless, this chapter provides a necessary framework that allows you to understand the utter chaos of the CCP prison system that I was thrown into.

Chapter 2:

An American Entrepreneur in China

"…strengthen control over the use of original-edition Western materials. We must by no means allow materials that spread Western values into our classrooms; We must never allow various attacks to defame the party's leadership and discredit socialism in the university classrooms.; it is absolutely forbidden to have any kind of speech that violates the Constitution and the law spread in university classrooms; it is absolutely forbidden for teachers to complain and vent in the classroom their grievances and pass on various negative emotions to students."[19] ~ *January 30th, 2015*

Yuan Guiren (袁贵仁):
China's 15th Minister of Education, 2009 – 2016

I founded and funded a business, during my fourth year in Beijing, as a 26-year-old. The company provided business and educational training courses for young professionals. Bear in mind that this meant familiarizing myself with everything from handling tax compliance to incorporation procedures, in Mandarin.

But that's the easy part.

Opening a restaurant as a foreigner? My friends did and made the mistake of being *foreign* showing up, in person, for inspections. They made the mistake of wearing suits too, which screamed wealth, to local officials. Their opening date was arbitrarily pushed back by Chinese authorities citing a range of vague "safety laws", unless of course, they paid bribes.

---

[19] Yuan, Guiren. Public Comments. Symposium of the Ministry of Education. Beijing. January 30th, 2015. Public speech

Welcome to doing business in China.

Business compliance firms have repeatedly warned foreign companies that investing in China is associated with a high degree of risk. One of the more predominant themes in these reports is that corruption is a systemic hallmark of the Chinese business climate,

> *"Corruption in China presents business operating or planning to invest in the country with high risks. The Chinese government, led by President Xi Jinping, is in the midst of a sweeping anti-corruption campaign that has led to thousands of arrests, nonetheless, corruption continues to negatively influence the business environment. Companies are likely to experience bribery, political interference or facilitation payments when acquiring public services and dealing with the judicial system.*
>
> *The judiciary in China carries high corruption risks for business. The Chinese Communist Party (CCP) rejects the principle of separation of powers and does not provide for an independent judiciary (Reuters, Feb. 2015). Judges receive guidance from the government and the ruling party regularly, particularly when it comes to politically sensitive cases (HRR 2015). Lower-level courts are particularly susceptible to outside influence and corruption, and they operate in an opaque manner (HRR 2015). Local governments appoint and pay judges, which can result in biased, vague or poorly enforced decisions (HRR 2015)."*[20]

Business in China operates through a concept known by locals as *Guanxi* which roughly translates into *relationships*. The Chinese generally explain it as a cultural norm that stems from the Chinese notion of face. This is another clever narrative meant to confuse and deceive foreigners doing business in "Earth's Middle Kingdom."

What is Guanxi then? Guanxi is legalized bribery. Chinese "scholars" will blow smoke in your face with nonsensical explanations about China's mysterious and complex culture. It's a medium to retain power by selling you propaganda that it's all "too complicated for simple minded Westerners to understand. How could you, your history is short by comparison and less appealing. You're barbaric and not part of Mr. Chi's heaven-sent Chinese master race."

Guanxi is a dressed-up term for normalizing bribery.

---

[20] China Corruption Report. (2020, September 30). Retrieved January 29, 2021, from https://www.ganintegrity.com/portal/country-profiles/china-corruption-report/

Why does the CCP need Guanxi? Ambiguity. Laws that have a nasty habit of being documented and subject to interpretation by a domestic population and the legal community. Personal relationships, on the other hand, are much more fluid and flexible. Relationships, unlike laws, can be terminated or amended at the drop of a hat. Laws can't be. Why deal with the litigious and rigid structure of a legal system when everything can simply be left in a convenient grey area?

This leaves the CCP in complete and unquestioned control of everything.

A key aspect of Guanxi is centered around gift-giving, with money being a popular medium of exchange. If money isn't being exchanged through one-medium or another, you're not building Guanxi. So where are these bribes expected to be paid? Everywhere,

"In March, as surgeons prepared to operate on the father of Mr. Liu in a county hospital in central China, hospital staff suddenly called him and other patients' family members over for a secretive meeting.

Under the pretense of needing "special fees" for experts coming from a larger city, the staff members of the Xihua County People's Hospital in Henan Province told Liu that they would require 1,500 yuan (about $225) to operate on his father, who had suffered a heart attack.

"These fees were not part of the medical bill," Liu told Henan Television.

Rather, they were part of what has essentially become institutionalized bribery.

In China, the service industry and bribes go hand in hand. This is especially apparent in hospitals, where patients lavish exorbitant sums of "red envelope" money on doctors to ensure high quality—or just adequate—treatment.

The phenomenon, which gets its name from the small, red, money-filled packets given to friends and family during the Lunar New Year, may not always involve the iconic holiday envelope. But bribery is firmly entrenched in the Chinese medical culture and has its roots in the structure of the Communist Party's health care system."[21]

---

[21] Hurricane, C., Congress, News, N., East, M., Politics, & News, C. (2016, August 16). In China, Don't Expect Health Care Without Bringing a Red Envelope. Retrieved January 29, 2021, from https://www.theepochtimes.com/in-china-dont-expect-health-care-without-bringing-a-red-envelope_2135182.html

And then there's China's media,

> "Chen Yongzhou...was taken in by authorities on October 18. Chen worked for the southern Chinese newspaper, the "New Express" in which he published a series of 15 articles about China's second-largest construction equipment company Zoomlion.
>
> He said he had been asked to write the articles and had received money for doing so. Some of the material he used in his articles, he "admitted," had been given to him by a third party and the rest of the story had been made up by himself.
>
> Zhan Jiang, a professor of journalism in Beijing, told DW that corruption in China's media sector has come as a great disappointment to the Chinese people and damaged their trust and support.
>
> Zhan has studied the problem of corruption in Chinese media for years. He has repeatedly called on journalists to refrain from accepting so-called red envelopes as bribes. Such envelopes, which traditionally contain money and are given as gifts - usually for Chinese New Year - are regularly handed out at company press conferences to guarantee positive coverage."[22]

The list is endless. Schools, government, politics; fill in the blank.

You might be thinking, "Well ok, that doesn't sound so bad. Bribery is legal in China, so what?"

China still has an extensively documented legal framework covering both the public and private sector. These laws cover everything from criminalizing 'corrupt' practices including, facilitation payments, money laundering, active and passive bribery, commercial bribery and anti-corruption laws.

But wait, isn't bribery legal in China?

It is, until it's not. Bribes may be perfectly acceptable or even expected within a specific industry. But for one reason or another, China will decide that a foreign individual or entity "did something wrong" and ambiguously throw the book at them even though this behavior is an industry standard for every domestic Chinese firm.

---

[22] www.dw.com), D. (n.d.). A little red envelope does the trick: DW: 30.10.2013. Retrieved January 29, 2021, from https://www.dw.com/en/a-little-red-envelope-does-the-trick/a-17194775

What about all the other domestic companies doing the same thing and pay the same bribes?

That's the beauty of ambiguity, the government is always in control and they can arbitrarily decide to accuse one company while ignoring all the rest who engage and operate in the same capacity.

You arbitrarily get to pick the winners and losers. Imagine what you could do wielding that type of ambiguous control over multi-billion-dollar global Fortune 500 corporations that employ millions of people.

Why would anyone ever do business in a country like that? There's only one answer, market size. Forieng investment into China comes with a laundry list of risks that can jeopardize everything from human lives to capital. But certain companies have simply decided that the benefits of the world's largest market outweigh the obvious risks and do it anyway.

Fundamentally, this is a corrupt business environment that I would advise most Westerners to steer clear of for a multitude of reasons. It's just not worth the headache and there's a litany of Western businesses that have tried and had to ultimately throw in the towel, including tech companies with billions in capital behind them,

> *"On Monday Uber said that it is selling its operation in China to a rival... Uber gets around a 20% share of the Chinese company, which will run Uber's Chinese operation as a separate brand.*
>
> *Much of the U.S. news coverage has centered on Uber capitulating to competition and getting schooled by its Chinese archfoe. Uber truly wanted to succeed in its fastest-growing market, one where taxi drivers outnumber their U.S. counterparts tenfold.*
>
> *I believe Uber is leaving China not because of interference from its rivals but because of interference from the state.*
>
> *In the end, it wasn't competition that spelled Uber's demise in China; it was impending national regulations. Under the new regulations, the data collected by Uber would come under the purview of the government. Uber would have to get both provincial and national regulatory approval for its activities anywhere in China.*

> *Moreover, foreign companies like Uber would be subject to even more regulation than their competitors. This national regulation was an impending disaster for Uber."*[23]

If you're foreign in China, you're knowingly held to a complete double standard.

My company worked with Chinese clients who sought to develop their education and careers. We created personalized curriculums, in English, that were specific to their desired career path. Once complete, we developed learning modules that would help them improve their English for university admissions or job applications.

In other instances, we partnered with Chinese companies to collaborate and focus on market development. This meant helping a company market their existing services, or we were contracted to train their customers or staff.

It's worth emphasizing that this business model already existed in the Chinese marketplace. In fact, the "English education industry" racks in billions of dollars annually in China. Furthermore, it's one of the few Chinese markets where foreign entities are legally allowed to operate unlike telecommunications or finance.

The main problem with China's system of English education is that English is often taught by non-native Chinese teachers. Because of China's authoritarian government, studying English in China is an incredibly dry and inefficient process.

Foreign culture, values and ideas have almost been entirely stripped from English language textbooks, classrooms and curriculum leaving students with an incredibly narrow understanding of the language they're trying to learn. The Chinese do not want "hostile" Western ideas influencing their population.

In December of 2016, President Xi Jinping spoke at a conference on Chinese ideology and politics in Chinese universities. In his speech, Xi instructed Chinese universities to "adhere to the correct political orientation." He also emphasized that Chinese schools must uphold the Chinese Communist Party's leadership, "guiding both teachers and students to be strong believers in Marxist theories and socialist values."

---

[23] The Real Reason Uber Is Giving Up in China. (2018, March 07). Retrieved January 29, 2021, from https://hbr.org/2016/08/the-real-reason-uber-is-giving-up-in-china

Xi's speech was attended by ranking Chinese leadership including military and propaganda officials, university leadership and members of China's elite Politburo Standing Committee. So, why all the fuss about education and universities in China? Well, China doesn't trust foreigners with Western ideals,

> *"China's education minister explained... 'Schools...are the prime targets for the infiltration of hostile forces.' For years, China's leaders have feared that they're losing their grip on the ideological loyalty of the country's youth...the forces wresting away young minds are cultural warfare waged through alluring foreign pop culture and the infiltration of 'Western values.'"*[24]

You are China's primary threat!

Remember, the Chinese population is already inundated about *your* hostile Western culture of imperialism. The Chinese have spent decades studying the West with the sole purpose of infiltrating it to control it. China is a country where government policies are enforced through the barrel of a gun. From the day a Chinese citizen is born, the notion of dissent is simply never allowed to exist. What does exist? Blind loyalty to the CCP and communist rule.

Anything less is not tolerated.

How does the Chinese construct and maintain such a rigid environment? Their education system! How does the Chinese education system differ from yours? A hardcore, rigid and strict indoctrination of communist principles.

What do Chinese kids learn in elementary school? They get dressed up in military uniforms wearing communist red star hats and recite CCP propaganda,

> *"Who gave us our happy modern life?" "Our happy life comes from the blood of revolutionary martyrs! From the Red Army", "Lotte (Lotte Group, South Korea), leave China! Boycott Korean goods! Protest THAAD (America's Terminal High Altitude Area Defense)! Love Communist China", "We are the new generation of little Red Army warriors... We march onwards with incomparable firmness.", etc.*

Compare that, for a moment, to the American elementary school curriculum.

---

[24] Fish, Eric. February 4, 2017. Why's Beijing So Worried About Western Values Infecting China's Youth? *Chinafile.com*. Retrieved: February 4, 2018, from http://www.chinafile.com/features/whys-beijing-so-worried-about-western-values-infecting-chinas-youth Xi, Jinping. Public Comments. 18th National Congress of the Communist Party of China. Beijing. November 8th, 2012

Repeat this stuff for the first 18 years of a child's life, name your country Earth's Middle Kingdom, and reinforce the idea that foreigners are not to be trusted and are responsible for every bad thing that ever happened to your population. What type of adult does that produce?

Look to Yuan Guiren (China's 15ᵗʰ Minister of Education) or Chi Haotian (Tiananmen Square murder mastermind) for reference.

This starts at the top of CCP governance and it is violently enforced all the way down to every last individual in China's massive population. This repressive communist education system is the brainchild of China's Communist Party. It's how they maintain control, because there is no way out of this country; aka a national prison system. But it doesn't stop after school. According to Chairman Xi, communism needs to become your political soul,

> *"General Secretary Xi Jinping pointed out that the belief in Marxism and the belief in socialism and communism are the political souls of the communists and are the spiritual pillars of the communists who have withstood any test. This is the fundamental requirement for the education of ideals and beliefs of party members and cadres."*[25]

Again, the goal here is not to critique or stereotype your average Chinese citizen. In fact, I feel for them. I can't tell you how many Chinese parents I met in Beijing who refuse to have their children placed in the same rigid education system that they survived and insist on the international model taught abroad.

At the same time, this information is necessary for Westerners to understand just how harsh the Chinese education system is and what its goals are. Westerners will often ask why the Chinese businesses copy and paste everything and lack 'common sense' or 'critical thinking.'

Make no mistake that you would turn out the exact same if you endured this system of communist indoctrination for the first 18 years of your life.

The other problem in Chinese English education is that all foreign influence is entirely stripped from the Chinese classroom. That becomes a huge problem for students when they are expected to learn foreign languages to perfection. For obvious reasons, countless Chinese students are frustrated

---

[25] Fish, Eric. February 4, 2017. Why's Beijing So Worried About Western Values Infecting China's Youth? *Chinafile.com*. Retrieved: February 4, 2018, from http://www.chinafile.com/features/whys-beijing-so-worried-about-western-values-infecting-chinas-youth Xi, Jinping. Public Comments. 18th National Congress of the Communist Party of China. Beijing. November 8th, 2012

that they can't attain a high-level of English proficiency. *It's not their fault.* It's that these communist classrooms and educators have stripped any notion of 'hostile' Western culture from the learning process. Despite spending countless hours studying English, Chinese students genuinely struggle to converse or understand simple nuances or prompts in English.

For a country like China that has spent decades pouring billions of dollars into education, specifically targeting English acquisition, the results have been dismal. China ranks 47th globally in English proficiency and is officially classified in the "low-proficiency" band, putting it's English proficiency on par with countries like Mexico, Egypt, Ethiopia and Albania.

Studying English in China would be like taking a music class where you memorize sheet music but never actually get to hear the song played. The entire beauty of discovering a new culture, arguably the best reason to explore and learn a new language, is entirely stripped away from Chinese students.

Ironically, English fluency in China is seen as a status symbol for native Chinese. High English proficiency is largely viewed as an extension of the quality of your education and intelligence. In China, your education is directly linked to your socioeconomic status. In a country where men must own a car, a house and have a good career before any respectable Chinese woman would consider marrying them, English proficiency, ironically, matters.

Bear in mind that it wasn't long ago, that learning English in China was banned by the government. Studying English as a foreign language was reintroduced around 1960, as Sino-Russian relations began to deteriorate. Unfortunately, the re-introduction of English to China's mainland would be short lived as it was once again banned six years later during the outbreak of the Cultural Revolution. For those of you that don't know, the Cultural Revolution was essentially a purge of Capitalists and Western values. As a result, China condemned the English language and the imperialists (Westerners) of English-speaking countries.

It wouldn't be until 1972 during Richard Nixon's historic trip to China, that diplomatic relations with the US would again be normalized. The seven-day trip was also monumental because it officially ended a 25-year period of no official diplomatic relations between the two countries. Shortly after Nixon's departure, the Shanghai Broadcasting Station began broadcasting a program called, 'Intermediate Broadcasting English.' Corresponding scripts were printed and circulated to a select group of lucky individuals that the CCP allowed to start studying English.

This is the environment I inherited, as a Westerner, to incorporate an educational consulting firm.

The company I founded in Beijing worked to remedy a lot of these underlying problems. Not only did we provide custom courses that were specific to our client's career goals, but we monitored and tracked their linguistic progress as well. Furthermore, we worked to transcend a lot of the barriers that existed in Chinese classrooms allowing students to engage with the English language in the same way as native speakers.

In doing so, English was no longer reduced to some rigid and agonizing language whose only function was meant for boring technical discussions on grammar. Instead the beauty of English as a language now had purpose, meaning and a cultural context.

The services we provided were miles ahead of the mundane English training centers you would find around major Chinese cities. These training centers usually had horrendous customer service, lacked individuality and yielded horrific quality.

Standard English training centers would often hire non-native English teachers, "illegally." Another massive problem in China is that it is incredibly racist, and they don't try to hide it. It's publicly acceptable and almost stated factually. It wouldn't be uncommon to find job ads placed seeking "native English speakers, or white Europeans that are non-native English speakers."

In other cases, English training centers would hire native speakers who didn't meet China's minimum teaching qualifications. These centers utilized painfully dated learning materials or didn't bother to measure or track linguistic development.

Education is heavily scrutinized by the Chinese government and foreign firms are often competing at a disadvantage against "domestic" companies, as in the case of Uber; making it nearly impossible to resolve these quality issues on a large scale.

As a result, many of the education problems outlined in this chapter still exist, unchanged, today.

For those of you who haven't done it, let me be the first to say that founding, funding and managing a successful company is harder than anything else you will ever encounter in life. It becomes significantly more complex to do in China, as a "foreign" 26-year-old non-native Mandarin speaker.

Navigating things like tax compliance, employment regulations, marketing on Chinese social-media platforms and contracts is hard enough if you're doing it in your own language. Try doing it in Mandarin. Remember, I'm not a billion-dollar corporation with endless assets at my disposal and team of Chinese investors. I was a a kid from California.

Despite all of these hurdles, my business became profitable within its first month and operated in the black every month thereafter.

In other words, what I was doing was working. I had never run a business before. I had no formal education in finance, management, or Mandarin. I personally funded this enterprise on my own dime. Furthermore, I was 26 years old. That's worth taking a moment to put into perspective, as an estimated 48% of foreign businesses fail and withdraw from the Chinese market within two years of establishing operations there.

Over the years in Beijing, I worked extensively with government officials, embassy staff, and Fortune 500 employees. I had also developed an awesome and international network throughout Mainland China and significantly improved my Mandarin every single year. Most importantly, I helped countless Chinese professionals develop their careers, improve their English proficiency and build their self-confidence.

That being said, I didn't plan on staying in China forever. I knew my tour would be coming to a close and that I was one or two visas' away from moving on to the next adventure. As they say, "Beijing is a humbling mistress." The pace and energy of the city has a way of grinding down your soul after a few years of working your tail off.

Somewhere along the way, before I could depart the country, I popped up on some CCP radar.

Despite the fact that I lived and worked in China legally, its arbitrary and ambiguous legal system eventually caught up with me. Having lived in China for a number of years, you hear stories of people getting caught up in the legal system. But that only happens to the troublemakers, I thought to myself. The drug users, the brawlers, and the foreigners working on tourist visas are the ones that get in trouble. As long as I steer clear of the obvious no-no's and you'll be ok, or so I thought.

How naïve of me. The signs were all around me and I should have known better, it's just that few of us are ever looking for them or paying attention. We fear the truth. Why wouldn't we? The truth is raw, unedited, direct and unflattering. Ignorance, on the other hand, is bliss. I should have been paying attention.

I should have been listening.

Before I moved to China, I was visiting my bank in California, back in December of 2011. I had to sort out a few financial issues before hopping on my one-way flight to Beijing. It was a busy day, and I patiently waited at the back of a very long line.

One by one, the tellers worked their way through the line, until I gradually made my way to the front.

"Sir," the next free teller called out in my direction. I looked up and saw a friendly face greeting me with a warm smile. I glanced up and saw my teller who appeared to be in her 70's.

I approached her desk and handed over my documents. I explained that I would be moving abroad for work, and that I needed to make a few changes. She had a very pleasant, kind and warm personality. I still remember our exchange vividly,

Teller: "…oh the weather has been so cold this week. Do you have any plans for the weekend?" she asked as she plugged information into the computer.

Me: "Not really, just packing a few more things before I take off" I replied.

Teller: "Well that's not so bad! Ok sir, I'll just need your signature here and… here" she prompted.

Me: "No worries. Will I be getting a copy of this? I asked.

Teller: "Sure thing! So, where are you moving for work" she asked.

Me: "Beijing, China" I replied.

She instantly froze and looked up immediately, catching my gaze, dead-center; as if I had just said I was going to a slumber party with serial killers. I'll never forget that look. It was a mix of disbelief, astonishment, confusion, concern, and shock all wrapped into one.

Teller: "China? You know that's a communist country, don't you?" she said in this, eliciting utter disbelief that I would voluntarily make this decision.

At the time, I didn't understand what she was trying to say. Sure, I recognized all of the words in her sentence. I had studied communism in high school classes and we covered China too. But in that moment, language was more of a barrier than an efficient medium of exchange. The English language simply wasn't capable of allowing her properly express what she was desperately trying to convey.

Me: "It's fine, it's 2011. The world's coming together and changing" I replied in my dumb, stupid, ignorant, twenty-something year old voice.

I had already traveled to so many countries. What does she know? Old people are just so judgmental. That is just the wrong attitude. Who still thinks that way? I have a great university degree. I'm an educated American citizen. I hold multiple passports. Doesn't she know what I've studied? I have an international family. I'm untouchable.

Uncomfortable truths are thrown in our faces every single day, but we often fail to recognize, acknowledge or embrace them. We don't want to. We want the world to fit into our perspective, not the other way around. It's easier to look away and recede into a world that makes us feel safe, and comfortable.

But I'll never forget her look or her words. What might I have learned if instead I took a minute to listen or inquire? But in that moment, at the height of my ignorance, my twenty-something years of blissful stupidity superseded her decades of wisdom. In fewer than ten words, she conveyed more truth than my arrogant twenty-something year old "educated" brain could ever hope to comprehend.

But at the time, I knew that I was right, and I knew she was wrong.

Hindsight really is 20/20. Looking back, I now see that I knew absolutely nothing, and she knew so much more than me.

Respect your elders and listen to them.

Chapter 3:

Interrogation

'Your only right is to obey': lawyer describes torture in China's secret jails

Xie Yang, a human rights attorney survived torture, prolonged interrogations and extensive sleep deprivation by the Chinese government. He was forced to "admit" that he had been "brainwashed" in Hong Kong and South Korea in an attempt to try and implement "Western Constitutionalism" in China. As a human rights lawyer he represented members of the Chinese Democracy Party, Christians, and a Chinese citizen who was shot and killed by the police, in court. The Chinese government charged Mr. Xie with "inciting subversion of state power and disrupting court order."[26]

Chinese Government's official response to Xie Yang's torture. Chinese Foreign Ministry Spokesperson Hua Chunying's press conference, December 28, 2017:

"Q: Yesterday, the German and US embassies criticized China over the handling of right activists' (Xie Yang) case. What is China's response?

A: China is a country with rule of law, and the Chinese judicial authorities handle cases in accordance with law. The individual countries you mentioned, by making such irresponsible remarks on our judicial authorities' normal handling of cases, blatantly interfered in China's

---

[26] 'Your only right is TO obey': Lawyer describes torture in China's secret jails. (2017, January 23). Retrieved February 28, 2021, from https://www.theguardian.com/world/2017/jan/23/lawyer-torture-china-secret-jails-xie-yang

internal affairs and judicial sovereignty. Their actions per se have violated the spirit of rule of law. China firmly opposes and will in no way accept that.

These two foreign embassies in China, as diplomatic missions, have no right to point fingers at China's internal affairs and judicial sovereignty. We hope the relevant embassies could accurately position themselves as regards their functions and do more to promote mutual understanding, mutual trust and cooperation, instead of the opposite."

Chinese interrogation is a very foreign concept to what we are familiar with here in the West.

In the US, we tend to envision an experienced team of witty detectives using the law to logically trap uncooperative criminals. If you've ever seen American crime films or tv shows, you're well aware that the police are laughably restrained in their approach thanks to this novel Western idea referred to as due-process. The police can't arbitrarily coerce the accused to sign an incriminating document in a foreign language.

China, on the other hand, adheres to a very different set of standards. It doesn't waste its energy or money on detectives or the cumbersome technicalities involved with due-process. Instead, China just cuts straight to the chase. And why not? It's much easier to just say, you're guilty or simply locking people up without having to charge them with anything in the first place or deal with cumbersome trials.

But hey, why stop there? Laws are selectively enforced by the CCP as well, so why not just have the police beat a confession out of the accused as well?

Chinese efficiency!

In the case of Mr. Xie, this is precisely what happened. It was reported that his Chinese guards routinely threatened to torture him to death and then started beating him until he began admitting to crimes that he did not commit. Other guards threatened that they would be able to torture Mr. Xie until he went crazy and that he would leave the prison cell crippled.

Understandably, Mr. Xie eventually wrote down a signed admission of guilt stating anything Chinese authorities ordered him to say. He got to that point where he simply wanted the torture to stop.

That, in a nutshell, is how the Chinese interrogate.

Before I took a deep-dive into China's entertaining take on interrogation, I was just another American working in Beijing. One of the learning centers I had signed a working contract with was in Guomao (国贸) which is regarded as Beijing's cosmopolitan and international hub.

Adult students would usually cram into these English learning centers at around 5 or 6 pm as they were getting off work.

On Tuesday, October 25th, 2016, a group of CCP officers randomly entered the English learning center where I was working, around 7 pm. Their captain, a slightly taller man wearing a distinctive brown leather jacket, trailed in behind them.

This company was working with young local professionals who sought to develop their careers by improving their English proficiency. Several of my students were VIP clients working at Fortune 500 companies while others were local government officials.

I was hired on because I was certified to work in Beijing, employed as an independent contractor, and had years of experience in this industry.

There were three other foreigners at work that day who had been employed directly by the company: a gentleman from Germany (Neil), Spain (Karl) and Canada (Conan) (who had recently arrived in China a few weeks earlier).

Conan was the oldest of the group in his late-40's. He had bright blonde hair, was an ex-cop who seemed to have hit a rough patch in life and had recently arrived in Beijing to start over. From the sound of his story, China seemed like his escape. Some sort of a mid-life crisis mixed with an opportunity to turn life's proverbial page.

That story wasn't out of the ordinary for a lot of older expats in Beijing circles. Beijing was the kind of big city metropolis anyone could get lost in. People from all over the world often reinvented themselves in Beijing, to become anything and anyone you could imagine.

Conan was divorced with two young boys. I never asked but it seemed like there was something forcing the distance between him and his kids. But it wasn't my business to know, and I preferred to keep it that way.

He was possibly the friendliest guy you could meet. His personality was always upbeat and optimistic, and he carried a smile that would shine from a mile away. Everyone loved him.

Then there was Neil, the German. Neil was somewhere in his mid-30's. He was unmistakably direct and somehow, came off as someone with a dead soul. At the same time, and unsuspectingly, Neil had the greatest sense of humor on the planet. It was painfully dry, and it would surface at the most inappropriate and hilariously unexpected times. RARELY would Neil ever let a joke out, but when he did, the entire room would burst into hysterical laughter because it was so random.

Most of the time, Neil was calm, quiet and reserved. My guess is that something happened to him when he was a kid. Whatever it was, it caused him to recede into the depths of his own mind and to some degree, he seemed happy and content there. It seemed like a defense mechanism for something in his past.

Neil never wanted to talk to you (or anyone) and he would let you know the second you opened your mouth that he had no interest in communicating with you. If anyone missed the initial cue, Neil would stare directly into your soul and blurt out, "stop talking." My favorite Neil line, "I hate everyone equally."

Neil came to work dressed smart, every single day, with his bright red hair combed perfectly off to the side. His professional attitude and calm composure won him the respect, or fear, of everyone that crossed his path.

Finally, there was Karl, the Spaniard. Karl was young and that is the easiest way to describe him. He was a young idealist who had the solutions to all the world's problems despite never having really held a job or paid taxes before. His own intelligence was not to be surpassed by anyone else and he would emphasize that in every single conversation.

Sure, he would tolerate a dissenting point of view from time to time, but only if he allowed it. This isn't to say that Karl wasn't smart, he was, brilliant in fact. But Karl's masterful brilliance was lost in theoretical ideals of what should be as opposed to what was realistic.

Compromise, concessions and cooperation were not in his vocabulary. He would go off on random tangents about how communism *could* work once we had, "technologically advanced robots and AI in charge of communes that were inhabited by genetically altered hybrid super-humans, etc…", I think you get the point.

As with most young idealists, Karl had good intentions and his heart was in the right place. But, as most young people and idealists eventually find out the hard way, "the road to hell is paved with good intentions." I will say I admired

Karl's passion, and his belief in a functioning hybrid human robotic communist commune system.

Karl was shaggy. I'm not sure how else to describe him physically. His dark black hair was long and uncut. His big round thick spectacles made him look cartoonish. He smelled weird, was unkept and his body would literally start to visibly shake out of rage in a debate when someone dared to disagree with his utopian vision for too long.

It was funny, sad and terrifying all at once. But that was Karl.

And there the 4 of us were, at work, watching as the police marched around the office, snapping up photos, taking video, and ultimately stopping our courses to begin questioning us.

Sadly, all of this was pretty standard in CCP China.

They interrogated us one by one, asking the usual questions, "What do you do in China? How long have you been in China? What kind of visa do you have?" etc.

Luckily, I had a legal alien work permit, documentation from Beijing's tax authority that my income had been properly taxed, a non-existent criminal record, a legal & unexpired Beijing residence permit, Beijing business incorporation papers, local police registration documents, etc.

I wasn't worried; my papers were all verified and legal. My work permit had been processed in Beijing and linked directly to my employer (the company I co-founded). All client funds were paid to my company and processed by a licensed Chinese accountant. Once our business and income taxes had been paid, paychecks were distributed through authorized government systems. There was nothing fraudulent or remotely illegal.

But don't take my word for it.

Here is China's Embassy in the US highlighting the protocol for foreigners employed in China:

"4. A holder of category Z visa must apply for a residence permit at the local public security authorities within 30 days of entry into China unless the Duration of Each Stay on the visa is marked as 30 days."[27]

And here's the U.S. Embassy in China:

"In addition to a valid passport and visa, all prospective teachers must obtain a Residency Permit within thirty days of their entry into China. One may not legally teach in China without both the Z visa and a valid Resident Permit. This is necessary whether one is classified as a 'foreign teacher' or a 'foreign expert.' Employers should provide assistance in obtaining this document."[28]

Finally, I was TEFL certified by Beijing's State Administration of Foreign Experts Affairs (SAFEA):

"TEFL in China is organized by the Information Research Center, State Administration of Foreign Experts Affairs (SAFEA), which is the presiding authority over TEFL training in China. Trainers are experienced and well-trained experts in education and related fields...Upon successful completion of this training you will receive the accredited TEFL in China Certificate, which is a valued qualification for foreign teachers in China...The Certificate is officially recognized as a qualification for teaching English throughout China, and it provides an excellent credential for entering the TEFL profession in China."[29]

With all this in mind, I wasn't the least bit concerned because I knew all of my papers were legit. Additionally, I had routinely encountered Beijing police raiding offices where foreigners worked, so I had seen the song and dance before.

Normally, CCP authorities would "shake-down" a business that employed foreigners over some arbitrarily written law and volley a few threats at the owner.

---

[27] Embassy of the People's Republic of China in the United States of America. March 22nd, 2017. How to Apply. Embassy of the People's Republic of China in the United States of America. *China-embassy.org*. Retrieved: February 4, 2018, from http://www.china-embassy. org/eng/visas/hrsq/.

[28] Pillsbury, Adam, Ed. 2009-2010. Teaching English in China. *China.usembassy-china.org*. Retrieved: February 4, 2018, from https://china.usembassy-china.org. cn/u-s-citizen-services/local-resources-of-u-s-citizens/index/teaching-english-china/.

[29] The TEFL in China Term. 2010. FAQ. *tefl.chinajob.com*. Retrieved: February 4, 2018, from http://tefl.chinajob.com/faq/index.html.

Remember Guanxi? Owners will generally fork over some type of payment, the cops leave, and business would go back to normal. It's worth emphasizing that this happens all the time in China, anywhere foreigners are employed.

According to a 2015 China Corruption report, 35% of Chinese companies reported having to pay bribes or give gifts in order to operate. The report also found that the incidence of bribery increased in regions where wealth and power were highly concentrated. In Beijing, that number jumped to 43% of businesses reporting that they had to pay bribes or give gifts to stay operational.

Therein lies the brilliance of this Chinese business and regulatory tactic. *Everything is legal and illegal at the same time.* If the Chinese want to call you on illegal bribes, they can, because there is always some arbitrary law on paper that they can say you've violated. On the other hand, foreign businesses are not going to win domestic Chinese business if you're not operating in the same capacity as domestic competition.

Damned if you do, damned if you don't.

At the end of the questioning, the police rounded the 4 of us up into a private room and said, "*Meet us at the police station tomorrow morning at 9 am, and we'll make a deal. Bring your papers (visas and passports).*"

We had heard of foreigners being interrogated at police stations before, but it certainly wasn't standard practice in my experience. I had seen police sweeps in the past, they usually started and ended in the office; not a police station.

We went home that night trying to figure out why we were being called in.

This should have been resolved by now. It usually is, I kept thinking to myself.

The four of us showed up at the police station the next morning, as requested, at 9 am:

北京市公安局朝阳分局出入境管理支队, *Beijing Municipal Public Security Bureau Chaoyang Branch exit management detachment*

The four of us arrived at the police station and hung out in the 'waiting room' for about an hour until the police separated us. I brought along every imaginable document that the Beijing government had provided over the years to ensure that I had all my bases covered.

One by one we were carted off into separate interrogation rooms where we sat at the end of unusually long desks. Two police officers sat opposite us, one of which could kind of speak English.

At the beginning of the interrogation, officers placed a video-camera on a table to ensure that certain parts of the interrogation were recorded.

My interrogator was your standard Beijing cop, featureless and emotionless. Any concept of individuality or critical thinking was removed a long time ago to ensure every part of this was merely procedural. And it was. From time to time, she wouldn't understand my answers in English which meant I would have to explain something to her in Chinese.

If I did bother to clarify or translate, this look of confusion and disgust would appear on her face, conveying what seemed to be, *"How dare you use OUR language, foreigner."* I guess she was capable of emotion; condescension.

They started with easy questions and gradually moved to more detailed ones, "Do you have a Chinese name?"

"小龙" (Xiao Long), I replied. It was easier for them to use our Chinese names.

"What is your job? How long have you lived in Beijing? How much money do you earn every month? What kind of company did you start? What contract do you have with this learning center? How did you obtain your visa? Etc."

All in all, I was interrogated for somewhere over 2 hours. I would answer, they would dig, I would answer they would dig; this was our song and dance.

Eventually, the "interrogation" came to an end.

The captain who had questioned us the night before suddenly re-entered the room. He kept accusing me of having "broken the law" (even though he wasn't in the interrogation) because I was *"working illegally."*

I explained that I founded a company (presenting the documents) focused on providing education consulting services. I went on to explain that I had to sign contracts and provide services to operate the business.

He didn't get it. It was as if I were explaining how a business worked to someone who had never heard of one before.

I went on to explain that the company with which I was working had signed a contract with my business to provide training services for their clients.

41

As expected, not a single Chinese national from that business was being interrogated.

I displayed all of the legal working permits and explained that Beijing's own government had legally and literally certified me to teach.

Nobody cared. Then again, I shouldn't have been surprised, that's how communist judicial systems operate.

Everything is legal and illegal at the same time.

China's government has a well-established history of targeting foreign firms for doing what domestic firms do, which is operating in a grey area. If you don't play by the rules, you're not competitive with domestic firms in the domestic market. If you do, you'll be competitive up until the Chinese government arbitrarily feels like collecting money from you. The CCP has a history of doing this with "international" Fortune 500 firms to send a message that no foreign entity supersedes the authority and strength of the mighty CCP.

The most notable example occurred in 2014 when Chinese courts fined GlaxoSmithKlein a record-setting three billion yuan ($489 million USD) over "bribery" charges. The British Pharmaceutical company accepted the fine but was largely seen as operating in the exact same manner as other domestic and international pharmaceutical companies operating in China.

International companies in China have leveled a long list of grievances against the Chinese courts arguing that the legal system is inefficient for settling disputes or challenging regulations. There are even reports of the courts leveling judgements against the Chinese government and state-owned enterprises but simply not enforcing the court's ruling.

Even if you win against a powerful entity in China, you lose.

And so the odd line of questions and statements from the police officer continued. One of the officers randomly blurted out, "You make too much money. Do you know how much we make?"

I shook my head, saying that I did not know how much their salary was:

"How much does a Vice Squad Police Officer make in Beijing, China? ¥107,000 to 128,000 CNY/Year (18,400.00 USD), Average Base Salary."[30]

I responded, "All of my taxes are paid, and I only collect a salary from my own company" handing over my tax documents from Beijing's local Tax Authority.

"That's not the law" one of them responded.

Me: "?????????"

It was a logic-free affair.

Despite my repeated appeals and refusal to go along with their narrative, the police department simply ignored my documents and said, "you broke the law."

They printed up a 30 page "summary" of my "interrogation" in Mandarin. We were coerced into fingerprinting and signing every page of the summary without access to a translator, without time to read through it, without access to a lawyer and without the opportunity to contact our respective embassies.

We literally had no idea what we were signing. The police forced us to sign and fingerprint every single page in the stack of documents.

We were told that we were guilty and had broken the law but that the punishment would not be severe. "Maybe just pay a fine," the police captain said. "Nothing serious. We'll contact you later."

And that was that. They were going to release us, for now. But we had no idea what that actually meant. As we've seen with China's legal system, China's police force operates under a similar level of corruption.

According to a GAN's 2020 China Corruption Report,

> *"Corruption in the Chinese police constitutes high risks for companies. Companies report that police services are unreliable in protecting them from crime and enforcing the law. Further, two-thirds of businesses report paying for security in China. Abuses of power among police officers were rarely prosecuted. Nonetheless, only slightly over one-tenth*

---

[30] ERI Economic Research Institute. 2018. Vice Squad Police Officer Salary in Beijing, China. *Salary Expert*. Retrieved: February 4, 2018, from https://www.salaryexpert.com/salary/job/vice-squad-police-officer/china/beijing.

of companies report that the road police impacted the circulation of goods by extorting bribes."[31]

If you're the CCP, how do you ensure that this ambiguous system of absolute control remains in place indefinitely? You need to have a citizenry that has no legal or physical recourse against a far more powerful and better equipped domestic police force. Independent judiciaries, human rights advocates, or an armed population dilute the government's perpetual monopoly on force.

These things that exist in America to keep the government in check, cannot exist in China, by design.

As a result of the lengthy interrogations, we hadn't eaten anything and decided to go grab dinner to discuss the utter chaos we experienced that day.

We decided to not contact our embassies yet as we had technically been "released" and didn't want to cause any more of a fuss, hoping the issue would simply resolve itself.

> *"Which questions did they ask you? Which interrogator did you have? Are we going to be detained? Will we be deported? Is it just a fine? Did they make you fingerprint the pages? Did your interrogator speak English?"*

Unbeknownst to me at the time, the gentlemen from Germany and Spain had been working in Beijing, illegally. Their visas were acquired in a different Chinese city and were meant to be used exclusively in Shenzhen, not Beijing. We assumed that I had simply been rounded up as some type of accessory to this.

Great.

Over dinner, one of the Chinese directors from the learning center (who had been appointed the police's point of contact) received a call from the police regarding our situation. They chatted for a few moments and she proceeded to hang up.

She looked up at us and said, "No problem. They said you can pick up your passports tomorrow morning at the police station at 9:00 am and that will be the end."

---

[31] China Corruption Report. (2020, September 30). Retrieved January 29, 2021, from https://www.ganintegrity.com/portal/country-profiles/china-corruption-report/

We looked around at each other completely *stunned*. I almost couldn't believe what she had just said, because I had this gut feeling that something felt off about this entire process. It can't be that simple and straightforward.

Why call us in to the police station in the first place then? Was it supposed to be ceremonial? Were they just trying to send a message? Would they gloss over Neil and Karl's illegal visa issues? Would they ignore me because my documents were all legal and board?

We looked around and breathed a collective sigh of relief. It was…unbelievable. I felt as if the weight of the world had literally been lifted off my shoulders.

Maybe this would all go away?

Maybe we were done?

Our conversation shifted to other topics while we happily sat there and finished our meals. It had been a long day and we were tired. Once we finished and paid the bill, we said our goodbyes and retired home for the night.

What would tomorrow bring?

Chapter 4:

Arrest (Part 1)

U.S. Department of State: Arrest or Detention of a U.S. Citizen Abroad

"If you are arrested overseas or know a U.S. citizen who is:

- *Ask the prison authorities to notify the U.S. embassy or consulate*
- *You may also wish to reach out to the closest U.S. embassy or consulate to let us know of arrest. Contact information for U.S. Embassies and Consulates overseas can be found here or by going to our individual country information pages.*

Consular Assistance to U.S. Prisoners:

- *When a U.S. citizen is arrested overseas, he or she may be initially confused and disoriented. It can be more difficult because the prisoner is in unfamiliar surroundings, and may not know the local language, customs, or legal system.*

We can:

- *Provide a list of local attorneys who speak English*
- *Contact family, friends, or employers of the detained U.S. citizen with their written permission*
- *Visit the detained U.S. citizen regularly and provide reading materials and vitamin supplements, where appropriate*
- *Help ensure that prison officials are providing appropriate medical care*
- *Provide a general overview of the local criminal justice process*
- *Inform the detainee of available local and U.S.-based resources to assist victims of crime*

- Upon request, ensure that prison officials permit visits with a member of the clergy of the religion of your choice
- Establish an OCS Trust, when no other means to send funds are available so friends and family can transfer funds to imprisoned U.S. citizens
- We cannot:
- Get U.S. citizens out of jail
- State to a court that anyone is guilty or innocent
- Provide legal advice or represent U.S. citizens in court
- Serve as official interpreters or translators
- Pay legal, medical, or other fees"[32]

The next morning, we returned to the police station at around 9 am, as we had been instructed. I was scheduled to work later in the day, so I was dressed in my button up shirt and tie, lugging my backpack around.

The four of us arrived, umbrellas in hand, on a noticeably cold and overcast Beijing morning. An officer greeted us at the door and marched us to a large meeting room, where we were told to sit and wait for further instruction.

We were seated opposite the room's entrance on a row of chairs that had been pushed up against the wall. We were positioned in the corner about a meter away from a giant meeting room table that hogged the center of the space. To the right of the door was a large window that looked out into the police station's parking lot.

And there we sat, waiting, for around 15 minutes before a Chinese officer finally marched into the room with a stack of documents.

Once again, we were instructed to sign before we could receive our passports. And sign we did. Signing documents in a police station is not optional in China. Once again, no explanation. No translation. No lawyer. No time to review the document. Nothing.

Who knew what we had just signed and fingerprinted?

One by one we signed our documents and handed them back. The unexpressive officer collected them and darted straight out of the room, without uttering a word.

Odd, I thought to myself.

---

[32] U.S. Department of State. 2018. Arrest or Detention of a U.S. Citizen Abroad. *Travel. state.gov.* Retrieved: February 4, 2018, from https://travel.state.gov/content/travel/en/international-travel/emergencies/arrest-detention.html.

And there we were, in some shabby police station in the center of Beijing, waiting for our passports and for all this to finally be over. And so, we waited.

5 minutes went by. Then 10 minutes… *Tick-tock. Tick-tock.*

Nothing.

Neil: Taking a long time to grab a couple passports isn't it?

15 minutes.

Then 20 minutes… *still nothing.*

Karl: Prolly gonna be overcast all day huh?

Me: Prolly. Any lunch plans?

Karl: Nah.

Something is wrong. Where are our passports? This shouldn't be taking so long.

25 minutes. 30 minutes.

Not a word.

The small talk had largely subsided at this point. We had been sitting in silence for quite some time as we could all sense that this didn't seem to be as simple or straightforward as we had anticipated. *Were we even here to collect passports?*

What had we just stepped into?

I failed to grasp that this is China's MO. Chinese authorities can say and do anything they want with impunity. Police corruption and brutality in China is the rule, not the exception. But don't take my word for it,

> "Deng Zhengjie was a farmer who made a living selling watermelons raised by his own hand. He died on July 17, having been beaten by six Chengguans (City Urban Administrative and Law Enforcement Bureau) and suffering brain damage. Witnesses said the Chengguans—thugs employed by city governments to enforce regulations—beat Deng with the steel counterweight used to weigh his melons.
>
> In China, the war between the Chengguans and the street vendors is a daily scene in most cities. Deng's case is just one typical example of those who "don't have money."

Then there's Ji Zhongxing's story which is also very similar. Ten years ago, like many Chinese from the villages, he went to Dongguan in southern China's Guangdong Province, the bustling center of economic reform, seeking a better life.

He began driving a Modi, a motorcycle taxi. One day, Ji Zhongxing and his passenger were caught by local security and beaten by seven to eight guards. Ji was left paralyzed. For the next eight years, he visited numerous state offices in vain.

Finally, on July 20, he decided to blow himself up at the Beijing Airport. While making sure his attempted suicide at least could not be ignored, he still managed to ask the people around him to evacuate. He survived, losing one arm, and nobody else was injured."[33]

The difference here is that there is no legal recourse like we are used to in the West. These instances of horrific violence don't receive media coverage in China. The rare exception is if you are killed in such an egregious manner by the state, as in the case of Mr. Deng, that it might catch the attention of Chinese netizens and hit critical mass. But even there, the state constantly monitors everything everyone says,

"The beginning of every June is one of the busiest times for Chinese censors. That's when the world — except China — commemorates the anniversary of the 1989 Tiananmen Square massacre in Beijing.

Internet censorship is tightened during this time of each year not only to prohibit discussion of the brutal crackdown on the pro-democracy protest that happened 27 years ago, but to erase the incident from Chinese history, especially among younger generations.

The impact of such suppression is staggering. Only 15 out of 100 Beijing University students could recognize the "Tank Man" photo, which is the global symbol of the bloody crackdown..."[34]

---

[33] He, Heng. July 25th, 2013. 'China Dream' a Nightmare in Reality. *theepochtimes.com*. Retrieved April 29th 2018, from https://www.theepochtimes.com/recent-deaths-show-reality-of-china-dream_201393.html.

[34] How China has censored words relating to the Tiananmen Square anniversary. (n.d.). Retrieved February 02, 2021, from https://www.pri.org/stories/2016-06-03/how-china-has-censored-words-relating-tiananmen-square-anniversary

Signing up for social media in China requires an authenticated government ID number that links directly back to you. In a country where millions of people are routinely abducted from their homes and forced into re-education camps based on what they post online, how far are you willing to push the envelope?

So, was I about to be arrested by the same corrupt system? *No way, they told us we were here to pick up our passports.* Then again, TIC ("This IS China", a common phrase among local expats for absurd situations that could only arise in China). They *can* do and say anything, I thought to myself.

That's precisely when something appeared off in the distance, instantly snapping the four of us back into reality. Through the window, a prison transport van with a steel cage slowly approached our window.

The vehicle's engine shut off and a group of Chinese officers slowly emerged out of the van with documents in hand. Once the group exited the vehicle, they began marching toward the police station's entrance, beyond our view.

We all saw it and proceeded to shoot puzzled looks at each other. Karl, who was sitting next to me looked over, and elbowed me in the arm, *"Maybe that's for us"*, he said laughing.

That's exactly when the warning sirens started going off in my mind, *I don't think we're here to pick up our passports.*

That's when the squad of Chinese police that had disembarked from the transport vehicle marched into our waiting room one by one. The initial police officer that had collected our papers followed in last. He looked at us from across the room, *"Up"*, he ordered.

We glanced at each other as there must have been some confusion. *Had he confused us for someone else? We're here for our passports...*

"Up!" He shrieked, again.

Well fu&k me. He's not kidding around.

And up we went. *"Come."* The four of us were marched out the door, through the waiting room and out into the parking lot where we were surrounded by a group of CCP officers, and lined up next to the vehicle.

The four of us stood behind the van, surrounded by Beijing police.

"小龙" (Xiao Long) the lead officer read off of one paper, my Chinese name.

He looked up at the four of us to see who that was. I raised a hand and he jotted something down on the paper, as if he were calling roll.

He proceeded to read two more Chinese names, referencing Karl and Neil.

Finally, he looked over at Conan…handing him his Canadian passport. "*You… go inside*", he said to Conan, pointing back into the police station.

We, particularly Conan, stood there baffled.

Lead Officer: You new, don't break law again. Inside!

Conan's eyes were locked in a gaze of confusion staring straight at the lead officer's face. I stood close enough to see his dilated pupils gazing around trying to figure out what was happening.

Unamused by the delay, a Chinese officer reached out, grabbing him by the arm and proceeded to guide him back inside. The rest of us were still processing the severity of the situation and what fate might await Karl, Neil and I. Conan clearly didn't want to rock our already shaky boat, so he peacefully followed his escort back into the station.

It was as if the officers decided they would leave one of us to *tell the tale* while the rest of us were going to become the proverbial example. I was happy that Conan wasn't going to have to deal with whatever was about to come our way. He had been through enough recently and he certainly didn't deserve to have another mess like this on his shoulders.

The three of us, however, remained outside the van as Conan disappeared inside the station entrance.

But that momentary bliss of seeing Conan go free, vanished instantly. We were still here, surrounded by officers. *If he is going free, what is going to happen to us?*

We stood there in silence as it slowly started to drizzle. A couple of the officers proceeded to unlock the cage in the back of the van. The lead officer looked back at me, Karl and Neil and simply said, "*in*" nonchalantly nodding his head in the direction of the cage.

We looked at each other even more confused. "*Are we being arrested*" Karl stammered in confusion.

The officer didn't understand. "*In*" he repeated.

"为什么？" (why?) I asked, in protest. 我的签证没过期了，也合法的. (My visa is unexpired and legal) I stammered.

"我们不知道." (We don't know) another guard replied in frustration, expressing that it clearly wasn't my place to speak or question the process. We didn't budge.

If you've never been forcefully directed into a tiny cage against your will, take my word for it, it's an incredibly unpleasant experience.

The guards were becoming visibly unsettled by our refusal to instantly comply with the "enter cage" demand. They were shaking fingers at this point, emphasizing that they wouldn't have a problem physically stuffing us inside, if needed.

We looked around at each other and we realized that this was a demand, not a request. I bit the bullet and went in first, and one by one, Neil and Karl followed inside.

No explanation. No discussion. No charges. No lawyer. No courtroom. No English. No embassy call. Nothing.

TIC.

Once inside, the guards locked the cage door behind us. There was an ominous *clank* as the harsh reality of detention immediately swept over us. That feeling of isolation and complete helplessness is a complicated feeling to explain to someone who has never been forcefully locked up against their will.

I had no criminal record nor had I ever had any type of encounter with the police. This was an entirely new and disagreeable experience. *Baptism by fire.*

I didn't know what to expect. We had no idea where we were going or what we were being charged with.

At least we were still together, but for how much longer? The officers stood outside, looking over the paperwork talking amongst themselves for a few minutes. Once they got the all clear, they climbed back into the van. The driver turned the key in the ignition as the engine roared back to life.

He backed up, put the car in drive and proceeded to exit the main gate onto the main road where we had arrived. The last thing we saw was Conan peeking his head out of the police station entrance with a stunned look on his face, as we turned the corner. *Here we go.*

Neil: Where do you think they're taking us?

Me: I have no idea.

Karl: Are we under arrest?

Neil: Maybe?

Karl: Well we're not handcuffed.

Me: Maybe they're just bluffing to try and pull a bribe out of the company. We have your foreign staff, pay us money or we'll keep them.

Neil: All this for a bribe? Seems excessive, no?

Me: Should we call our embassy?

Karl: No...we aren't formally under arrest, I think? Let's not muddy the waters until we know what's happening.

Neil: This might all be for show. If we pull the embassy card now, maybe they'll send us to prison to prove a point?

Me: I don't know, I've heard if you're involved with the police in any way in a foreign country, you're supposed to contact your embassy immediately.

Karl: Can the embassy do anything if we are under arrest? We fall under Chinese jurisdiction anyway, right?

Me: I don't know...I'm going to call the US embassy and ask.

Neil: Don't! Not yet. We don't know what's happening.

Me: Well we're locked in a cage; how is this not arrest?

Neil: We still don't know where we're going.

Karl: What if we call all our embassies at once?

Me: I don't think they can collectively do anything.

Neil: Well they haven't taken our phones yet.

Me: Sure, but what if they do and then we can't contact anyone?

Karl: There is international legal protocol, they must contact our embassy.

Me: It's China, they don't care about international protocol.

Neil: Maybe they won't. But we still don't know where they're taking us...

There we were, a German, an American and a Spaniard...stuck in the middle of Beijing traffic, sitting in the back of a prison transport vehicle, surrounded by Beijing police, and locked inside of a cage. It sounded like the start to a terrible joke.

"What if our van gets hit from behind", I thought to myself? Maybe we'll die in this cage? What if they 'accidentally' lose the key? What if they run the car indoors and we die from carbon monoxide poisoning? Do they even know what carbon monoxide poisoning is? Where are we going? How long could I survive here? I have a protein bar in my backpack, but how long can I survive off of that?

My mind started racing at a million miles a minute. Every possible, horrific life-ending scenario was popping up in my mind. I'm not even claustrophobic, but being locked in a cage this way, under these conditions, was fundamentally terrifying.

The psychological effect on people facing false arrest and detention is pretty intense.

According to one study, "The Psychological and Legal Aftermath of False Arrest and Imprisonment" in the *Journal of the American Academy of Psychiatry and the Law*, false arrest victims face an elevated risk of suicide with the first 24 hours of incarceration. Furthermore, the detainee is likely to lose a sense of time as the process of being wrenched from your normal environment and plunged into a prison cell is a highly traumatic, "Kafkaesque experience." The extreme nature of the false arrest process can also cause psychiatric dissociative disorders.

Dissociative disorders can range from memory loss to suicidal behavior.

Bear in mind these are symptoms that can occur when someone is falsely detained in their own country, with due-process, familiarity of the detention system, and dealing with officers who are speaking in a language that they've known all their life.

This was fundamentally worse.

I had never been locked up in a cage before. I had no idea where we were going, or how much trouble we were in. It took every ounce of energy to simply stay calm, focus on my breathing and maintain composure.

Where are they taking us? How long are we going to spend here? What are the charges? Are there charges?

We had just been thrown head first into the undefined and unpredictable maze of China's underground and corrupt legal system for which there is no rulebook...by design. No paper-trail. No structure. No precedent. No rules. Luckily, our phones were still in our possession.

What on earth do we do?

Chapter 5:

Arrest (Part 2)

U.S. Department of State, Country Information: People's Republic of China

"The Chinese legal system can be opaque and the interpretation and enforcement of local laws arbitrary. The judiciary does not enjoy independence from political influence. U.S. citizens traveling or residing in China should be aware of varying levels of scrutiny to which you will be subject from Chinese local law enforcement and state security.

Criminal Penalties: You are subject to Chinese laws. If you violate Chinese laws, even unknowingly, you may be expelled, arrested, or imprisoned. Certain provisions of the PRC Criminal Law – such as "social order" crimes (Article 293) and crimes involving "endangering state security" and "state secrets" (Article 102 to 113) – are ill-defined and can be interpreted by the authorities arbitrarily and situationally. Information that may be common knowledge in other countries could be considered a "state secret" in China, and information can be designated a "state secret" retroactively.

Arrest Notification:

- *If you are arrested or detained, ask police or prison officials to notify the U.S. Embassy or the nearest consulate immediately.*
- *The Chinese must notify U.S. consular officer within four days; however, this does not always occur in a timely manner.*
- *A consular officer may be the only authorized visitor during your initial detention period.*

+   *Bail is rarely granted.*
+   *Detention may last many months before a trial."*[35]

We had been riding around in the cage for about ten minutes now, but it felt like we had been locked inside for ages. There was this odd mix of emotions we were trying to balance, confusion, anger, frustration, and outright concern. My brain flicked into "survival mode" and I just felt my senses push into overdrive; I was hyper-aware.

According to one study, "Doing Time: A Qualitative Study on Time Perception During Detention" published in the *Netherlands Journal of Psychology*, Western societies have a unique fascination with making the most of their time. With this concept in mind, the restricted freedom and idleness of detention causes the passage of time to seem "unbearable, slow, and snatched away." The passage of time in a cage becomes a painfully unpleasant burden for detainees to endure.

The process of detention is incredibly traumatic, especially for those who are experiencing it for the first time. The freedoms that we normally enjoy are instantaneously restricted or entirely eliminated. You feel psychologically trapped in the most uncomfortable way imaginable. Your sudden exposure to this external threat induces psychological trauma, further altering our perception of time.

In a separate study, "Subjective Time Dilation: Spatially Local, Object-Based, Or A Global Visual Experience?" published in the *Journal of Vision*, the passage of time is one of the most immutable aspects in the world. Concurrently, the passage of time also appears to be a fundamentally subjective and malleable experience. How often have we described time as "flying by" when we are having fun or "crawling by" when we're feeling bored? This phenomenon also occurs to an extreme degree when someone experiences a traumatic event, as time appears to slow dramatically.

But there was nothing we could do.

This was our new reality and it simply came down to a matter of self-discipline. Could we adapt to our new environment?

       +

---

[35] U.S. Department of State. August 3, 2017. International Travel > Country Information > China. *Travel.state.gov.* Retrieved: February 11, 2018, from https://travel.state.gov/content/travel/en/international-travel/International-Travel-Country-Information-Pages/China.html.

This is laughably unnecessary, I thought, as I looked around examining the metal bars. *Did they think we were some type of violent criminals? Had they mistaken us for someone else? Was this some sort of Chinese prank tv show?*

My anger was shifting back to the lack of civility in this process. Why had we initially been told, "come pick up your passports and that will be all." *Did they lie because they were worried, we might flee? Where would we even go?* Without so much as a warning, or explanation, that situation instantly evolved into, "get in the cage."

But why the sudden change? Why not be honest about what was going on in the first place? This is China.

Time grinded to a halt and being stuck in sluggish Beijing traffic compounded the feeling. Passengers and drivers in the surrounding gridlock looked on curiously at the three foreigners locked in the back of this cage. We were a fascinating spectacle for Beijing commuters.

Neil, Karl and I decided to cut our conversation short because we knew that anything we were saying was probably being monitored, if not recorded. In the unpredictable and ambiguous environment of the CCP, anything can be manipulated in their favor.

The officer next to you who *can't* understand a word you're saying, likely speaks fluent English. Chinese citizens who manage to flee this authoritarian system and land in the West, are still monitored 24/7 by CCP operatives:

> *"In New York's Chinese communities' people are wary of each other, afraid of honestly voicing their opinions. They know that what they say and do is being watched by individuals loyal to Beijing, and there are consequences for stepping out of line. "They said they can make me disappear," said Judy Chen, 55, recalling an encounter in New York with what she believes were Chinese agents.*

> *"It's very common knowledge," Chen said. "If you speak about the Chinese Communist Party, even among co-workers, they'll tell you to watch what you say." She added, casually,,that Chinese residents in New York will sometimes report people to the Chinese Embassy if they make comments critical of the Chinese regime.*

> *The Chinese regime has a well-organized system for controlling Chinese communities around the world. "Chinese operatives and consular officials,"*

it adds, "are actively engaged in the surveillance and harassment of Chinese dissident groups on U.S. soil."

According to Tang Baiqiao, founder of Democracy Academy of China, 'all the Chinese people know it.'"[36]

One thing you learn after you spend a few years in China is that the legal system has no protocol or precedent, by design.

I spent years describing the Chinese incarceration process to Americans and Europeans, and I'm usually flooded with a list of "but" questions. For example, "But couldn't you call a lawyer? But couldn't you contact your embassy? But couldn't you request a translator? But couldn't you...fill in the blank." We are so accustomed to a legal system replete with human rights and fail-safes that the idea of those not existing is alien for us to process.

"Legal" decisions can be made on the fly by CCP officials thanks to the arbitrary enforcement of laws, regardless of what laws are written on paper. The simple notion of implementing objective or uniform enforcement of the law is a completely nonexistent idea. And why would there be? That would mean allowing foreigners to operate on a level playing field with the Chinese. *By CCP standards, that would be a fundamentally stupid idea. Remember our friend Chi who believes the Chinese are the "superior" race to the Nazis?*

Therein lies China's strategic advantage if you ever decide to operate on their turf. The Chinese are always a few steps ahead because they've never *actually* agreed to anything, in the sense that Westerner's "agree." The enforcement mechanisms that you and I are used to in the West exist superficially in China. Sure, this can work to your advantage, until you end up locked in a cage.

The entire notion of something as basic as signing a "legally binding" contract in China is seen as a cumbersome "Western" endeavor, more ceremonial than legal. I've met plenty of Chinese who think Westerners are gullible for believing that a piece of paper would dictate business or government decisions.

The Chinese perspective on contracts shouldn't be surprising given the fundamentally corrupt legal system, absence of an independent judiciary, and anti-foreign sentiment that is preached by the CCP education system. Chinese

---

[36] Philipp, Joshua. July 7th, 2014. Chinese Expats Monitored, Harassed in NYC. *theepochtimes.com*. Retrieved April 29th, 2018, from https://www.theepochtimes.com/chinese-expats-monitored-harassed-in-nyc_790894.html.

businesses are well documented as "not abiding by the contract" or "changing contractual terms after they have been agreed."

According to the 2018 China Business Climate Survey Report conducted by AmCham China, 75% of respondents felt that foreign businesses were *less welcome in China than before*. An additional 63% of respondents cited that their 2018 increase in investment would be lower than their increase entering into 2017. Additionally, 60% of respondents cited "inconsistent regulatory interpretation and unclear laws" as the top business challenge for foreign companies operating in China.

Litigation is also largely seen as a foreign concept and not as readily pervasive in Chinese culture. Due to the ceremonial nature of contracts, Chinese firms don't really hire teams of lawyers to comb through details or waste months debating the use of the word "is" or the meaning of article X.

Chinese people and companies come first, always. Period.

It's no surprise then that the primary complaint (55%) made by American businesses operating in China was "prohibition/restrictions on market participation" followed by "enforcement of rules and regulations." So why does China so vehemently oppose the West's "egalitarian" business environment?

Complete, top to bottom, and thorough government oversight and control of everything. Remember, the CCP's goal is complete ownership and unilateral domination. Sadly, China doesn't only distrust foreigners; it also distrusts its own population.

The emergence of China's Social Credit System has been used to monitor every aspect of Chinese society. Imagine a credit score that isn't just ranking your financial behavior, but every single decision you make. The government adjusts your *personal citizen score* based on the websites you visit, who your friends are, adherence to government regulations and the type of content you access online. Based on those ambiguous parameters, your citizen score would arbitrarily move up or down, dictating your ability to access credit, a plane ticket, a mortgage, the type of hotel you can stay at, or the type of school your child can attend.

I'm not kidding.

Despite hearing about these things while I lived in China, I never stopped to think about a worst-case scenario. Detention was not something that ever crossed my mind as a realistic concern.

And yet, here I was…in the cage.

Luckily, I still knew where I was geographically.

We had turned onto 光华路 (Guang Hua Lu) which was a main road adjacent to Beijing's central artery, 建国门外大街 (Jian Guo Men Wai Da Jie). I was familiar with the area because I took this road, west, all the time traveling from my home to see clients in and around 远洋光华国际 (Office Park) and 世贸天街 (The Place), two very central and popular Beijing attractions. Suddenly, the van turned once again, and we were heading down a familiar road.

It was a bit of a shortcut I would take walking from Office Park to 中海广场写字楼 (another office complex) near Jianguomen's Outer Road.

After about 100 meters, the van pulled into an even smaller side road, crammed between two buildings. Surprisingly, there was another police station hidden on this tiny little side road that I hadn't noticed before. That's where the van came to a stop:

建国门外派出所 (Jianguomen Gate Outer, Police Station)

The police shut off the van, exited the vehicle and disappeared inside. Neil, Karl and I looked around at each other trying to piece together what the next step of this journey might be.

Was this our stop? Were they picking up some new prisoners for transport? More paperwork? Was anyone going to explain what was going on?

We waited for another 5 to 10 minutes until the police re-emerged outside. One of the cops pulled out a set of keys and unlocked the cage door.

Finally. Anywhere but here.

The cop motioned for us to exit. I didn't hesitate and practically leapt at the door. I stepped down through the back of the vehicle and emerged back into freedom. *THANK GOD! And I was an atheist at the time.* We probably hadn't spent more than 25 to 30 minutes in that cage, but It felt *AMAZING* to finally be let out of that steel box.

One by one, Neil and Karl stumbled out behind me. Once we had all gathered around in front of the police station, the guards motioned for us to follow them inside.

This station was far more run down than the other one. It was depressing to just step inside...*imagine working here every day. What a nightmare. I remembered the police officers' question, "do you know how much our salary is?"* The paint was chipping, the furniture was worn, the lighting was dim, and the overall environment just seemed...miserable.

Here we go again.

The guard led us through a central door that was opposite the main entrance. It branched off into a hallway with some faded cement ramp that led to a tiny room about two meters by two meters wide.

This used to be a jail cell?

It was missing a door and there were just large metal hinges attached to the frame. There was a tiny barred section on either side of the entrance, but the actual door seemed to have been torn off. It looked like a poor man's drunk tank. *The oddities continued.* There was a locker pushed up against the side of one wall, where it seemed like the cops stashed some of their personal belongings.

It was like a holding cell that doubled as a locker room?

Along the back there were three chairs...or at some point, there had been three chairs...that were mounted into the wall. Two of them were missing the "seat part" so it was more like two prongs protruding out from the wall, next to a single "functioning" chair.

This looks like a torture room.

We were marched into the drunk tank/storage room and told to stay put. It was tiny, damp, and filled by three other Chinese guests who also appeared to be detained. There was a female somewhere in her 30's and two other men.

One of the men, who also appeared to be in his 30's, seemed to know the woman. They weren't talking. The other gentleman was some older man who appeared to be in his 60's. He was handcuffed and sat there by himself in the only non-wall chair.

As we got settled in the police started to make their way back toward the central hall. "Why are we here?" I asked again in Chinese. "You're being assessed" the guard shouted without so much as a look in my direction. He disappeared around the corner before I could say another word.

The cell guard was sat just outside of our cell. He was an old man who was wearing a different uniform than the police who dropped us off. His uniform was unkept and tattered which seemed to match the conditions of our new environment. He sat there with a smile on his face playing some game on his phone.

"Why are we here?" I asked him in Chinese. "I'm not the police." He replied without looking up. "What are we being charged with," I responded? "And how long will we be here?" I asked. "I'm just a guard. I don't know you" he responded waving his hand to signal that the questions needed to stop.

The other Chinese nationals in the cell looked at each other in confusion. I wasn't sure if they were shocked that I took that tone questioning the guard or if they were surprised that I could speak Mandarin.

Neil, Karl and I finished examining our surroundings and looked up at each other.

Neil: Holding cell?

Me: I guess so.

Karl: What did the guard say?

Me: He has no idea why we're here

Neil: Isn't he police?

Me: I don't think he knows what's going on. He says he's just the guard. Look at his uniform. I'm gonna call the US embassy.

Neil: No! Not yet. What if this is just for show while they pull a bribe from the school. Ha, we got your teachers, now pay up.

Me: I think we're detained. Isn't the protocol that we contact our embassy if we are detained abroad?

Karl: Yea, but we haven't been 'charged' with anything yet. Let's not muddy the waters.

Me: Watters seem pretty muddy after the cage.

Neil: That might have just been for show.

Karl: Well at what point should we call and notify them?

Me: We still have our phones. What if they confiscate them? Then we can't call even if we want to.

Karl: Aren't they legally required to notify if they detain a foreign national?

Me: It's China, they don't follow 'protocol'.

Neil: Ok, well give it some time first and see where things are in like an hour or two.

Me: If I'm still here in an hour, I'm definitely going to call.

Karl: Do you think they're keeping us here that long?

Me: Maybe? I haven't been detained in China before.

Neil: I knew a guy who was arrested for working illegally, and they held him until his school paid a fine.

Me: Wouldn't a bribe have already been paid?

Karl: I had a roommate that was caught working on a tourist visa a few years back. They made him pay a fine and let him go after signing a confession document.

Neil: Is that what we signed in the first police station?

Me: I still think we should call our embassy. Maybe they can do something collectively to petition our release. It is still daytime and they're in their offices.

Neil: Not yet. Let's just wait this out for now.

Chapter 6:

Processing (Part 1)

Chinese 're-education camps' for Uighur Muslims run like 'concentration camps', says Amnesty

The United Nation's Committee on the Elimination of Racial Discrimination (CERD) estimates over a million ethnic Uighurs and other Muslim minorities have been detained in Chinese re-education camps without being charged or tried.[37]

Chinese Government's official response to CERD's report on Uighur re-education camps. Chinese Foreign Ministry Spokesperson Hua Chunying's press conference, August 30, 2018:

"Q: Some US lawmakers called for the US government to impose sanctions on Chinese officials responsible for "human rights abuses against minority Uyghurs in China's Xinjiang". What is your comment?

A: ... The Chinese government protects its citizens' right to freedom of religious belief and people of all ethnic groups enjoy freedom of religious belief in accordance with the law. We hope the US side could recognize and respects facts, discard prejudice and stop doing or saying anything to undermine mutual trust and cooperation between the two sides.

---

[37] China's Muslim 'RE-EDUCATION centres' are run LIKE 'concentration camps', AMNESTY researcher says. (2018, December 16). Retrieved February 28, 2021, from https://www.independent.co.uk/news/world/asia/china-muslims-re-education-camps-amnesty-uighur-religion-human-rights-watch-a8678156.html

> *I would like to advise those US lawmakers, who are paid by taxpayers'*
> *money, to focus on doing their job and serving the Americans, instead*
> *of poking their noses in other countries' domestic affairs, acting as some*
> *kind of "human rights judge" to make groundless accusations, or even*
> *threatening to impose unreasonable sanctions."*

Me: It's been like five or six hours you guys.

Neil: We should probably call.

Karl: We still haven't been charged with anything.

Me: We agreed on an hour.

Neil: Even if we call, they can't do anything.

Me: Embassies are still supposed to be notified.

Karl: The other detainees were released, we might be?

Me: The police aren't answering any of our questions.

Neil: They could tell us how long we'll be here for.

Me: If our embassies work together, wouldn't they be able to do something?

Karl: I'm pretty sure we're being processed for detention.

Neil: Do your phones still have battery left?

Me: I'm at like 40%.

Neil: I'm at like 30%. What if they confiscate our phones?

We had been standing in this cold, isolated, enclosure for somewhere around 5 hours at this point staring at the barren and tainted cement cinder block walls and dirty lockers. It was somewhere around 3:00 pm now and we were frustrated. The room was cold. There was no food. No information. No explanation. No charges. No translator. Nothing.

Welcome to cage number two.

The old guard seated outside gave us an occasional laugh. He would gleefully wave his phone around as he scored points playing his game. Aside from that, he still refused to speak to us.

Police would pass through the hall beyond our holding cell from time to time. They didn't want to stop and chat either.

Hour, after hour, after hour went by…but we were still starved for information. My repeated attempts to get answers, in Chinese, were largely ignored with a disapproving look of, "We don't answer to you foreigners."

As time crept by, we took turns sitting in the one available chair. We tried messaging contacts in and around Beijing to see if anyone could help. People were responsive, but there wasn't much they could do. In China, citizens don't involve themselves in police and government matters. Even the police fear the government:

> *"A policewoman from central China's Henan Province was recently arrested when visiting her daughter in the provincial capital Zhengzhou. Mistakenly accused of being sex workers, the woman and her daughter were beaten, tortured and detained for hours by local police.*
>
> *Not only did this poor policewoman suffer the punches of her male counterparts, when she attempted to persuade them they were making a mistake by showing her own police ID they laughed at her. And when she requested to see the policemen's credentials, they told her that their uniform was all the ID she needed to see.*
>
> *If the victim had not been a policewoman and the media not reported the story, the police would have quietly filed the incident, which would have been considered as an ordinary, negligible affair. Not only would the policemen not have been punished, they would most likely have been praised internally for being "resolute" or "loyal to the party."*
>
> *There is also the idea that the police force is one big family that protects its own, allowing them to do what they please."*[2]

Sometime around 4:00 pm a group of Chinese officers marched into our holding cell. "Phones" was all that was said, with an outstretched arm in our direction. *Oh boy…there goes our only option of communicating with the outside world.*

I handed it over, but the officer refused. "你的密码 (your password)?" Oh great, *they want our unlocked phones. What have Karl and Neil been up to? Drugs? Prostitution? Gambling? If they've done something wrong, do I get lumped in and charged as well? Why wouldn't I…this is China…there is no legal precedent.*

As usual, the password wasn't a request, it was an order. There was a group of Chinese police staring us down in a tiny cell. There wasn't much wiggle room. *Password entered, phone handed over.* The others followed suit. And out they walked, with our unlocked phones in hand.

Me: Well, there's that.

Neil: Oh boy…I wonder if we get them back?

Karl: So, you guys haven't done anything particularly *wrong* recently have you?

Me: Yea, murder? Just twice though.

Neil: Black-market heroin fueling the drug trade.

Karl: Fabulous!

Me: So now what? When we get our phones back, I'm definitely calling. This is absurd.

Karl: This doesn't seem like it's going to end soon.

Neil: Seems like they're preparing us for detention. There's no reason to hold us this long.

Me: Or confiscate our phones.

Another hour crept by. Nothing.

I was fed up. I marched right past the old guard playing games on his phone and out of the cell towards a group of police. It just felt good to be out of that damp, dark, depressing holding cell…even though I had only walked about five feet. It was a *relief!* Simply having the opportunity to make a decision again was refreshing.

"Why are we in here?" I demanded in Chinese. The police weren't thrilled, and once again stared me down. "I want to call the US embassy right now." I demanded in Chinese. "Go back" one of the officers said. "We've been in here for over six hours, why are we here?" "Back", the same officer demanded, raising his finger, pointing at the cell. "I want to contact the US embassy right now" I demanded again, "I'm NOT a Chinese citizen."

The guards weren't pleased with that one.

They started physically moving in my direction with a number of them starting to bark orders. This momentary allusion of freedom was refreshing… but short-lived.

I got the message and quickly receded back into the holding cell. *But they got the message as well.* I made it clear that I wanted to get in touch with the *American embassy* and that I *wasn't* a Chinese national. It wasn't much, but it had to hold some weight.

Another 30 to 45 minutes went by until a group of Chinese police marched back in with our phones in hand. *Finally, I'm going to call,* I thought. They handed over our phones and walked out. I looked up the American embassy's phone number in Beijing and stored it in my phone. I dialed the number, but for some reason…the call wasn't going through.

Odd, I thought.

I had a clear signal and my 4G was working. It's just that the call wasn't going through.

Me: You guys getting a signal?

Neil: I'm still not calling. This might be the end of it. What if they release us after all of this?

Karl: I'm pretty sure we're being detained.

Me: You're holding on to false hope Neil. I don't think this is going where you're thinking it is.

Neil: Call if you want. I get it. I'm not going to.

Karl: It holds more weight if we all call.

Neil: I don't think it matters.

Me: My call isn't going out.

Another hour went by. And then another. The battery life on our phones was fading. No food. No water. No explanation. No communication with the outside world. I was hungry though; *I guess I had that?*

For those who haven't been arbitrarily and forcefully detained, it's hard to explain the many things that flood your mind. Arguably, the hardest part is the first few hours because the instant, and unexpected, transition from freedom to detention is impossible to put into words. Basic things we generally never think about, like the freedom to move or basic privacy...are all instantly stripped away.

If you're detained in the U.S., you are *legally protected* in a million different ways. Bail, a lawyer, a phone call, medical assistance, food, *someone that speaks your language*, a Miranda Warning, human rights groups, etc. Informed Chinese citizens are aware of these differences in the US. They will chuckle at the idea that anything we do is remotely categorized as "punishment."

What is there to fear from the police in America? They are more restrained than the criminals.

Not in China. This absence of uniform due-process compounds the already high levels of anxiety, stress and confusion that have overloaded your brain. Locking humans in cages has destructive psychological effects on mental health and has been studied extensively.

One such study was performed back in the 1950's, "Vertical-Chamber Confinement of Juvenile-Age Rhesus Monkeys. A Study in Experimental Psychopathology" in the *Archives of General Psychiatry*, placed rhesus monkeys inside a custom-designed solitary chamber nicknamed 'the pit of despair.' The pit was shaped like an inverted pyramid, with slippery sides, making it impossible to climb out of the central chamber.

The University of Wisconsin psychologist Harry Harlow found that after a day or two of putting the monkeys inside the inescapable chamber, "most subjects typically assume a hunched position in a corner of the bottom of the apparatus. One might presume at this point that they find their situation to be hopeless...profoundly disturbed, given to staring blankly and rocking in place for long periods, circling their cages repetitively, and mutilating themselves."

Detention changes you instantly.

At this point, it was around 7:00 pm. We were starving and one of the guards was nice enough to respond to our request to eat. He brought us a tray of food from the police canteen. It wasn't much but the three of us scarfed it down *immediately*.

We were closing in on the ten hour mark when a new group of Chinese police marched back into the holding cell. "You are being detained. Let's go." One of them ordered. We glanced at each other disapprovingly. Karl was shaking his head in frustration staring straight at the ground. On one hand, we were happy to be leaving this depressing cell. *Then again, what might come next?*

Cage three?

Well at least we know something now. Sadly, that was a victory at this point...access to information. Moving forward, even with limited information, did make me feel somewhat relieved. Nonetheless, this long-awaited answer yielded an infinite number of new questions:

How long will we be detained? Where are we being detained? What happens after detention? Will we be detained together?

Fu&k it, let's just get going. We picked up our gear and proceeded to exit the cell. Once again, the swarm of Chinese police officers entered to escort us back to the main entrance. I shot one last glance back at the empty cell as I made my way forward.

Beyond the front doors we were greeted by Beijing's freezing cold winter conditions. Day had faded into night and our police swarm led us toward yet another transport vehicle. *Back in the cage?* As we got closer, I realized it was a *normal police van! Thank God! NO cage this time.*

One of the police officers opened the door and ordered us to sit down in the back of the van. What the vehicle lacked in cage, it more than made up for in sheer police force. There seemed to be around two police officers for each one of us...*just in case the nonviolent foreign teachers got a little out of hand and tried to break free? And escape where...exactly?*

We were back on the road at this point as our van disappeared into a cold and black Beijing night. Once again, we had no idea where we were heading or what would come next.

Me: Well now we know. I'm calling my embassy.

Neil and Karl didn't offer a single word of dissent this time and immediately followed suit. It seemed like the police had been through the "foreigners in detention" drill before. They were aware of our next move and surprisingly, let us proceed to call our respective embassies.

I didn't know if our phones would be confiscated a second time or how much time we had left on the road, so I needed to get this done immediately. I had a million things racing through my mind.

Does my roommate have my parents phone number? Do I call my parents first? Do I get my parents in touch with my business partners? Do I call my brother to tell my parents? Should I get any other family in touch with my roommates? What time is it in the US? Is the US Embassy in Beijing open? Do I also call the Swiss embassy (Dual-citizen)? Should I call both and have them coordinate? Can the US embassy call my parents? Who should I notify?

My first call was to the US embassy in Beijing which has a special emergency number for US citizens in China. I dialed the number and ended up on the phone with a very calm and experienced female Consular Officer from the US embassy in Beijing. It was really odd, but I could actually hear the desperation and concern in my own voice...this was my one lifeline to the outside world.

What on Earth do I say? There is no rulebook for this kind of thing:

Me: I've been detained, and my name is Steven Schaerer. I'm a US citizen. I've been working in Beijing for nearly 5 years. I've spent all day detained in a holding cell without any official charges.

U.S. Embassy: Ok, sir please remain calm. I've got you. Please read your name back to me.

It was SO good to hear an American accent on the other end.

Me: First name: Steven, S-T-E-V-E-N. Last name: Schaerer, S-C-H-A-E-R-E-R. I'm a US citizen from California. They're saying we're working illegally, but I have a company here in Beijing with a legal/unexpired work visa. I overheard the guards saying we'd be detained for around 2 weeks?

U.S. Embassy: Ok, are you with anyone?

Me: Yes, I have two colleagues here with me. A German national and a Spanish national who are on the phone with their embassies right now. It seems we're all being detained under the same charges.

U.S. Embassy: Ok sir and what is your visa number, do you know where they are taking you?

Me: My visa number is XXXXXXX and it seems like we're heading south. I've overheard them mention DaXing District a couple times. They've mentioned processing us and detention. I'm guessing our personal items will be confiscated. Is there anything you can do, or I should know?

U.S. Embassy: Sir, we'll notify the relevant authorities here in the embassy. Embassy representatives do have the right to petition for a visit and we'll do our best to send someone from the embassy out to come see you. Remember to stay calm, we're aware of the situation. You do fall under Chinese jurisdiction, so we can't pry you out, but we certainly can petition the relevant Chinese authorities to keep us apprised of your condition and make sure everything follows Chinese legal protocol. Try to notify your family members as well.

The rest of the conversation was a blur, but I got off the phone pretty fast when I realized everything I could possibly say or do had been done. I felt partially relieved knowing the embassy heard from me directly. Next call was to my parents. "Hey mom and dad, I know it's 4:00 am but I'm about to be detained for an indefinite period of time in a communist country on the other side of the planet. Good morning!"

In the background, there was a whirlwind of Spanish (Karl with his embassy) and German (Niel) with the German embassy.

Me: Hey dad.

Dad: Hey, it's late. Are you ok?

I had clearly woken him up. I could hear it in his voice.

Me: I'm being detained in Beijing. They said I'm working illegally. I guess I'll be held for around 2 weeks, but I don't think I'll be allowed to call you in that time. I'm being arrested with a colleague from Germany and another guy from Spain. I've already contacted the US embassy. You can contact my business partner John and my roommate Adam at this number XXXXXXX.

Dad: What the fu&k??????!!!?!?!?!? What?!?!?!???!??

Mom: You're being arrested?!!

Me: Yes, I'm being arrested. I'll be detained for two weeks then released. Here are my roommate's numbers, the US embassy in Beijing, and my business partner.

Dad: Are you ok?

Me: I'll be fine, you know that. Just talk to the embassy, John, Adam and my brother. Don't worry if you don't hear from me for a couple weeks. I can take care of myself. I have to go now. Love you, bye.

Mom: Love you too, we'll call the embassy right away.

Time to call my brother. The Swiss embassy. My business partners in Beijing. My roommates. Same conversation. Same surprise and shock, every single

73

time. My goal was simple. Get all of these people in touch with each other immediately. There had to be a strong network working on this.

Once the calls were made, my phone was at around 10% battery life. I decided to shut it down. Who knew what surprises lie ahead? I felt a bit relieved having all these people in touch with each other and with the US embassy. Together, they were a powerful force and it put me a bit at ease.

There was nothing more I could do.

What the f7ck happens now?

Chapter 7:

Processing (Part 2)

Tibetan Monk Tortured for 3 Decades in China's Prisons Dies

The United Nation's Committee on the Elimination of Racial Discrimination (CERD) reports that Tibetan Buddhists are routinely charged under vague, broad and unclear definitions of terrorism and separatism in Chinese legislation. The report also highlights concerns about reports of Tibetan Buddhists being tortured, subject to travel restrictions within and beyond Tibet, restricted from learning the Tibetan language, barred from language translations during court proceedings and discriminated from employment.[38]

Chinese Government's official response to report highlighting CCP's torture of Tibetan Buddhists. Chinese Foreign Ministry Spokesperson Liu Jianchao's press conference, December 11, 2008:

"Q: Yesterday, the Free Tibet Campaign issued a report, saying that torture prevails in Tibet because the local government deliberately ignores the law that prevents torture. Do you have any comments?

A: We have taken note of relevant report. We believe torture is an infringement on human rights. To prevent and punish torture is the common responsibility of all countries in the world. The Chinese Government resolutely opposes torture, and Chinese law prohibits torture.

---

[38] Tibetan monk tortured for 3 decades in China's Prisons dies. (n.d.). Retrieved February 28, 2021, from https://www.voanews.com/south-central-asia/tibetan-monk-tortured-3-decades-chinas-prisons-dies

> *I wonder whether the organization you mentioned has any evidence to prove there is torture in Tibet. If there are specific evidences, we are ready to carry out investigation. But we don't accept groundless accusation."*

"小龙" (Xiao Long, Chinese name)! 来 (lai, come)!

Stop number three for the day. Another police station…

I marched forward, complying with the officers demands. Over the course of our 12-hour detention, this was the first time I didn't know where we were, geographically. *I was officially lost.* I knew that we had been traveling south and I had overheard them discussing Beijing's DaXing District.

We sat through the rest of the car ride in silence. One by one, our frantic calls to family, embassies and local contacts slowly died down. One by one, reality overtook us as we came to terms with the fact that *our fate would now fall into the hands of the Communist Chinese Party.*

Yay.

It was somewhere around 9:00 pm when we arrived at the next destination… another police station. Our police-swarm escorted us out of the transport vehicle and inside. As soon as we entered, we took a hard left and marched through a hall into the far back of what seemed to be an empty building. The lights were entirely shut off, and we didn't encounter another person the entire way. *Maybe this place was only used for processing?* This facility seemed to be far better than all the rest. Modern equipment and a sleek design; it seemed new.

At the end of the hall, we turned left and were escorted into a room. As the motion detector lights flickered on it became apparent that this room was used for collecting biometric data. In the center of the room there was a desktop computer sat on top of a swivel desk. There were several contraptions and machines scattered along the perimeter of the room…scales, scanners, pads, and machines I didn't recognize.

The way the room was setup immediately made me think of alien abduction stories. Abductees would describe how they were lifted into a UFO's medical bay where aliens would experiment. To be fair, we had technically been abducted as well, except this was the human version that ran off a Windows platform.

One of the officers separated from our escort swarm and plopped down right in the middle of the room at the central command desk. He instantly got to work as the computer as the screen sprang to life, and other machines in the room simultaneously flickered on. Another officer walked over handing him a stack of papers with our information plastered across it: mugshots, personal data, etc.

The biometric room was significantly bigger than our holding cell had been, around five meters wide by five meters long? The officers had ordered the three of us to stand by the door, where we waited patiently. Interestingly, it was around this time that the officers came to the realization that the three of us posed absolutely no threat to anyone.

A couple of the officers even seemed sleepy. They were probably frustrated that six of them had to work the late shift and drag three harmless foreigners around Beijing all night. *They took this opportunity to take a break.* They kept around four police officers in the room to maintain a numerical advantage… *just in case.* This gave one of the officers the opportunity to grab some water while another ran off to the bathroom.

While the younger officers were out, the lead officer at central command was becoming increasingly annoyed. He was having problems operating the abduction software. A couple of the other more tech savvy officers slowly closed in to try and assist, which seemed to frustrate him more. We stood by and waited as he re-started the machine for a second time. Karl was tired, and quickly growing impatient.

Karl: Is any of this necessary?

Me: No. But they sure think it is.

Karl: Can't they just detain us and let's get this thing over with?

Neil: It's going to take however long it takes.

Karl: This is idiotic.

Me: We don't have much of a choice. What are you going to do?

"小龙" (Xiao Long, Chinese name)! 来 (lai, come)!

Guess the machines are working.

They were done trying to translate at this point. "Hand" the officer instructed in Chinese. I approached what seemed to be a hefty fingerprint scanner that was sat next to the central command desk. I placed my hand on the device and followed the instructions. That didn't satisfy one of the police officers, however, so he wrapped his hand around my wrist and forced it down. It was a simple move to assert his authority over the situation.

Karl's not going to handle this well, I thought.

One by one the machine scanned my hand, then each individual finger, then the right side of my palm, then the left, and finally the bottom. *Well...they have that now!*

"Foot" the officer at central command bellowed.

Another officer moved me along to the next contraption which sat square in the middle of the room. This one was laid across the ground, adjacent to the desk. Putting two and two together I realized that this was some sort of weight distribution sensor. "Stand still", the guard ordered in Chinese.

One of the officers stepped on the platform, demonstrating that I needed to stand on the footsteps that were painted on the floor pad. I followed suit, stepped up, and well...stood. I looked over at the central command desk and saw the officer clicking his mouse, until he motioned for me to step off.

The "wrist grab" officer looked over at me and said, "one step, right foot" following with a quick demonstration. *So, this one measures the weight distribution of my gait?* "3, 2, 1" the guard counted backwards in Chinese, "go." And "go" I did, taking one step onto the platform with my right foot and then stepped off.

"Again" shouted the guard from central command. *The sensor apparently failed. Shitty abduction technology.* I re-oriented myself at the front of the sensor and waited for his countdown, "3, 2, 1...". Once again, I stepped. Once again, *the sensor failed.*

This is going to take a while. I looked over at Karl who was visibly flustered at this point. *He hadn't even gone yet.*

After a few more tries, they got it to work. Same process for the left foot. Once the "gait sensor reading" was complete I was directed by wrist-grab officer to stand on the weight scale. I hobbled over and stood on the scale until they got my measurements. Lastly, they had me stand by a chart on the wall to measure my height. They snapped a photo and voila...that was all. Weight, height, and fingerprint scan? That made sense. But the weight distribution of my gait?

Are they investigating a crime scene?

They asked me to step back and stand by the door, next to Neil and Karl.

Neil was called next which meant Karl had to wait longer. *He breathed a deep sigh of despair.* Once again, he was visibly frustrated, shaking his head at the ground. *Patience wasn't a Karl virtue.* Unsurprisingly, the sensors and scanners failed on Neil a few times as well. The scanner didn't like his hand, and the weight sensor struggled with his step. Ultimately, Neil powered through like a champ and was sent back to stand next to me at the door.

Finally, it was Karl's turn…he wasn't a fan of the wrist grab…but you could tell he was mustering all his strength to try and deal with it. Every wrist grab prompted him to roll his eyes and shoot frustrated looks at Neil and I. The weight-gait thing crashed on him too prompting the central command officer to restart the computer, again.

Karl was visibly breathing heavily in frustration at this point. Funny enough, Karl was a "big government" type of guy. Today was Karl's lucky day. He was getting a heavy overdose of government.

Surprisingly, Karl managed to finish without causing some type of altercation with the police. Neil and I were legitimately concerned about him lashing out, not fully understanding the consequences of his actions, and getting all of us into more trouble. By the time everything was wrapped up, it was around 10:00 pm.

There's not much more they could possibly know about us at this point.

One by one, the police shut off the machines and switched off the lights in the room. Once again, the cops marched us out of the room but were nice enough to let us use the restroom and grab some water on the way out. While I was peeing, I glanced around the bathroom to see if there was anything that I would be able to utilize through the rest of this odd Chinese abduction. *Yup! Toilet paper.*

I collected a few sheets and snuck them into my coat pocket. *You never know.* Out we marched, back to the van, where we piled in. We turned right out of the parking lot and made our way back to the main road, once heading further south.

Where now?

We had been on the road for about ten minutes or so when I thought, why not strike up a conversation with one of the officers? I overheard a lot of their chatter at this point, but I figured it would be a good opportunity to do some recon. None of them spoke more than a few words of English, or so we were led to believe. The two officers assigned to me were younger and seemed to be around my age, in their mid to late 20's.

These two guys were surprisingly nice. There was some tension from the lead officers as a result of their willingness to converse with me. The rest of the police-swarm didn't say anything but looked displeased at the three of us talking. At the same time, they could sense that we weren't violent criminals, so they kind of let it go:

Me: Do you know where we are being taken?

Officer 1: You'll be taken to a detention center in DaXing District.

Me: Why are we being detained?

Officer 2: Illegal employment.

I had already argued with the cops enough throughout the day that I was innocent, which produced no meaningful results. These guys were willing to talk, which was more than I could ask for. I wasn't about to start arguing my case, surrounded by six cops going 70+ mph on a dark freeway:

Me: How long will we be detained.

Officer 1: Should be 14 days.

Me: For all three of us?

Officer 1: Yes.

Me: How are the conditions in the detention center.

Officer 1: Not bad. It's short-term detention and this is where the foreigners are brought so the conditions will be better than where the Chinese are brought. It has food and it's heated.

'Not bad'…food and heat. So, we won't be starved…that's…positive? Wonder what the Chinese conditions are like?

Me: Will we be held together? Is it like a room?

Officer 1: I'm not sure.

Officer 2: I don't think so. There are other detainees, probably separated.

Me: So, like a prison, or like a room?

Officer 2: It's locked and monitored.

It seemed like they knew where we were going but it didn't seem like they had seen the interior of the detention facility.

Me: So, after 14 days, we'll get to leave?

Officer 1: Maybe, it depends on your situation. Usually deported though.

Me: Deported????

Officer 2: Yes, but depends on the case.

Deported?! For starting a company??

Karl: Did he just say deported?!?

Me: I guess it depends on the individual case.

Neil: That seems a bit harsh, no?

Karl: If we get deported, are we banned from returning?

Neil: I mean, Karl, technically you and I are on illegal visas.

Me: I'm not. I have a legal work visa.

Neil: Well, maybe just Karl and I will be deported.

Karl: This is absurd. The companies processed our visas. Why aren't they being charged with anything? That's how all these Chinese companies operate in Beijing.

Neil: Those are Chinese companies, they're not foreigners. Different standards, you know that.

We had been on the road for about thirty minutes when we finally arrived at destination four. This time we were driven underground into an expansive parking garage. This seemed to be another restricted government area. The police keyed in a special code and proceeded to drive around to some large underground hanger.

Down here, we were wholly closed off from the rest of the world. This place gave me the creeps. It was too isolated, empty and desolate. They could say and do just about anything they wanted to us down here.

That wasn't a reassuring feeling.

The van was parked, and we were unloaded and marched through a door into a short hall. There were two elevator shafts and the guard pressed the button. The elevator arrived, and we went up to the second floor of the building.

We exited the elevator, surrounded by our police swarm, and entered a huge hallway that was crammed with people. I couldn't see a single foreigner; everyone was Chinese. The hall was dimly lit, with chairs that were bolted into the ground lined up and down the walls. Doors dotted both sides of the hall.

I was shocked at how many people there were as it was almost 11:00 pm. Police officers, handcuffed criminals, families, kids...all on full display. *Processing center*, I thought. *I guess we'll finally receive our charges?* The cops marched us up the hall where we were told to wait. The two cops that seemed to be in charge marched off with their papers leaving the other four with us.

We drew a lot of attention as the only foreigners in this massive complex, as we were escorted around by our police-swarm. It was as if the entire hall stopped to stare at us as we waited. "What are these foreigners being charged with? What did they do?" seemed to be the questions on everyone's mind.

We don't know either guys.

After around five minutes, the two police officers returned with more papers in hand and ordered us to march towards the opposite end of the hall from where we originally entered. This time we were brought all the way to the end of the corridor and turned left into another big waiting room. Everyone stopped and stared at us.

The walls of the room were dotted with plastic blue chairs that were bolted into the wall. Most of them were occupied aside from a handful in the corner, which is where we were ordered to sit. Toward the front of the room was a large group of desks bolted into the ground. There was a team of three officers wearing clean-cut blue uniforms trying to orchestrate chaos at this central desk. Their tables were flooded with documents and they were clearly overworked. Arresting officers were constantly approaching them and lobbing a volley of questions in their direction. At the same time, family members of other detainees were busily trying to get their attention.

The entire thing was utter chaos.

I'm honestly not sure how they got anything done.

After around ten minutes of sitting and waiting, our police-swarm ordered us to stand up and marched us over to one of the desks. A female officer stood up and approached us in her finely pressed blue uniform. The look on her face screamed that she was overworked and tired. She proceeded to look at a new stack of papers she had just been handed and proceeded to call out our three names in Chinese. Each name corresponded to a different form with our information and pictures on them.

Desk Officer: Sign here.

Me: What am I signing?

Desk Officer: You broke the law, worked illegally and will be charged to 14 days in Chinese detention.

She pointed down at the paper where it said 14 days in Chinese.

One last try.

Me: I have a legal and unexpired work visa in Beijing, legal work permit, and founded a company here. I am not illegally employed as my work permit is linked to my business.

Desk Officer: You will spend 14 days in detention then be released.

Me: No lawyer? No translator?

Desk Officer: No. Sign here.

It was late. I was tired. At this point, it had become painfully clear: *nobody gave a flying f7ck.* In China, the desk officer says you're guilty...you're guilty. That's that. *They could have charged us with murder for all we know.*

I signed the document. It wasn't a question, it was another order. Neil and Karl followed suit. Both tried to ask similar questions and they too, were roundly rejected and ignored. She collected the papers and the officers marched us back to the elevators, and down into the parking garage. *Back into the van.*

Well, we're officially "guilty" now.

We hopped back on the main road for what seemed to be the last time. We continued south for another twenty minutes or so until we exited onto the offramp, driving further and further off the beaten path. *If they wanted, they could say we tried to escape, kill all three of us and no one would ever figure out what happened.*

Unmarked gravesites, end of story.

I tried to stay positive and shifted back into survival mode. *Figure it out, develop a plan, and push through this. Stay positive. It can't be that bad.* "It's where we put the foreigners" after all, the officer said. *Probably something uncomfortable to sleep on. Maybe we will be able to stay housed with each other? Maybe we'll make some friends and have a good story to laugh about afterwards? Maybe it's just foreigners. Maybe we'll get to keep our phones and stay in touch with family. Maybe it'll just be like a vacation in a really bad hostel?*

At this point, I knew that we had been driving through DaXing District for some time now as it had been plastered all over the road signs.

It felt late. We were closing in on midnight, and around fifteen hours of detention at this point. We were tired and hungry. And the hours of stress and confusion were kicking in.

Our van slowed down after the last turn and came to a stop. We were parked outside of something that a massive steel gate that seemed like the entrance to a military fortress. It must have been at least 20 or 30 feet high.

The outer perimeter had high fences with barbed wire and armed guards on patrol.

Not a hostel. Not even a detention center. I quickly realized this was a pretty intense prison compound.

Karl, Neil and I looked around at each other. We were all thinking the same thing.

WTF is this?!

The van pulled up to the exterior gate to talk to the guards stationed outside. They let them know they were transporting detainees and showed them our paperwork. The guard went back inside to his control room and the massive gate doors slowly rumbled open. Just inside, a second large gate opened in quick succession, and our transport van pulled through. There was a single road through the center of what seemed like the prison's central courtyard. It was full of dead or dying foliage.

At the end of this road was a single row of parking spaces sat right in front of a massive structure. To the left there was another multi-floor building that ran perpendicular to the main building.

Around the perimeter of this main structure stood 12 to 14-foot walls protruding everywhere with barbed wire. *I wonder where they house murderers? I wonder what the conditions were like in the place they don't bring foreigner detainees?*

We exited the van and entered the main building.

Attempting to re-trace the exact location of where this compound was geographically located was just about impossible to find online. Chinese search engines repeatedly came up empty. It took extensive research on Chinese forums to find the actual address of where we had been taken. CCP officials want these locations to remain hidden.

After an exhaustive online search, I eventually found the exact location of this prison compound. What popped up on the actual map? Absolutely nothing. You can find it if you know what you're looking for through satellite imagery, but you can't get a name for the location, a description, an address, or much of anything.

This location didn't exist. Not to locals, not to foreigners. We didn't exist anymore.

Our van parked just outside the main building and we were escorted straight into the lobby. The lobby looked, surprisingly, stunning. It was decorated with potted plants, sleek marble tiled floors, and a large reception area filled with oversized black sofas. The ceiling was super high, a large electronic display board was hung along the back wall, and everything was freshly painted. If you hadn't been told, it would be almost impossible to know that you had just entered a detention center.

Maybe this won't be so bad after all. Maybe this really is a "nice" place for foreign detainees?

At this point three of the officers walked off to process our paperwork with the guards at reception. Opposite the large lobby's grand reception desk was a holding cell...*which looked like a fish tank for humans.* This one didn't have any bars, but it's two forward facing walls that were made from what seemed to be thick, bullet proof glass.

Inside was a row of neatly lined up chairs, bolted into the ground, as we had seen earlier. But the room didn't scream "detention." *It almost seemed welcoming.* Two of the officers sat us down and stood guard until the paperwork was finished at the front desk.

Me: This doesn't look bad.

Neil: I have a feeling the rooms won't be like this.

Karl: Do you think they're rooms or cells?

Me: Maybe rooms with barred windows?

Neil: It doesn't seem like there's a lot of people here.

Karl: Well it is past midnight.

Me: Do you think it's only foreigners?

Karl: Maybe, isn't that what the guy said earlier?

Once the paperwork was processed, the police returned and said we had to do a medical check.

Again?? Didn't we just do this?!

I volunteered to go first. *We'll just get it done with.* I was marched across the hall, alone, into another medical room.

It wasn't pleasant by any stretch of the imaginations as it reminded me of what psychiatric facilities looked like in movies. Barred windows. Sad white walls with chipping paint. A closed metal door. This was a substantial change from the elegance of the main lobby just outside. I entered inside with one Chinese police officer and a female nurse, who had a facemask on.

Medical checks can be awkward when they're done in your own language. It's an entirely more unique experience when it's done in a foreign language and you have no idea what to expect. I knew general body parts in Mandarin… but I didn't know specific medical terms.

"Pants off" the nurse said in Chinese. That much I understood. I pulled them down and she did a quick inspection of my genitalia. I guess she was looking to see whether there was any obvious sign of an STD? She marked something down on her paper and instructed that I pull my pants back up.

Straight to the point, this one.

"Sit down, arm out." That much I understood. Blood pressure or blood sample, I thought. She came over with a familiar looking blood pressure band and wrapped it around my arm. *They're really being thorough.* She squeezed the little ball and slowly released the pressure to get the reading. She jotted it down on her paper, stood up and walked over to her desk.

This doesn't end.

She walked back over and told me once again to extend my arm. I put two and two together and realized that this would probably be a blood sample. The nurse grabbed my arm, found the vein and popped the needle straight in. No explanation. No countdown. No mention on the total number of vials that would be taken. No words really. Just, *in the vein we go.* Luckily, I don't have much of an issue with needles, but still, this was too much. I'd been detained all day, stressed out of my mind, hadn't eaten, dehydrated, tired…I'm honestly surprised I didn't pass out.

Deep breaths.

I sat there, tired, as I watched vial one slowly filled up with my blood. *On we go.* She removed the first vial and replaced it with a second bigger vial, until it too, filled up. *Maybe this is how they'll do it. Drain me to death by taking all my blood.* And then, magically, she stopped. That was it, I guess? *Do I get a cookie?* Without warning, the nurse pulled the needle out and handed me a cotton swab to stem the bleeding. *I guess she got what she wanted.*

That must be it, I thought. *What more could they possibly need?*

Nope, there was more! Once she had stored the blood samples I was instructed to walk into another room where a second nurse was waiting. As I was walking out of the main room, I saw the officers go out to fetch Karl to begin the joy of whatever I had just completed. In the next room there was an odd contraption that looked like binoculars had been welded onto a microscope.

Retinal scan?

The nurse got on his computer and turned the contraption on. He instructed me to look into the binocular lenses. Somehow, there was a reflection that allowed you to target the center of your eye for the photo or scan they were about to take. "Hold still" the nurse said and clicked his mouse. I could see the image he had just taken pop up on his computer screen.

What's next, a rectal exam?

Luckily, there was no rectal exam. I was told to wait in the retina scan room until Neil and Karl finished. One by one they trickled in giving me odd looks, to verify whether I had just gone through the same tests in the other room. Karl came in after me to do his retinal scan.

Once again, they had to restart the retinal scanner twice for Karl. He looked as if he was about to run head first into a wall. On one hand, his inability to simply be patient was comedic relief. On the other hand, a part of us was worried that Karl might actually lose his temper. He was young and impatient…*not a good combination. We weren't sure if the guards had picked up on any of this yet.*

Eventually, the machine worked, and all three of us managed to complete the retinal scan. Even Karl. Apparently, that was the end of the medical check.

The police re-entered the room and marched us further down the hall, away from the lobby, and into a large room on the opposite side of the corridor. The room was large, primarily empty and had a few prison guards inside. It seemed to be where our police swarm would be handing us off to the guards.

There were several large bins in this room that had been pushed up against opposite sides of the walls. We were instructed to go to the first row of bins on the left side of the room and pull one item out from each bin. The first bin was full of blue and yellow prison jackets. The second had matching pants. The third had blue slippers. The fourth had what appeared to be bulk size plastic moving bags.

So much for personal possessions?

Once we had one of each, we were marched back to the center of the room. "Take off your clothes" one of the guards instructed. Neil, Karl and I looked around at each other.

Really? Really though?! We JUST did this in the medical bay.

"Take off your clothes" the guard barked again. I took off my jacket, then shirt, and threw them to the floor. Next my pants came off, with my long johns, and socks. Finally, I stripped off my underwear and just stood there. Over fifteen hours of detention, nearly 1:00 am and now I'm standing in what appeared to resemble a psychiatric ward, naked.

Wonderful. Even I was starting to understand Karl's level of anger.

The guards ordered us to spin around, and spin we did. "Underwear" the guard ordered. We put our underwear on. Off to the side of the room, there was a metal detector that I hadn't initially noticed, upon entering. The three of us were lined up on one side of it (in our underwear) and marched through it.

Just in case we wanted to sneak drugs into prison…in China?

Once that was done, we walked back to our pile of stuff on the ground and were ordered to pack all of our personal belongings into the tote-sized plastic bag. We were handed a pen to write down our name. Finally, we were ordered to put on our new matching prison uniforms.

Lovely.

A few moments later, Neil, Karl and I stood there looking around at each other as we were getting acquainted with our new prison gear. *At least I still have my underwear?* A mildly warm, pre-worn jacket, bright blue pants and matching blue slippers. Plastered across the back of the jackets were the words, 拘留所 (JuLiuSuo, Detention Center).

We were instructed to gather all our personal belongings, which had been crammed into our moving bags. We were marched out of the room and turned left back into the hall. At the end of the hallway, we turned left once more and were marched into what appeared to be a massive storage room.

This one was full of what seemed to be hastily built metal shelves. Row after row after row of shelves, full of these plastic tote bags with other inmates personal belongings.

I guess there's a lot of people here?

At the end of the room, there was a bit of space and where we were told to stash our bags. We placed them down and parted ways with everything we had initially been arrested with. We were marched back out of the room, with nothing left and back into the metal detector room. This time we were instructed to go to the bins on the opposite side of the room. These bins were stuffed with worn, unwashed, blue blankets. "Grab two" the guard ordered in Chinese.

I tried to rummage through a bit to find some that were in better shape, but they were all pretty beat up from extensive use. I pulled two out and made my way back to the center of the room. As I waited for Karl and Neil to grab theirs, I took a closer look at the two blankets I grabbed. One of them was sort of ok, the other clearly had blood stains on it. I thought about asking to grab new ones, then realized it probably wouldn't make much of a difference as they all seemed to be in the same general condition.

Hopefully blood wasn't the worst type of stain?

Blankets in hand, the guard drew our attention back onto him, informing us that we could purchase a plastic baggie with toiletries. *I hadn't even thought about that up until now.* He pulled a couple items out to show us that it included a toothbrush (the size of a pinkie finger), a tiny tube of toothpaste (the length of a sewing needle), a couple pads of toilet paper, a roll of tiny shampoo packets, a bright red cup, and a tiny plastic tupperware container.

"50 RMB" he said.

Me: Can we use WeChat wallet (mobile pay service)?

Guard: Only cash.

Karl: I have a credit card?

Guard: Only cash.

Well FU$K, nobody mentioned needing cash for this fuc%ing bag during the past 15 hours or I could have pulled some out of an ATM!?!?!!

Neil: I have cash, but it's in my wallet. Can I go grab some?

Guard: ???

The guard didn't speak any English. I translated and let him know that Neil had cash in his bag.

Guard: I will escort him there.

Me: Please tell me you have an extra 50? I don't have any cash on me. You know I'll owe you.

Neil: It's your lucky day…I have around 400 on me right now. Karl same thing?

Karl: Yes, please. I owe you big time.

The guards escorted Neil out of the room and back to his personal belongings leaving Karl, myself and other guards in the room.

Karl: Wonder what happens if you don't have cash?

Me: I think you just get stuck in there without anything.

Karl: That would be really, really fu$ked.

Me: Barter with the other detainees, I guess

Karl: I suppose so.

A couple minutes later, Neil and the guards returned to the room, cash in hand. He handed off the 150 RMB to the guard and he handed out three plastic baggies to each of us.

Thank God for Neil, I thought.

"*Come*" he ordered. The three of us followed him and the other guards out. *On to wherever we'll be staying for the next fourteen days.* We walked back through the hall, past our arresting officers in the lobby, a couple of whom were asleep on the sofas. *I don't blame them.* We found ourselves opposite the fish tank at the grand reception desk where we were handed off to another group of guards.

Our names were read, paperwork was sorted and one by one we were told to wait at the door at the back of the reception room.

Once everything was in order, we were marched behind the reception doors and into another wing of the building. And that's precisely when everything changed.

The nice, clean and pleasant décor of the lobby disappeared immediately. This new area smelled old and stale. The paint was faded. The lighting was dim and flickering. It wasn't pleasant. *What a stunning transition.* The elevator doors to our right swung open and the three of us were marched inside.

The guards were emotionless and had no interest in conversing with us. This just seemed like another routine and frustrating part of the day for them, especially at 1:00 am. It wasn't better on our end either. The three of us were tired, frustrated, stressed, confused, angry, hungry, thirsty, worried, and every other negative adjective.

Hopefully this day is coming to an end soon. I need to sleep.

The guard pressed the button for the second floor, and up we went. *Ding.* Once again, the elevator doors swung open and out we marched around a corner and down a hall. Our surroundings hadn't changed much, and if anything, it got worse. We passed a row of empty rooms that looked like they were meant for interrogations. Inside, these rooms there were single chairs isolated at the center and bolted to the ground. They had restraints across the lap. It seemed to be an interrogation room that doubled for torture.

Where are we going?

Finally, we got to an oversized metal door that seemed to occupy the entire entrance into another hallway. The oversized comfy couches with the LCD displays were long gone. This new and unwelcoming environment screamed "prison." The first door was followed by a second metal door that the guards were unlocking. Beyond both doors was a long hollow corridor with barred windows and doors.

The walls were covered in a depressing and faded light blue and white paint. Every window was completely barred. Everything looked worn and dated, dark and tired.

Karl: So, prison cells?

Neil: So it seems.

The guards marched us past the first two cell doors on the right. *Who knew what might lie on the other side?* I was starting to realize that it wasn't the run-down hostel room I was hoping for. Far from it.

Once we got to the third cell door, the guards stopped us. "小龙" the guard called my name. I stepped forward, blood stained blanket and plastic baggie in hand. "来."

Here we go.

I could feel my heart pounding. I could tell that my body just fed me what felt like its last kick of adrenaline. The guard unlocked the large metal door. Behind it, another large barred door. I could hear commotion on the other side, but I couldn't see in. I stood next to the cell door, facing the faded blue and white wall. The guard unlocked the second door and pushed it open, motioning for me to step in.

Without thinking, I took my first few steps into the cell.

Cage number three.

As soon as I had fully stepped in, I realized that neither Neil nor Karl would be joining me. For the first time, they were separating us. The gravity of the situation hit me: *I would soon be on my own, detained in a communist Chinese prison cell, halfway around the world from home.*

I tried to look back to say goodbye to the others before they were hauled off to their cells. All I caught was a quick glimpse of Neil as the second door was being closed. "Enjoy prison" I heard Karl shout, with his awkward chuckle right before the large metal door slammed shut in my face.

Those were the last words I heard from either of them. I was very much alone now. Stranded in a communist prison cell that couldn't be found on a map, halfway around the world from home. *Fu&k me, right?* I stood there, blood stained blanket in hand, adrenaline pumping, and one phrase repeating in my mind.

Enjoy prison. Enjoy prison. Enjoy prison...enjoy...prison...enjoy...

Chapter 8:

Detention (Prison, Night 1)

"Police in China can do whatever they want; after 81 days in arbitrary detention you clearly realize that they don't have to obey their own laws. In a society like this there is no negotiation, no discussion, except to tell you that power can crush you any time they want - not only you, your whole family and all people like you."[39]

Ai WeiWei: February 26ᵗʰ, 2012

Chin up, chest out, deep breaths and be confident.

FU$KKKKKKKKKKKKKKKKKKKKKKKKKK

I have no idea what the FU$K I'm doing. FU%K I'm LOCKED in a PRISON CELL. FU&K. FU&KKKKKKK. AGHHHHHHHH. I'm LOCKED IN A FU$KING COMMUNIST PRISON CELL. IN FU%KING CHINA. FU%%%%KKKKKKKKKK.

It's that moment we've all seen played out a million times in movies and tv shows. The actor or actress stepping foot into the very foreign world of a prison for the first time. Not once, did I think that I would ever be experiencing this in real life.

I realized that I had been standing there, frozen, for just a second too long. My brain was trying to process everything that was happening, and trying to get a handle on my new surroundings. I had just been separated from Karl and Neil. I was alone in a communist cell on the other side of the planet in a

---

[39] Ai, Weiwei. 2001 – 2018. Ai Weiwei Quotes. *Brainyquote.com*. Retrieved: March 11ᵗʰ, 2018, from: https://www.brainyquote.com/quotes/ai_weiwei_470204.

black-site prison compound. I had no idea where I was. I didn't know what was happening.

I couldn't focus. I was terrified.

My brain slowly started to catch up. I noticed a bathroom on my left and then there were, wooden, tables to my right?

Nope, those were the beds. Table beds? So many eyes...everyone is staring at me. FU&K, there's a sh!& load of people in here.

What are THEY in here for? What crime did they commit? I see one foreigner. This is clearly not the foreigner center. Dude's standing up by himself in the corner... at night? Why is he wearing that bright orange hat? Everyone seems to be in bed, but nobody's asleep. A couple dudes are standing, just staring at me. Everyone's staring at me.

Why the FU%K is everyone staring at me.

Mostly everyone is Chinese. There's another foreigner. WHAT THE FU&K DO I DO. WHERE THE FU$K DO I GO?! Is this like prison in America? Is this different? I've seen the Wire. Do I need to fight? DO I establish myself by punching someone in the face? Do people kill each other in Chinese prisons? Fu&K everyone is still staring at me. Are the foreigners cool with each other? Where the FU&K do I go?! Do I kick it with the foreigners? Will the Chinese be cool? At least I can communicate with them.

FU$KKKKKKKKKKKKKKKKKKKKKKKKKKKK.

This is the abridged and calm version of the absolute terror and chaos that flooded my mind at that moment. I was hungry. They took my blood. I was thirsty. I was tired. I had no contact with the outside world. I had been stripped of all my personal belongings. I didn't know where the fu&k I was. *I had never felt more alone in my life.* Like cage one and two that day, there were no instructions. *There's no damn rulebook for walking into a prison cell. Survive. I guess that's the only rule.*

I was terrified. Fake it. Fake it. Fake it. I put my chin up and looked around the room as if I owned the place, eyeing everyone in the cell with a blank stare. It wasn't my best performance, but I'd give it a solid 7 out of 10 for the condition I was in.

Hopefully, that would do for now.

I'm not the strongest guy but I do have a relatively solid build. The jacket was bulky, so no one could really tell just how muscular someone was with it on. I am somewhat tall, though. That height plus what people refer to as my naturally, "serious" face sent some type of message around the room.

At least I hoped that's what it did.

The proportions of the cell dimensions are hard to describe. The cell itself was small given the number of people it housed, maybe thirty feet long by fifteen. The walls were painted a light blue and divided half-way down ending in a depressing gray tone.

Our blankets were worn, stained by any number of human fluids and dyed an abused off-blue color. Right behind me stood the large, reinforced metal-cell door that served as the only entrance and exit for this hellish landscape. There was a barred window on the far wall, opposite the door, that sat in the middle of the division between the gray and white paint. To my immediate left is where the cell's "bathroom" door was located. The bathroom itself was maybe six by eight feet long.

The bathroom door and wall were made of some type of strong, durable glass. This ensured that the entirety of the bathroom was always visible, which I'm assuming was some type of safety precaution.

The bathroom had a single, moldy squatter toilet, with an equally sad sink right next to it.

Home sweet home.

I looked around at the walls and every square inch had various words, names, numbers and symbols carved into it by ex-prisoners. Directly in front of me and there was a short stocky black foreigner wearing a bright orange hat staring at me. The look on his face was utterly emotionless.

Welcome to prison?

He stood in the tiny walking space between the wood plank "beds" and the wall…just staring at me.

Well this is confusing. Why the fu%k is he wearing bright fluorescent orange hat?! Why is he the only person wearing that hat? How did he get a personal bright orange hat in the cell? Does that mean he's dangerous? Is that the warning hat they put on dangerous offenders in China? Why is he just standing there? Why isn't he asleep? Why is he motioning at me to move over?

Do I trust him?

I didn't have much of a choice. Everyone else was in bed. Some were disinterested and tried to get back to sleep. Other Chinese inmates carried on talking about the new foreigner in the cell. *What is he going to do next? Is he crazy? Is he violent? I could see they were trying to figure me out as well.*

Fu&k it. I didn't have a choice and I couldn't stand here all night. I walked over in his direction.

Prisoner: You can put your stuff here.

He pointed to an empty container space built into the bottom of the wood planks. I placed my plastic bag down there.

Me: Thanks.

Prisoner: Where you from?

Me: U.S. You?

Prisoner: Senegal. What's your name?

Me: Steve. You?

Prisoner: Muhammad. Steve from America. Nice to meet you.

He reached out to shake hands, eying me the entire time. *He was trying to figure me out. So was I.* We shook hands, maintained eye contact…and that was that.

Me: Nice to meet you too. What brings you here?

Muhammad: They tore up my visa on a bus. Said I'm visiting illegally. You?

Me: Similar. Work visa. They said I'm working here illegally. It's bs.

Muhammad: Yea, it's one fu$ed up country. Try and get some sleep. You hungry?

Me: Nah, I'm alright. *I lied. Can I trust anyone?*

What kind of food was it? What do we even eat here?

Nobody was asleep yet. Muhammad budged one of the Chinese inmates on the bed in front of us to make some space for me, motioning for him to move over. As he was getting that sorted, I took the opportunity to glance around at the other inmates.

How many people are locked in here with me?

There seemed to be around 8 or 9 wooden plank beds in total. Each one seemed to have been designed with enough space for a grown man to lay down on their back and sleep.

I did a quick count. *13?! There were 13 inmates lying down on planks designed for eight people.* One guy in the bathroom plus Muhammad and me. *Sixteen inmates, total.* I re-examined the wooden planks...there was no space. Each bed was made for one person and there were 14 people, including myself. *Do the math.* People were literally piled on these things practically laying on top of each other. Legs were crisscrossed, arms were crammed next to heads... *welcome to Communist detention.*

Somehow, Muhammad managed to get a sliver of space for me in between two Chinese inmates. *I have no idea how he managed to do that.* I looked at the other two inmates to see how they had prepped the area with their two human-stained blankets. Ideally, I'd get a pillow, a blanket, and a mattress.

Great, I have two blankets that are smaller than me.

I decided to go for the mattress and blanket combination. Sleeping on cold wooden planks seemed like it would be the worst option. *I can do without a pillow?* I laid out my blanket down the hard wood surface in between these two, now-separated, inmates. I took my slippers off and placed them underneath the wooden structure. I climbed up and laid down in the same direction everyone else had been facing: *feet up against the wall, head by the crammed walking space.*

I grabbed my lesser-blood-stained blanket and threw it over my body.

You couldn't, literally, imagine being more uncomfortable than this. *I'm not going to get any sleep tonight.* The hard wooden plank pierced through the thin blue blood-blanket that I folded over to use as a mattress. *The mattress idea seemed to be a useless endeavor...but there's no going back now.* The guy to my left was trying to sleep, and I certainly wasn't going to budge him awake to re-adjust anything. *I was the new guy.* I didn't want to piss anyone off at minute nine. *At least the blanket was keeping me warm?*

What time do they turn the lights off? Do they turn the lights off?

The massive fluorescent lights above were unnecessarily powerful and kept the entire room brightly lit. *It would be impossible to sleep with those things on.* There was an elbow in my spine, a wood board dug into my bones, and inmates still staring at me. *Fu&k it, I needed sleep.* I looked up at the clock and shut my eyes. *I can't do this.* I kept my eyes shut. *Try. Try. Try.* Keeping my eyes shut. I'm going to power through this. *I can't do this.* I looked up at the clock.

It's been about 30 seconds. FU&KKKKK!!

My mind and body were both painfully tired, so I thought getting to sleep would be the easy part. *Despite how incredibly tired I felt, I couldn't sleep in any capacity.* BURP. Somewhere close by, an inmate let out a deep belch that seemed to rock the foundation of the wooden planks. *Oh boy.* Another inmate asleep under the window immediately got up and slid it open through the metal bars. *Well at least we can open it? Too bad it's barred outside. I'd probably try and escape. I'm not even kidding. How many floors down? 2 or 3? Is a broken leg worse than this?*

PRRRRRVVVTTTTT! Somewhere else a massive fart ripped.

Hahahah! Another inmate started laughing.

HELL. *This is HELL I thought. It exists, and I've been thrown in, feet first. Now, other inmates were discussing the fart.*

Sleep was supposed to be my escape after this impossible day. *It didn't seem like I was going to get any.* Muhammad was still standing, leaning up against the wall with his bright orange hat.

Does he just not sleep?

I looked up to my right, down the walking space towards the metal door. Another guy with a bright orange fluorescent hat was pacing back and forth by the bathroom. *What is it with these hats? Why are the lights still on?*

BURRRPPPPP! Another one...more laughter. *Fu&kkkkkkkk?!* Some of the inmates started discussing the burp. Noise was noticeably amplified in here. *You could hear everything.* There was nowhere to escape. You couldn't avoid it. The lights. Being lodged in between two strange inmates. The non-stop laughter. The elbows. The wooden planks and bloody-blankets. *What was this?*

Ok, just try. Try and sleep. Force it. I pulled the blanket up over my head, trying not to move too much. I didn't want to disturb the guys next to me. I hid under the blanket. I was buried underneath. I felt like I had finally escaped.

"SHOU DAOSI HAW DOAU OAI!" *WTF?!* I jumped up. *There's a speaker in the room?!* Some muffled voice screamed an inaudible command through a speaker. I hadn't noticed it earlier, but there it was perched in the corner and mounted on the ceiling. Up in the corner of the room, high up above the door was a camera and a large, old-school, speaker. *I guess this is how the guards keep watch? And the speaker lets the inmates know they're being watched?*

Muhammad leaned up off the wall and started moving toward me.

Muhammad: Your blanket. Can't cover your head during sleeping hours.

Me: *??????!!?!!!? Oh…ok.*

How did he know that? How could he understand that muffled sound through the speaker?

I pulled the blanket down and turned to my side. The hard-wooden bed dug into my bones. *FU&K. FU&K. FU&K. This was impossible. Make it work. Make it work.* LUCKILY, the inmate next to me had a roll of blanket scrunched up by my head. It was just lying there. He seemed to have more than two blankets.

I'll have to figure out how he managed that.

I bunched it up next to my head and formed a makeshift pillow. It wasn't great, and it wasn't particularly comfortable…but it was better than having my head drooping down, out of alignment, onto the wood. I wouldn't be able to really move but whatever; *it's better than where I was ten seconds ago.*

I put my head down but the wood was still digging straight into my hip. *WHEEZE. Oh FU&K. WHEEZE. WHEEZE. SNOREEEEEEE! AGHHHHHHHHHHHHH.* A few guys down, one inmate magically managed to fall asleep in the midst of this chaos. He was a rather large fellow and he was out cold. His snoring sounded like a freight train. *GARGLE. FLAP. WHEEZE.*

DAMMIT!

I looked up at the clock, only around three or four minutes had gone by. It literally felt as if three or four hours has passed. *How the FU&K do people survive in here? How is Neil doing?*

HOW IS KARL DOING?!

The lights. The farting. The snoring. The wave of cold air from the window. The wood digging into every bone in your body. The cramped space. The giggling. The talking. The orange hats. The people who weren't asleep. The speaker. The staring. The inability to move freely. The burping. The noise. The uncertainty of who you were locked up with. *Were they violent? Were all of them violent?*

All of this made sleeping impossible.

I forced my eyes shut again. I'll at least pretend to sleep. It was sometime after 1:00 am already. I was tired. My brain, my body and my soul needed rest. I could feel my body struggling, but my brain couldn't stop. It was desperately trying to alert me to all of the possible threats. The unknown sounds. The unknown people. This unknown environment.

That's what it was; the unknown.

My mind was screaming, stay up and defend yourself, you idiot! My body wasn't really listening. It needed a break. It needed sleep. *I felt my mind and body battling each other trying to resolve an unsolvable problem. I felt like I was watching myself from above. It was almost as if I was experiencing all of this in the third person.*

I kept my eyes shut. I couldn't sleep, but I kept them shut. I had to at least pretend. I lied there with my eyes shut for as long as possible, but my brain was still wide awake. It alerted me to every unknown disturbance. My mind was forcing my body to pump out any last reserves of adrenaline that were still available. My mind was overloaded. But I had managed to keep my eyes shut.

This was such an odd sensation. I had never really experienced anything like this before. I was painfully tired, but I couldn't fall asleep regardless of how hard I tried. *How long could I do this for? Does my brain consider this sleeping? My eyes are shut, but I am still conscious of my surroundings. Is there such a thing as 5% sleep? 20%?*

I couldn't sleep. I had done this for as long as physically possible. I looked up at the clock. It felt like hours had gone by. *It was only about 25 minutes. FU&K THIS.* But there were no options. There was no way out.

Find a way. Find a way.

I went back to the makeshift pillow and forced my eyes shut again. It wasn't any better. My brain kept me up. There were too many unknowns. I *desperately* needed sleep. I could feel my heart pounding. Unknown sounds.

Unknown smells. *The unknown was everywhere.* My brain was alert to every-thing. Subconsciously, there was danger all around. *My brain was trying to keep me alive and kill me at the same time.*

I needed it to shut down. *The lights. The sounds.* I couldn't make them stop. I'll try the blanket again. Maybe not over my entire head this time. Just over my eyes. A couple other inmates were starting to fall asleep already. *Maybe the guards kept less of a watch as the night dragged on?* Ever so slowly I snuck the blanket over my eyes. Ok. I'm there. *Mission accomplished.* And then I waited. And waited. And waited. *No speaker. No announcement.*

For now, the light was significantly dimmed from my vision. This wasn't per-fect, *but it would do. Finally, one variable in my control.* That's how this battle would be won. *One tiny variable at a time.* I laid there with my eyes shut on my uncomfortable makeshift pillow, still waiting to be screamed at by the speaker.

It didn't come. Maybe I'm in the clear? Lesson learned…*don't cover your entire head with the blanket.*

Ever so slowly, I was adapting. I was thrown into a new environment and I had to adapt. *There was no other choice. This was raw survival.* That's how this war would be won. *One battle at a time.*

Dimming the light helped. It didn't put me to sleep immediately but it gave me a meaningful sense of control. All my freedoms had been stripped from me today but controlling the light…*that meant something.* My eyes were still forced shut. My mind was a bit more at ease. I wasn't asleep, *but this was noticeably better.*

The noise and smells became slightly more tolerable. I could hear other inmates getting up to go to the bathroom. I stayed frozen in this forced sleep mode for a while. The added combo of a makeshift-pillow plus the lack of powerful lights flooding through my closed eyelids helped significantly. I went for as long as humanly possible in this faux-sleep mode. Eventually, I looked back up at the clock, *it had been an hour.*

That's better.

I forced my eyes shut again. This was doing something. I wasn't really sure what, and it certainly wasn't as good as sleep, but it *felt* helpful. At some point in this process I actually managed to doze off. I still felt partially aware of my surroundings, but it worked.

KCSHHH. My eyes shot open. Someone slammed the bathroom door as they were walking out. *Dammit. I was actually asleep this time.* I looked up at the clock...4:45 am. *Thank God, I got around two hours of sleep.*

I still felt horrible, but fu%k it. *That's sleep. I'll take what I can get.* I needed to pee. *Time to see what this bathroom is all about.* Ever so slowly, I made my way up and out of the bed. *I felt weird.* I was groggy, dizzy and sleepy. I threw my bright blue prison slippers on and walked over towards the bathroom. A couple of the other inmates were up and pacing around. Others that weren't asleep looked up to see what I was doing.

I opened the door and made my way inside. The bathroom was tiny. To the left was a sink which was right next to a single squatter toilet. Directly in front of me was the "shower" aka the remnants of a small battered garden hose that had been forcibly applied to a spout on the wall. There was moldy green netted matting covering the floor.

There was an obvious growth of black mold under the sink. Stains by the squatter. Who knew where the shower hose had been. *One of each for 16 people?* It'll be interesting to see how this works out during the mornings.

I stood there peeing, staring at the tile wall in front of me. My brain was processing everything incredibly slowly. I looked up and to the left and saw two of the Chinese inmates were staring at me from bed. Once paced by into view looking me up and down until he had turned around. *I guess they're bored? Not much else to do in a prison cell then watch people pee.* I finished up and kicked the leaver at the back of the squatter to flush. I crept back out of the bathroom, making sure not to slam the door to not disturb the other inmates. I made my way back to my tiny space and kicked my slippers off.

I stepped back up onto the bed and got back into my cramped position in between the same two guys. *Let's try this again.* I shut my eyes underneath the blanket and willed myself back to sleep.

How long can I physically survive this?

Get back to sleep.

You need sleep.

Try and sleep.

How long can I survive this...

Chapter 9:

Detention (Prison Day 1, Morning)

Torture Methods Used to Persecute Falun Gong Practitioners in Henan No. 3 Forced Labor Camp (Part 1)

"A United Nations report highlighting the practice of torture and human organ harvesting against practitioners of Falun Gong found that the process has been forcefully inflicted upon Falun Gong members throughout China making organs available for transplant operations. Vital organs including human hearts, kidneys, livers, and corneas are systematically harvested from Falun Gong practitioners (reportedly without anesthetics) who are generally killed in the process." [40]

Chinese Government's official statement regarding <u>Facts About the So-Called 'Shen Yun' Performance by the 'Falun Gong'</u>:

"The so-called "NTDTV" and the "Divine Performing Arts" are controlled by "Falun Gong" cult. They have been staging the so-called "Shenyun" Performances in the U.S. in recent years in the name of promoting Chinese culture and showcasing the oriental charm. But in fact, the performances were filled with cult messages and implied attacks against the Chinese Government.

Li Hongzhi himself claimed openly that it was he who instructed the various "Falun Gong" groups to organize the "Shenyun" performances aimed at "showcasing the practitioners, salvation and telling the truth"

---

[40] Torture methods used to Persecute Falun Gong practitioners in Henan No. 3 forced labor CAMP (Part 1): Falun Dafa. (n.d.). Retrieved February 28, 2021, from https://en.minghui. org/html/articles/2013/7/10/140957.html

rather than entertainment for the ordinary people. Clearly, the so-called "Shen yun" is not a cultural performance at all but a political tool of "Falun Gong" to preach cult messages, spread anti-China propaganda, increase its own influence and raise funds.

Such show denigrates and distorts the Chinese culture, and deceives, makes fool of and even brings harm to the audience."

Bah nah nah nah nah nahhhhh...WTF?!. WHO the FU^K is playing music?! WHY is music blaring from a speaker???

?!?!?!?!!? Fu&k...it's morning. What time is it? Where am I? Oh right...F&K this isn't a dream...I'm locked in a prison cell...in FU&KING CHINA...

I sat up from my cramped sleeping position. My body was aching, my back was sore and my vision was blurry. Others were sitting up too. Something was happening. *What is this? Is this the morning alarm?* Everyone was getting up and packing their blankets away...*what do I do?*

What's going on?

I guess I pack my blankets away too? Sh!t, how are they folding it that way?! I don't know how to fold it that way?! Am I supposed to know how to do that? Why are those two placing the blankets at the head of the bed...like pillows? Fu$K I'm still tired. How many hours of "sleep" was that? What do I do with my blankets? What time is it? Do I fold and put them or also do the blanket thing? Does it matter? Do I get in trouble if I do it wrong?

Fu^k it's only 6:30 am.

Right on cue, there was Muhammad.

Muhammad: American, fold it like this...

Thank GOD for this guy! Muhammad sat there and folded up my blanket in the same way as other inmates. Within a few seconds, blood stained blanket number one was properly folded and placed neatly at the head of the bed.

Me: Hey, thanks man.

Muhammad: No worries. The other one, you just toss with the others.

He wasn't wearing the orange hat anymore? Now it was hung up on the wall?

I walked over to the edge of the planks towards the main cell door. There was a tiny narrow space in between the furthest wooden plank frame and the wall. That seemed to be where blood-blankets were kept during the day; in a pile on the floor. *So much for assigned blankets.* I threw my second blanket into the pile hoping I would be able to retrieve it later.

I wonder if the other ones have fewer blood stains?

There was a long line along the wall by the bathroom door. *I guess this is the morning bathroom rush?*

I paused to look inside as I was walking back toward my "bed" area to collect my pinkie-length toothbrush. There were around six inmates crammed into the bathroom at once going through their morning routine.

Two guys were hovered over the sink, brushing their teeth. Standing right next to them were two guys who were peeing into the one squatter toilet at the same time.

Well that's efficient.

Right behind the two guys peeing in unison were two other guys sharing the shower hose with a third waiting his turn behind them. One of them seemed to be using it as a backup sink to brush his teeth. The other guy was using it to wash his hair. They worked in unison, taking turns, handing the hose off to each other. The guy brushing his teeth took a big swig of water out of the hose, gargled, and spit next to where the hair washing guy was standing.

The contents of his rinsed mouth splashed all over the other guy's feet *who surprisingly didn't seem to care much.* His mind was too focused on washing his hair to care about backwash splashing all over his feet. *Is there a time limit? Efficiency, not hygiene, seemed key for the morning bathroom rush.*

Well this is fun.

I reached for my plastic bag, pulling out my toothbrush, toothpaste, and bright red cup. *I guess that's what I'll need for now?* I got in line towards the back. *I'm the new guy, I'll wait my turn.*

Maybe I won't have to double pee into the squatter toilet if everyone is already finished?

As I waited, I looked around to get a better idea of who I was locked up with. I counted fourteen Chinese inmates, and two foreigners. There was one other black inmate in the cell, aside from Muhammad. Foreign inmate two was one of the first people out of the bathroom in the morning. *He seemed to have his routine down.* He had this look of carelessness and confidence on his face as if he had spent years here.

A seasoned veteran.

I was still standing in line as he marched confidently out of the bathroom. He glanced over at me, disinterested, as he passed by. *Another one,* was the impression I got from the look on his face, as if he had seen a dozen of me come and go. *Why bother with a new name?*

He walked to the far back corner of the cell, sat down and started singing to himself. The upper part of his body was rocking back and forth as he sang what appeared to be Christian hymns with his eye's buried into his hands. *I guess this is his routine? How long until I get to that point? I wonder how long he's been here for?*

I wonder WHY he's in here?

Slowly, the line moved forward as people were finishing up in the bathroom. As I moved forward, I looked up and inspected the walls. From the floor all the way above my head the walls were covered in writing. Past inmates had carved their stay into this cell's history. Every imaginable language, number, name, date, and country covered the four cell walls. Countdown calendars, next to "Ukraine's been here", next to something in Arabic, next to a Chinese name, next to "God can't see you here."

It was fascinating and terrifying at the same time.

Over to my left were two particularly loud Chinese inmates that were practically screaming at each other. If you didn't know what they were saying, you would have thought they were seconds away from coming to blows. Ironically, this was just a casual discussion about the food.

It's simply how they communicated with each other.

They were also some of the first people out of the bathroom and were now sat in the middle of the wooden beds. Based on how their composure and interaction with the other inmates, they seemed to be in charge of the cell. It's not that they were particularly big, or even stronger than anyone else, they just had this kind of confidence in the way they carried themselves.

The main guy looked like Squidward from the Spongebob tv show. They had a painfully similar facial structure. I referred to him as *the Godfather*. He appeared to be somewhere in his late 40's, bald, kind of thin, and also had this *I've been here a long damn time don't fu&k with me* attitude. He was easily the most noticeable person in the room, as the guards had shackled him in a way that I had never seen anyone shackled before. He was cuffed, left ankle to right wrist, with a chain connecting the two, far too short to let him stand up straight. Therefore, he was always hunched over. This short chain not only prevented him from standing upright, but from simply being able to walk normally. He got around by hobbling, half bent-over, almost as if he were crawling. He was the only person cuffed in the cell this way.

I wonder what he did to earn that?

Luckily, the Godfather was a reservoir of positive energy. He seemed to always have a smile on his face when communicating with others. *And he was always communicating with others.* His number two, who was surprisingly louder, reminded me of Gollum from Lord of the Rings. They looked exactly the same. The main difference between this dude and the Godfather was this dude was insane, and very short tempered. Luckily, he was small, but that seemed to make him overcompensate everything he did. He seemed to follow the Godfather's cues and looked up to him in a weird way. *The lieutenant* was younger, somewhere in his early 30's and around 5'4."

People were naturally drawn to the Godfather. When he spoke, people listened, and he had an innate way of capturing people's attention with his captivating stories. Conversely, everyone hated the lieutenant. *He was a poor man's copycat.* When the Godfather spoke, people seemed to stop and enjoy listening to a loud, but charismatic voice. When the lieutenant spoke, seemingly demanding attention, nobody cared. But he *didn't get it*, which caused him to act out even more and scream which just pissed everyone off even more.

Bear in mind, you're locked in this prison cell with him. In the lieutenant's mind, he was hilarious, smooth and respected. Nothing could've been further from the truth. Chinese and foreign inmates seemed equally annoyed by his crass behavior.

The lieutenant had clear signs of severe and untreated mental issues (hyper-aggression, extreme instability, and depression).

I turned my attention back to the bathroom. Things had cleared up a bit and there only seemed to be three or four inmates inside at this point. I waited for the sink to clear so I could brush my teeth. There was one guy standing at the sink, another peeing, and one guy brushing his teeth by the hose. *There was an unmistakably strong scent of urine in the air*, but luckily, there was a tiny barred window in the back of the bathroom that was open. It wasn't much, but it helped mitigate what would have been an otherwise impossible smell that would make most people vomit. The guy at the sink finished up and headed out of the bathroom.

Finally, my turn.

As I stood there brushing my teeth, the number of inmates in the bathroom continued to dwindle. Everyone was sitting down outside getting ready for whatever the day ahead would bring. *I still felt super tired.* A couple of guys looked through the glass at me as I finished brushing my teeth. They probably saw me arrive the night before but were still curious about their new foreign cellmate. I finished brushing my teeth, peed and headed out of the bathroom. *That was easy enough. Sure, the sink was disgusting, the room smelled like piss, and I'm sure there was urine splattered all over the floor, but I survived without vomiting.*

I walked over to my bed area and placed my toothbrush, toothpaste and cup back in the bag.

Muhammad: American. Water. You get the water?

Me: Uh…what?

Muhammad: The water brother. In the morning, they give us warm water. It's nice. Soothe your spirit for the day. Get yourself a cup American.

Fu&k it, why not?

Me: Oh, yea thanks. The sink, right?

I had noticed a separate spout by the sink that literally seemed to be steaming. I wasn't sure what it was for, so initially left it alone.

Muhammad: Yes. Get it fast, they turn it off soon.

I turned around, plastic cup in hand and headed back towards the bathroom. *Pretty sure this water isn't filtered. Dirty Beijing tap water…but it's all we had.* I got my cup of warm water and proceeded out of the bathroom when I heard:

The Godfather: 老外！是哪里儿的人呢？ (Foreigner! Where you from!?)

Great…I'm on their radar now.

I wanted to draw as little attention as possible and try and keep to myself. But I knew I was going to have this conversation sooner or later, *let's hope they're cool with Americans?*

I looked him straight in the eye with an emotionless response:

Me: "我是美国人，来自西海岸。你知道旧金山在哪里吗？你是哪里人？" (I'm American, from the West Coast. You know San Francisco? Where are you from?).

Every Chinese inmate froze in place and stared at me as if I had magically transformed into a hippo. Other Chinese inmates looked over, seemingly in disbelief, and proceeded to stare at me. I knew what they were thinking. I had seen that look on Chinese faces for years. It's unmistakable, and I can recognize it from a mile away...Fu&K, this one speaks Mandarin.

He knows what we've been saying.

The Godfather: American huh? Why are you in here?

Thank God I didn't actually do anything bad or immoral. What type of reception might await me in here had I actually done something against the CCP or a Chinese citizen?

Me: They are saying I am illegally employed in the country.

The entire cell was listening to our conversation. For the first time in my life, I was speaking, in Mandarin, to a prison cell full of Chinese inmates.

Universities in America don't have lectures on this one.

The Godfather: Expired visa?

Me: No.

The Godfather: Illegally obtained your visa?

Me: No.

The Godfather: So why are you here, American?

I guess he's probably heard every story from the other inmates at this point.

Me: I have no idea.

I was terrified.

But I refused to let it show. There aren't textbooks written on how American inmates in Chinese prisons are supposed to engage a room full of inmates. *Make it work.*

HAHAHAHAHAHAH! For some reason the Godfather spontaneously burst out laughing.

The Godfather: "Well, welcome to detention!" he said chuckling to himself.

Me: Thanks. What about you?

The Godfather: Drugs. Like most others.

Me: I see.

The Godfather: How long will you be with us?

Me: Fourteen days. You?

The Godfather: Oh, that's easy enough! Me? 180 days. Enjoy your warm water.

Me: Thanks.

That was good enough for now. I wanted to ask more questions. There were a million things I was still trying to figure out. I wanted to know why he had a wrist-ankle shackle on as well. But I knew better than to dig for information in here. Time will tell, I thought. This is a need-to-know environment, and I certainly don't need to know. I probably wouldn't want to.

Maybe the fact that they know I speak Chinese will be helpful? Does it establish some type of mutual respect?

As our conversation died down, others started back up. *Now they know who I am.* They knew I wasn't in here for anything serious, but that I had been called on some nonsensical technicality. *Hopefully that would be enough for them to leave me alone.* I walked back towards the back of the cell, with my cup of warm water. Muhammad was right, *it was nice.*

Muhammad was seated at the back of the cell by the window with the other black inmate. The cell seemed to be completely segregated based on racial lines. *Well where the fu*k do I go? I'm not black or Chinese?* It's not like there was ample space either. Muhammad seemed to be keeping an eye out for me in the cell, so I figured I would go stand over by him.

The other black inmate wasn't singing to himself any longer and had struck up a conversation with Muhammad.

Black inmate: Welcome passenger. *He spoke some English. "Passenger"?*

Me: Hey man. What's your name?

Black inmate: Agyei. But you can call me Soldier.

Me: Cool man. Where are you from?

Soldier: Ghana.

Me: What brings you here?

Soldier: Drugs. I didn't use any. They just arrested me with other black people in the club.

Me: Sh!t. *I had heard of this before in China.* Did they drug test you?

Soldier: Not me, others. They said they found some in my jacket. I didn't bring a jacket.

Me: How long have you been in here for?

Soldier: Sh!t. *He paused to look up and count.* 33rd day? 34th? Something like that.

FU&K 33 days?! Can they just do that to anyone?! Will I be in here for over a month?!

Me: 34 days?! How long is your sentence?

Soldier: One month. But no one comes. My visa situation is complicated. I have two passports. They sent the wrong embassy the first week. Haven't seen the other embassy yet.

Me: Do they let you call? Have they mentioned when the other embassy is coming?

Soldier: No calls. Can't call. Nobody comes. Just waiting. Waiting here in hell. Here with all the crazy people. This place is crazy. Crazy, crazy, crazy, crazy, crazy, crazy, crazy, crazy fuc&ing crazy ass backwards people.

I heard keys outside the door and whipped around. *Was this another scheduled part of the day? Who would appear on the other side this time?* The outer cell door flew open. A guard stood at the door, next to what appeared to be a couple of nurses disguised in masks. Three or four inmates immediately shot up, cramming around the inner-barred metal frame trying to get to the medical staff first.

The nurses yelled out a couple Chinese names and one by one the inmates would reach through the bars for medication. Once they had taken their pills, the disinterested nurses slammed the outer cell door shut and moved on, opening up the next cell door in the hall and repeating this process.

Interesting. So I guess medical checks are the first part of the morning routine?

I was slowly learning about my new environment.

The Godfather: Line up! Line up!

Everyone stood up and seemed to get in place, taking a seat on their respective wooden plank areas.

Once again, I was confused. Do I have a space? Is there a place I'm supposed to go? What's going on? Why is everyone lining up?

Muhammad: "Sit here," he ordered. "Morning inspection."

Just outside, we could hear the echo of other cell doors being opened up and slammed shut by the guards. I sat down between Muhammad and another Chinese inmate. Everyone was sitting down at this point, staring in unison, at the cell door.

After around five minutes of waiting, our outer cell door flew open one again. Three Chinese guards were standing outside, staring in.

My cell-mates began chanting instantly in Mandarin: "ONE, TWO, THREE...!"

Everyone stood up immediately as the count got to three, staring straight ahead at the carvings on the wall.

I had no idea what the fu&k was going on.

I responded a bit slower than everyone else, but I tried to watch and follow their lead. The guard barked orders at the first inmate which immediately prompted a headcount to begin among the inmates starting from at the door.

"ONE!" The first inmate shouted in Chinese. "TWO!" the next followed in quick succession.

Well, this I can do.

And the numbers kept rising until it got to me, "FIFTEEN!" I shouted out in Chinese. Then the counting stopped. Soldier and Muhammad leaned over, looked down towards the door, smiling and waving at the displeased guards.

I guess they don't know Chinese?

Muhammad and Soldier seemed to have the routine down and didn't seem the least bit concerned.

The guard nodded back and looked down at his paper. *Headcount done.* Another guard stepped forward, paper in hand. He shouted out a name in Chinese. "HERE!" One of the inmates yelled back and proceeded to sit down. *Roll call?* This continued until the guards had screamed every inmate's name and every inmate was seated.

Guard: Be good today. Breakfast is coming.

SLAM. He shut the door. Outside, we heard the guards move down the hall, opening the adjacent cell door to continue this process with the next group. *The tension in the room was gone.* The inmates withdrew from their rigid, respectful postures and collapsed back into more comfortable positions. A couple guys laid down on the wooden planks to try and sneak in some more sleep. Others stood up and began to pace around, continuing on with their conversations. One inmate dove straight into the pile of blankets on the floor which appeared to be out of the camera's angle.

Is he allowed to do that? What next?

I started looking around the room for the first time in the daylight. There were several large signs posted high on the walls and one of them seemed to be an extensive list of rules. *It seemed to outline behavior that was and was not appropriate?* It was a long list with painfully small print. One list of rules was posted in Chinese, and the other in English.

I'll read through that later. Don't want to get through all the fun in a single day now do I?

Next to the rule list was a daily schedule poster, also posted in English and Chinese.

I quickly glanced through the list which read *something* like this:

6:30 am: wake-up.

6:45 am: medical staff.

7:00 am: roll call.

7:30 am: breakfast.

8:00 am: morning exercise.

9:00 am: education and learning.

10:00 am: outdoor activity.

11:15 am: rest.

11:30 am: lunch.

12:15 pm: nap time.

1:15 pm: nap time end.

2:00 pm: outdoor activity.

3:00 pm: education and learning.

4:30 pm: dinner.

5:00 pm – 9:30pm: evening activity.

9:30 pm: bathroom.

10:00 pm: sleep.

At least we get to go outside? There seems to be a lot of activity time? Wonder what we learn about. I wonder what the activities are?

I continued to glance around the cell and saw a large red plastic bucket sitting in the corner. It was about two feet deep and a foot and a half wide. Almost as if one cue, one of the Chinese inmates ran over, picked it up and hauled it off into the bathroom. He started hosing it down on the piss-covered floor and began cleaning it with the bathroom shower hose. He carried it back out and sat it next to the door.

I wonder what that's used for?

115

Once again, I heard keys rattling outside the cell door and once again, the outer metal door flew open. This time there was a guard standing next to a man with a large, solid-metal, food cart. *Breakfast?* The same Chinese inmate ran over to the cell door, picked up the red bucket and placed it on the ground, right in front of the door. The inner barred door had a square opening cut-out just above the ground, just high enough for the bucket to fit into.

The food cart guy walked over and shoved a giant metal funnel into the square cut-out. The tip of the metal funnel slide down into the red plastic bucket. He walked back over to the food cart and picked up a large and heavy metal canister.

He waddled back over toward the cell door with his giant canister cradled in both arms. He proceeded to dump a soupy-yellow liquid from the metal canister through the metal funnel, pouring the sloppy mixture directly into the red plastic bucket.

Breakfast...?

When the last of the yellow slop had finished dripping out through the funnel, the same inmate picked up the giant red bucket and heaved it up on top of one of the far wooden planks.

Muhammad: Grab your plastic. Breakfast, American.

I watched as the other inmates swarmed the bucket. The bucket-inmate ran back over to the door to pick up a large brick of "饅頭" (man tou). Mantou is a fluffy, sourdough bread roll...except it isn't fluffy, doesn't taste like sourdough, and has the same texture as cardboard. And that's under good conditions. This is prison mantou. This was more of a flavorless, nutritionless wafer brick.

At least we aren't going to starve...technically?

I made my way over to the bucket as other inmates were peeling off their individual mantou brick from the larger mantou brick-sheet. One by one, my cellmates were using a plastic container that was floating around in the bucket to scoop the sloppy-yellow mixture into their individual plastic containers.

I peered into the bucket and saw what appeared to be an inedible yellow gruel. *I instantly recognized it as what was supposed to be a Chinese variation on porridge.*

Porridge is a pretty common staple for Chinese breakfast that I would occa-sionally eat in Beijing during my morning commute. Under normal conditions, it was alright. This was the watered down flavorless and nutritionless yellow prison version.

I couldn't eat it. I could hardly even look at it. Surprisingly, the other prisoners didn't seem to mind.

Soldier seemed used to it at this point and scooped up a big helping into his plastic container. It looked…I mean, you'd couldn't pay someone enough to eat that stuff.

And I was starving.

It's worth taking a moment to put this into context. When you live in China long enough, you discover how to eat a bunch of random stuff that isn't considered *normal* in the West. After five years in Beijing, I had literally tried everything including, pig brain, cicadas, donkey, chicken heart, and duck blood. I had seen, and eaten, some incredibly odd things.

And I couldn't touch this stuff. This was worse. Way, way, way, way fu&king worse. I stood up and walked away.

I took a flavorless brick and walked over to Soldier and Muhammad who were both squatting by the planks as they ate. I stopped and looked around. *Why am I the only person who isn't squatting?* As I was staring at the yellow piss porridge, I failed to realize that everyone was squatting down over the planks. Individual plastic containers and cups were placed on the edge of the wooden planks, and everyone was eating from a squatting position around the bed frames?

Me: We aren't allowed to sit?

Muhammad: Something about squatting while we eat. Sometimes they yell through the box, so we squat. Less yelling.

Well this is loevely.

Muhammad and soldier saw that I had refused an individual helping of the yellow…death liquid.

Muhammad: You need to eat.

Me: I'm good man. Not super hungry right now.

Muhammad: It's not that bad.

Soldier: You need to stay strong in here. This place is crazy. Crazy, crazy, crazy fuc&ing people. Crazy, crazy, crazy, fuc&ing country.

Me: I will, just uh…just not right now. Maybe lunch.

They glanced at each other for a moment, disapprovingly, and continued eating. They didn't try to force the issue. I doubt I was the first person they had seen reject this food.

Everyone comes around sooner or later, I guess? Hell, they probably had to clear the same mental barriers when they first arrived.

Once again, I would have to adapt to survive. In the back of my mind I knew that eventually I would succumb and end up eating this stuff as well. *Just not now. I wonder what we get for lunch?* I squatted down in line, gnawing on my flavorless brick and sipping warm water.

Day one…I thought to myself…Day fuc&ing one…

Chapter 10:

Detention (Prison Day 1, Early Afternoon)

Canadian held in China questioned daily, no lawyer, can't turn off light: sources

"The United Nations Working Group on Arbitrary Detention released its Country Visit report on China regarding civil and political rights in 2004. Among other findings, the report found that Chinese deprivation of liberty fails to meet international standards and norms. Specifically, the time that alleged criminals can be held in custody without judicial approval is too long, administrative detention can't be challenged and the lack of a precise definition surrounding the concept of 'endangering national security' (applied to a broad range of offences) were among some of the report's key findings."[41]

Chinese Government's official response to allegations of human rights violations, including arbitrary detention, regarding the arrest of former Canadian diplomat Michael Kovrig. Chinese Foreign Ministry Spokesperson Hua Chunying's press conference, January 14, 2019:

"Q: According to reports, Canadian Prime Minister Justin Trudeau said on January 11 that China has arbitrarily and unfairly detained

---

[41] Blanchard, B. (2018, December 21). Canadian held in CHINA Questioned daily, no lawyer, can't turn Off Light: Sources. Retrieved February 28, 2021, from https://www.reuters.com/article/us-china-canada/canadian-held-in-china-questioned-daily-no-lawyer-cant-turn-off-light-sources-idUSKCN1OK07Q

two Canadian citizens, and is not respecting diplomatic immunity in the arrest of former diplomat Michael Kovrig. This is something that they are engaged in right now both with Chinese officials and with their partners around the world, and there is a need for all countries to do like Canada and to respect the rule of law and the independence of our judicial processes. What's your comment?

A: I have seen relevant reports. The relevant Chinese departments have handled the case in accordance with the law and the accusation of "arbitrarily" detaining Canadian citizens is totally unfounded. As for the issue of immunity, I would suggest relevant person in Canada to read and study the Vienna Convention on Diplomatic Relations and international law first before making any comment, instead of making himself a laughingstock with specious statements.

Michael Kovrig is not entitled to diplomatic immunity under the Vienna Convention on Diplomatic Relations by any measure. He is not currently a diplomat. Michael Kovrig used an ordinary passport and a business visa to come to China, who has been taken compulsory measures by relevant Chinese state security organ on suspicion of involvement in activities endangering China's national security. He doesn't enjoy immunity in accordance with the Vienna Convention on Diplomatic Relations and international law.

As to the Canadian side's claim that all countries should respect judicial independence, I believe this is quite right if only the Canadian side itself could first prove its judicial independence with concrete actions."

The keys were rattling against the door again.

About an hour had passed since breakfast and the scheduled "exercise time" was an utter let-down. After reading the sign, I stereotypically pictured an outdoor prison yard that we see in American movies. I pictured myself doing a few pull-ups and running around the yard or something. A breath or two of fresh air would be nice and hey, maybe we'd even get to play basketball.

Nope.

ASDOH OJDIASJ SDOSD UHSODJ! One of the guards screamed through the speaker in that inaudible muffled voice. The inmates stood up, as if on command, and began pacing around the small walking aisle next to the wooden planks one large, sad, circle. Door to wall, to door, to wall, over and over and over and over again...pacing in this endless circle of despair. We continued on for about 15 minutes until some inmates started to lose interest. One by one, inmates got bored and just kind of stopped.

That certainly isn't the "outdoor" exercise advertised on the cell wall poster. Is everything in here a lie?

SLAM! Once again, we heard the outer corridor metal door slam shut. *Guards approaching.* Everyone that had been casually sprawled around after our group-pace, immediately rushed over to the planks and sat upright.

Be on your best behavior for the guards, apparently?

Within seconds, the keys unlocked the outer cell door and a group of guards were gathered outside. One of the guards approached the door with a stack of papers in hand. He proceeded to read off a name. One of the inmates stood up, responding, "here!" in Chinese. Pleased, the guard checked off something on the document and continued to shuffle through to other papers.

He proceeded to shout another name, and then another with inmates responding in quick succession as their names were called.

Guard: Grab your belongings!

The three inmates dispersed and proceeded to scuttle about searching for anything that belonged to them. One rushed over to his bed area grabbing a plastic bag while another ran over to pick up two blankets in the pile. Once the three Chinese inmates had everything in hand, they marched over to the entrance and stood in line.

A second guard rushed forward to unlock the door, and the three inmates marched in a single-file line out of the cell and into the hall. The guards ordered them to stand facing the cell door with their backs to the barred hallway window. The three complied immediately, awaiting further direction. The lead guard closed the inner door and proceeded to slam the outer door shut.

Just outside, we heard the guards continue calling prisoners out of the neighboring cells. Once they rounded up everyone, the inmates were marched back to the main hallway door. SLAM! The door shut. *Well at least there's more space in the cell now.* It wasn't a massive change, but three bodies down from 16 to 13 was a noticeable and positive change.

That should speed up the morning bathroom rush?

Soldier: Freedom.

Me: Are they being released?

Soldier: Yes, they are free now.

Muhammad: Their time is complete. Now they go.

Me: Wait, so Chinese inmates get to leave when their sentence is up?

Soldier: Yes, but not foreigners.

Me: How does it work for us?

Muhammad: Depends on your case. Hard to say.

Me: Have either of you seen foreigners released?

Muhammad: No, I just got here before you. Only my third day.

Soldier: Yes, I've seen two go. The foreigners, the Chinese, we all leave. If you survive this place. Crazy, crazy place. Crazy, crazy people. Crazy fuc&ed up country.

Me: So, you've seen a foreigner leave here?

Soldier: Yes, one from Indonesia. He was in here for over almost two months. Supposed to be two weeks. Caught with drugs. Stopped eating. Wasn't doing well. Also, a Russian. But he was only in here for 5 days. Fight or something.

Me: What does it depend on?

Soldier: I guess your country. Probably what they will do with you next. Some get released back into the city, others are deported.

Me: How do you know if you're getting deported?

Soldier: Immigration tells you, whenever they have time to visit you.

Me: How do you know when immigration comes?

Soldier: You don't.

Me: So, we're indefinitely detained?

Soldier: Correct. Immigration only arrives once your sentence is over.

FU*K. How long will I be in here for? How long will Soldier be in here for? How long can they keep you in here for? Is there a max? How long have they kept foreigners here in the past?

Me: And if immigration doesn't come? You just get released back out?

Soldier: They always come. We all seem to get deported. That's real freedom. Away from this fu*ked up country. Never coming back. Go live a happy life back home. So many crazy, crazy people here. The guards, this country...no love. Africa has love. Not like this. Here you can see the hate in their hearts and the way they look at us. No love. Just hate. Crazy, crazy people...

This was one of the first times Soldier had opened up in any way and you could just see the broken look on his face. If eyes are the windows to the soul, his had escaped a long time ago and there was just nothing left in this guy.

The time he had spent locked up in this cell had clearly worn him down. I honestly didn't know how he had managed to hold up after that much time in this nightmare environment. *Would I be in such good shape after 30 something days of being locked up?*

Would I even still be alive?

On one hand, Soldier's story terrified me. *Fu&k, what if I'm in here for over a month?* On the other hand, seeing Soldier survive and power through this sh!tshow provided some degree of hope.

If he can survive this, then fu%k it, so I can I.

Hearing that he had seen other foreigners released was a relief. The Indonesian's timeline didn't sound great, but it was good to know he got out. I tried to compare my situation to his, hoping someone would understand a visa technicality should be less serious than a drug charge. *Hopefully I'll do less time than two months?* I sat back down pondering this new information, staring straight ahead at the carvings previous inmates had etched into the wall.

Another hour slowly passed, and I was still sitting there on the bench...thinking.

There wasn't anything else to do.

It was another smoggy day in Beijing so all you could see through the window was a thick and constant gray. A couple of the inmates had a card game going in one corner of the cell. I didn't want to impose. That was their thing, it made them happy. *Keep them happy. There's a lot more of them than there are of you.*

Others were still pacing back and forth from the window to the door. Some were lying down on the wooden planks trying to sneak more sleep or just pass the time. One inmate receded back into the blanket pile for more rest.

SLAM! Once again, we heard the hallway cell door slam shut which meant the guards were coming back. Once again, everyone shot up and scurried to sit properly at the end of the planks. The inmates seemed terrified of being caught out of position. It seemed like the expectation was that you were to be seated or standing in the pacing area at all times.

No exceptions. No sitting. No sleeping. I wonder what happens if they catch you out of place? Is that why Godfather is handcuffed wrist to ankle?

We heard the guards march to our cell and start jiggling the keys to unlock the door. The two guards flipped through paperwork and called, "小龙!"

Why are they calling my name? Am I being released? No, that's impossible.

I shot up and looked over at the guard.

Guard: "Come!" he barked in Chinese.

I froze for a second, looking around at the other inmates, before I snapped back to reality and started walking toward the door. The other inmates had an equally confused look on their face as they watched me approach the guards. *Does the American get to go?*

Why are they calling *HIM* out by *HIMSELF?* The guard unlocked the barred door and let me out. He ordered me to stand against the hallway wall. The other guard reached over and shut the cell doors, leaving the other inmates locked away.

Guard: "美国的大使馆。" (MeiGuoDe DaShiGuan) American Embassy.

THANK GOD! The cavalry has arrived! MAYBE there was SOMETHING they could do. Maybe I could plead my case. At least they would KNOW I'm HERE. I get to talk to an American! I can get them in touch with my family. Have they been in touch with my family?!

Just the thought of being able to hear an American accent, let alone speak to the American embassy in Beijing was the most refreshing feeling in the world. *I was sleep deprived. I was starving and depressed. I felt like death.* But this fantastic news instantly put a smile across my face. Just walking outside of that horrific prison cell was a relief.

124

This was the best I had felt since being detained.

I looked up and down the hall. Other foreigners, including Karl and Neil were being pulled out of their cells and lined up as well. *It seemed like they had people from every single country here.*

Fu&k, I wonder how Karl and Neil are managing to hold up?! How is their cell? How are their cellmates? Are the conditions the same?

Karl and Neil spoke around the same level of Chinese as each other. It was enough for them to get around, but not enough to hold much of a conversation. *I wonder if that was helping them in their cells with the other inmates?*

Karl was being held two cells down from me. Neil was being kept just past Karl's cell. We looked down and saw each other giving subtle nods and a smile. Their hair was a mess, their faces seemed to show that they had also struggled through the night, *but at least they were up and about.* That was good enough for now.

We all survived night one. Another positive development in an otherwise impossible situation.

Once the guards finished rounding up the foreign inmates, we were marched in a single file line to the hallway exit. One of the guards unlocked the door and we were marched outside into the larger lobby that we had entered through the night before. This time, we took a hard left into a stairwell and were marched down into the first floor. I wanted to rush over to Karl and Neil to inquire about their first night, but I didn't want to alarm the guards either. They didn't know me and I wanted to stay off their radar.

At the bottom of the stairwell we were marched outside into a cold, smoggy Beijing day. Temperatures for that time of the year in Beijing hover around 40 to 45 degrees Fahrenheit in the late morning hours. Nonetheless, I was thrilled to be outside of that horrid prison cell. It was the best feeling in the world!

I looked around at the cold-dead courtyard full of decaying trees and dying foliage. Seeing all of this during the day gave me an entirely new perspective. For the first time I was clearly seeing the high-wall enclosure we were trapped in. There was barbed wire strung across the top and walkways for the armed guards patrolling the perimeter.

There was no way anyone was getting through that.

I could see tall buildings off to the west, just beyond the walls. It looked like a new apartment complex being built and I heard construction off in the distance. To the north of the wall was some other shorter building, possibly an older apartment complex. We were marching east up the central road leading towards the massive metal gates that our transport vehicle had initially entered through.

I didn't really have the time to stop and count but there seemed to be around fifteen foreign inmates in this group. As we closed in on the main gates, we took another hard left following the guards to a building that sat adjacent to the main entrance. This building was technically inside the compound and there was a little red door on our side.

One of the guards opened it and marched us inside.

Stunning, my jaw nearly dropped. Like the main lobby, the interior had gorgeous decor and was beautifully designed.

Impressive artwork was hung about the walls, with sleek décor lining the interior of the room. There were several large wooden tables divided into separate meeting areas with the same oversized black sofas that were scattered around the main lobby.

I was stunned at the sudden transformation. Why does this keep happening? Who designed sub-human torture conditions 100 meters in the other direction, and yet this place seems to be full of beautifully decorated offices and lobbies? Who the fu&k planned this? Who the fu&k approved this? What is the fuc&king point?

To my surprise, there were a couple of other foreign inmates already seated inside, waiting. *There's more?* I gazed around. We were standing in a central room that branched off into a hallway which led to the main entrance. Additional meeting rooms seemed to line the hallway with other inmates sitting and waiting.

Guard: American?

Me: Yes?

Guard: *There*, he said pointing to one of the couches in the central room.

There were already two other inmates sitting down on opposite ends of the couch he was directing me to. I walked over and sat in the middle of a white and black inmate. Both seemed to be in their early to mid-30's. The white inmate was tall and lanky while the black inmate looked short and stocky.

Me: "American?" I asked, looking over at each.

Inmate one: Yea. Alabama.

Inmate two: Yessir. New York.

Alabama: You

Me: "California. What are you here for?" I asked looking over at the first inmate.

Alabama: Fight at a bar.

Me: Damn. How long do you get for that?

Alabama: Three days.

Me: You getting deported?

Alabama: Nah, I don't think so. Sounded like an in-out thing.

New York: How long you in here for?

Me: 14 days.

New York: Damn. What did you do?

Me: They say I'm working illegally, but nothing really. My visa is legit.

New York: Expired though?

Me: No. It's completely legit. Not unexpired, legal. Just bull$h!t. You?

New York: Supposed to be 7 days, but got it reduced to 5. First offence.

Me: What for?

New York: Smoking weed. But I'm working a teaching job for a state-owned firm. Boss is government. They like me, made a few calls. They got my sentence reduced.

5 days for drugs?! 3 days for a fight?! Fu&k me, lesson learned. If you're a foreigner in China, don't start a business. Use drugs or get in a fight instead.

Alabama: Lucky fu&k. Your cell sh!t too?

Me: Yea. Eating out of the bucket?

New York: Fu7k that sh!t. Can't eat it. Looks like piss.

Alabama: How bout the squatter?

Me: Sh!ts fuc7ed. One squatter for 16 inmates in my cell.

Alabama: Fu&k me, you got 16? How long you been here for.

Me: First day today. You?

Alabama: Two, I'm out of this bit&h tomorrow.

New York: Lucky fu&k. I still got 5 days. Just arrived yesterday morning.

Me: Better than two weeks.

Alabama: Yea, that's some serious sh1t. I can't sleep on those fuc&ing planks.

Me: Yea. Place is a nightmare.

I paused as they continued talking to look around the room.

There were foreign inmates everywhere.

The guards seemed to segregate everyone by country. Some sat alone in different areas of the central room while larger groups were rushed into the bigger hallway meeting rooms.

I looked over and saw Karl sitting on the adjacent sofa all by himself. He couldn't really see me from how the couches were angled.

Guess there aren't any other Spaniards. He seemed to be doing alright. Had he managed the first night ok all alone? Well, he's up and alive, I guess? That's something.

I couldn't see Neil. I guess he had been sent into a separate room along the corridor. There were a lot of prison guards in here, monitoring and watching every last thing we did and said. I noticed a few police officers that stood out from the crowd as they were wearing a different set of solid black uniforms.

As more officers flooded in, I realized that the police had cameras on their tactical vests. The body-cameras had little red lights to indicate that the device was recording. I looked around and realized they had placed small video recording devices in various corners as well to monitor the entire room. Fu&k, I'm sure the couches even had recording equipment embedded in them.

Every last little thing was being recorded, and not for the reasons police record in the US. They weren't monitoring to protect us.

That's when we heard the main entrance doors fling open. At the far end of the hall there was an exit, into freedom. But it wasn't meant for us to go out. Instead a flood of suits and dresses streamed in; also escorted by guards. Badges hung around their necks with country designations, stacks of papers in hand, satchels flung over their shoulders. The embassy consular officers had arrived.

THANK GOD. Who is the American?

Embassy consular officers were being marched in all directions to meet their detainees. A flood of different countries emerged including, Germany, Nigeria, India, Spain, France, and others. I couldn't make them all out. One by one they found their detainees and started up what can only be described as painfully complicated conversations. Last, but not least, the American Embassy's Consular Officer appeared.

He was a tall black guy that looked to be around his mid 40's. He stood around 6'6" (1.98 cm), wearing a dark blue tweed suit, thick glasses, and was completely bald.

US CO: Howdy boys. Well gentlemen, what brings you here today?

He spoke with a deep southern drawl.

Alabama: Adventure.

New York: Weed.

Me: I literally have no idea.

US CO: Alright boys. My name's Randy. From Texas originally, pleasure to meet y'all. I am a Consulate Officer for the United States Embassy in Beijing and I'm here to see you through this. Yes, I've seen this before and yes, I know, it is far from ideal. Know that you will get out, all three of you.

Randy couldn't stop smiling. He was a wave of fu&king positive energy. We needed this.

Me: Have you seen the inside though?

US CO: No I have not. They don't let us back there. I've heard it's not great and I understand the conditions are subpar.

Me: It's a fu&king nightmare. Eating out of a bucket. One squatter toilet for 16 inmates.

New York: Sh!ts fu&ked.

US CO: Gentleman I understand it's difficult and I assure you we'll cross that bridge. First things first. Let me get your names and information.

He handed us a stack of papers.

US CO: Boys these documents do two things. One, they confirm who you are, so we can get your personal information on file. Two, they legally allow us to speak to the people you specifically cite on page two. Gentleman this is your only connection to the outside world. If you have loved ones that you want us to communicate with, you can list their full name here with their contact information on the following line. According to US law and privacy regulations, we can only communicate with people that you verify on this document. Take a minute to write down your information, and their contact details.

We all started writing. Full names. Passport numbers. Addresses in Beijing and the US. Our dates of birth. Everything was listed there.

Page two: Parent's full names. Their phone numbers. Brother's name. Fu&k, what's his number?! Dammit.

Me: I don't have a number, can you still find a way to contact him? Or through a separate contact that's listed?

US CO: No sir I cannot. I can only get in touch with the specific name and numbers listed on that paper.

Me: Even with their full name?

US CO: That is correct sir. I can't get in touch with someone that doesn't have a correct number provided by you.

Who still memorizes phone numbers?!

We finished filling out the forms and handed them back over to Randy.

New York: So now what?

US CO: Well gentlemen, there's good news and bad news. The good news is we know you're here and there are a few things we CAN do for you. We CAN provide you with a list of local attorneys, but the honest truth is, your sentences are short, and they generally can't change the length of stay anyway. You're welcome to try. Would anyone like the list?

We looked around at each other. It seemed like we all had the same experience. Nobody gave a fu&k about what we said. We could probably get an army of ten lawyers and we'd probably end up staying for three months instead of a couple weeks. The consular officer had a tone in his question emphasizing how useless it would be to try.

We all shook our heads declining the offer.

US CO: Alright. We CAN petition the Beijing Prison Administration to have a consular officer from the US embassy visit you although this is generally a one-time thing unless your sentences are significantly longer. We don't usually get to see prisoners twice in a month and by looking at all three of your charges, you should be out of here before the month is up. Hopefully.

Fu*k...hopefully?!

US CO: We can petition that you receive appropriate medical care and are being treated in a humane way and not subject to torture. Are you in need of any special medication or being subjected to inhumane treatment?

Alabama: Define torture.

New York: No, but we probably will soon with the piss they're serving us out of a bucket.

Alabama: The polluted Beijing tap water fu&ks with your system.

New York: The dude taking a sh!t and then preparing the meal bucket without washing his hands fu*ks with your system.

US CO: So that is a yes or a no?

We looked around at each other once again. "No," we replied in unison.

US CO: Ok. The Chinese criminal system is everything that you've experienced up until this point. I don't think I need to say much more than that. Gentlemen at this moment you fall under Chinese legal jurisdiction and are not subject to US law. The US Embassy in Beijing nor the US government, in any capacity, has the authority to intervene in the Chinese legal process. As criminals, you will serve your full term. We cannot remove you from your cell or state that you are guilty or innocent. We cannot provide legal advice or serve as official translators.

Additionally, there are important differences here in the Chinese legal system versus what you are used to back in the US. The Criminal Law and Criminal Procedure Law of the People's Republic of China do not include presumption of innocence, the right to remain silent, or the right to an attorney. Again, you've experienced a sufficient amount of the Chinese legal system at this point to understand how things operate. So, here's what will help you: deference, cooperation, and a good attitude. Does everyone understand?

We nodded in agreement. "Yessir," *we replied.*

US CO: Alright Alabama, let's start with you.

Time for one-on-one. I sat back and looked around as they carried on their conversation. I was still trying to take it all in. The prison cell. Being a "criminal."

Talking to a consulate officer about whether I was being tortured. It was a lot to process.

Alabama wrapped up his conversation quickly, as he was going to be out in a day or two, so he didn't seem super phased. New York didn't seem super concerned during his one-on-one either because he had help from the Chinese government via his employer. He had already been told that his sentence would be reduced and that he would not be deported.

I had my one-on-one last.

US CO: Alright California. What's happening with you.

Me: Two weeks for absolutely nothing.

US CO: Your visa isn't expired?

Me: Nope.

US CO: Legally sponsored by your legal employer…which is your company?

Me: That is correct.

US CO: Beijing work visa? Acquired by the PSB?

Me: Yup.

US CO: Written contracts for your company's clients?

Me: Yessir.

US CO: It is what it is.

Me: Indeed. So, what's this process look like?

US CO: Well, assuming you're well behaved, you'll serve the full 14 days. At that point you fall under Chinese immigration's purview.

Me: How long does that process take? Am I being deported?

US CO: You very well could be. It has happened before, but I can't say with any degree of certainty. Could take a week or two for immigration to settle your case but usually it's under a week.

Me: A week or two, plus my sentence? So, I could be looking at a month in here?

US CO: Again, I can't say with any degree of certainty. It's a case by case basis. It's possible, but I've also seen people go after a couple days for deportation. Just depends.

Me: Ok, so I'm not going to be in here for like, two months.

US CO: That is highly unlikely given your charge of illegal employment.

Me: Highly unlikely?

US CO: I haven't seen it for something like this. I would say no. Anything is possible as you've seen thus far but I wouldn't expect it.

Me: So how do I know if I am getting deported or not? Is it possible that I won't be deported?

US CO: Again, either is possible. They make internal decisions during your sentence. Immigration will come around eventually to give you a warning if you are being deported.

I had a million questions. I didn't have much advanced warning that we were going to meet with our embassy officials otherwise I would have been better prepared. But I was still incredibly tired. I could feel that my mind and body had experienced high levels of stress and anxiety. There's just nothing in the world that could prepare you for anything like this. I knew I was forgetting important questions. It was hard to focus. My brain still needed sleep. I was trying to take advantage of the situation...I didn't want to regret failing to ask something important. I knew I was forgetting a lot. I was still hungry. I was trying to focus...

I drug the conversation out as far as it would allow. I didn't want to go back to the cell and I wanted to arm myself with as much knowledge as possible. The ambiance of the room, despite the video cameras recording my entire conversation, was also a welcome break from the cage. I finally understood why they did it, the transformation.

It was part of the show for the international embassy officials.

Inmates were suffering horribly a couple hundred meters in the opposite direction, and over here we were surrounded by expensive wall art and over-sized sofas. *Very Chinese.* Nonetheless, it was nice to sit on a cushy sofa and not a rock-hard wooden table, even for just a few minutes. It was comforting chatting with an experienced American embassy officer that could help provide context in this nightmare scenario.

I told him the message I wanted passed on to my parents. I told him about my family. We talked about life back home. I explained the cell conditions, the sleeping situation, and everything else. He had probably heard these stories a million times before, but he was still kind enough to listen.

I couldn't have asked for a better consular officer to show up.

I'm not sure how much time passed nor was I even really paying attention at that point. Thirty minutes? Forty five? At some point, the guards decided that it was time for the conversations to end. *Time's up.* They walked around to all the different areas abruptly cutting off conversations. Randy motioned at one of the guards to come over. He pulled a pile of American magazines out of his satchel.

What a fu&king hero this man is.

In absolutely flawless Mandarin, he proceeded to inquire,

US CO: We have provided some reading materials for our American inmates. I would like to hand it over to them, if you could inspect it please?

Guard: Let me see.

Randy handed over a *Time Magazine, National Geographic,* and *Rolling Stone.*

Please, dear God. Oh, please oh please let me take any one of them in the cell.

The guard looked it over, front and back. He shook his head.

Guard: No.

Man, FU&K YOU. I wanted to stand up and snap his jaw off…*it's a FU&ING MAGAZINE YOU PIECE OF SH!T. FROM A FUC&ING US EMBASSY CONSULAR GENERAL!?!?!? WHO THE FU*& ARE YOU?!*

But I sat there in silence. *In my mind I was repeatedly punching the guard in the throat. These conditions were changing me. My fuse was starting to run short.*

US CO: Is there a problem with the reading material?

Guard: I'm not allowed to give him special privileges. The other inmates aren't receiving magazines.

US CO: I wasn't aware of the policy.

Guard: It's the rules.

He knew better than to argue.

Randy was a seasoned veteran. We both knew this was another ambiguous "no." *No rules were being broken.* Which way is the wind blowing? Today it blew in the "no" direction. *This is China.* The guard handed the magazines back and Randy who returned them to his satchel.

US CO: Sorry man. I tried.

Me: It's all good sir, I appreciate the effort. It is what it is.

US CO: Alright brother. Stay strong and we'll get you to the other side. We know you're here, you'll get out. Remember that. We'll get in touch with your family and let them know you're getting through this and in good spirits. But now it's your turn. Next couple of weeks are on your shoulders, you got that?

Me: Yea I got it brother. God bless.

US CO: God bless. Stay strong. We'll see you on the other side.

He was trying to be positive. I could tell by the tone in his voice and the look on his face that people struggled in here. I wasn't surprised given the horrific conditions. I thought of Soldier. Dude was tough as nails for making it as long as he had. I'm willing to bet others didn't. I wonder if Randy had seen people not survive? As reassuring as he was, you could tell he was trying to read you just as much. Trying to gauge whether you were the type of person that would pull through or not. Had I sold him one way or the other?

We stood up and shook hands. He turned around, satchel strung over his shoulder, and headed towards the other consular officers that were congregating at the end of the hallway. *I wonder what their conversations are like?* Other inmates were wrapping up their meetings. I was marched toward the door, and once again stood in line with the other inmates. I looked over as the last consulate general stood up and walked towards the hallway exit. *That was that.*

Well, we've done everything there is to do. Now this sh!t is on me. Survive.

We were marched back out the red door and through the cold decaying courtyard. *Enjoy this while it lasts. Who knows how long it'll be till you're back outside.* We entered the side door of the cell block and the guards marched us up the stairs and through the cell corridor. One by one we were lined up alongside our respective cells. The guards started at the first door, corralling the inmates into their cells. *SLAM!* First door shut. Then they moved to cell two.

SLAM! Second door, shut.

I looked over to my left as the guards approached my cell. My turn. Phil and Neil were staring down the hall at me now, as if we were waiting in line for a firing squad. So were the other inmates.

Back to reality. How long will it be till I see another American? When will I see Phil and Neil again? Will I spend another 2 months in this sh!thole like the Indonesian guy? Will I be out in two weeks? Will I be deported? Will Neil and Karl make it through? Can I survive 2 months here? Can I survive 1 month here? Fu&k, another night on those wooden planks. So fuc7ing tired. So many inmates. Are they safe? So much noise. No sleep. The piss food. Fu&k I'm hungry. The dirty tap water. Fu&k.

I couldn't shut my mind off.

The guards had arrived. One of them flung my cell door open and somehow, my mind voluntarily walked my body inside.

I could feel part of me hesitate. I could feel my body subconsciously wanting to fight back. My brain recognized the danger in front of me. I knew it wasn't safe. I knew I would rather be anywhere on Earth than inside that cage. What were the odds of me ending up here? How stupid was I to come to a country that treated people like this?

But it was a simple calculation. *Non-compliance would certainly be worse.* That was all I needed to know. I stood there, back inside my cage, as the first door locked behind me.

"China? You know that's a communist country, don't you?" Those wise words from the old woman at the bank. *Despite all my degrees, passports, international travel experience...she knew so much more than I ever could have hoped by simply having more experience than me. Now I fuc7ing know what she meant.*

SLAM! The outer-metal door slammed shut behind me.

Back in the cage...and this time, it's for real.

Fu&k.

Chapter 11:

Detention (Prison Day 1, Afternoon)

'CRACK, CRACK AND MY BACK BROKE' Former prisoners reveal horrific torture taking place in Chinese prisons

"The United Nation's Committee Against Torture (CAT) monitors the implementation of the UN's 'Convention against Torture and Other Cruel, Inhuman or Degrading Treatment or Punishment' amongst state parties. On February 3rd, 2016, CAT concluded its fifth periodic report on China's implementation of the Convention. The Committee expressed 'grave concerns' regarding the arbitrary charge of 'endangering public security' where the law doesn't stipulate that family members must be told the reason or location of a relative's detention. Access to a lawyer is routinely rejected in cases involving this type of offence which has been found to correlate with a 'high-risk' of torture.

The Committee also expressed deep concerns regarding China's unprecedented detention of over 200 human rights lawyers, four of whom remain unaccounted for. Human rights lawyers are being detained for carrying out their professional responsibilities of holding the government accountable over cases of alleged torture. The Committee concluded that these restrictions may deter human rights lawyers in China from addressing reports of torture for fear of reprisal."[42]

Chinese Government's official response to CAT's report about China's implementation of the Convention Against Torture.

---

[42] MEGAN PALIN, F. (2016, September 16). Former prisoners REVEAL horrific torture taking place in Chinese prisons. Retrieved February 28, 2021, from https://www.thesun.co.uk/news/1799086/former-prisoners-reveal-horrific-torture-taking-place-in-chinese-prisons/

Chinese Foreign Ministry Spokesperson Hua Chunying's press conference, December 10, 2015:

"Q: The UN Committee Against Torture issued a report about China's implementation of the Convention Against Torture yesterday, expressing concerns about the existence of torture in China. What is your comment on that?

A: China is firmly opposed to torture. In the process of pursuing all-round progress of law-based state governance, China has deepened judicial reform and put human rights under more protection, making well-recognized and tangible progress in its anti-torture campaign.

China is resolute in its position against torture. With the advancement of state governance in accordance with the law, China will make greater efforts for better performance in its fight against torture. We have also noted that some opinions held by the UN Committed Against Torture are based on uncorroborated information. It is hoped that the committee could stick to its mandate, improve its way of work and review China's implementation of the convention in a more comprehensive, objective and impartial way. The Chinese side will carry forward its communication with the committee based on equality and mutual respect for the realization of the purposes of the convention."

Fu&k, I was starving.

Unfortunately, I had just missed lunch, but the scheduled nap hour was supposedly about to start. *I desperately needed to catch up on sleep too.* My brain was a jumbled mess which made my mind feel physically disconnected from my body. I reflected on my conversation with Randy for a bit and felt somewhat reassured. The detention process had worn me down and I was mentally drained.

How long can I last in here?

I walked over to Soldier and Muhammed who were sitting down near the window chatting. There was a small group of Chinese inmates on the door-side of the wooden planks door discussing the orange hats hung on the wall. The Godfather was hunched over by the bathroom door, screaming some story at a small group of inmates. His captivated audience encircled him and hung on every word as he described a violent prisoner he had once encountered.

The Godfather was the most charismatic guy in the entire cell-block, and was a gifted orator.

Baaa naaa nan aa na naaaa! That music started blaring through the speaker again. Everyone got up, rushing over to the blanket pile.

Seems like that's their go to song for sleep time? I looked up at the large schedule hung on the wall. I guess it's at least 25 percent accurate?

I stood up and made my way over to the blanket pile. There didn't seem to be any method to the madness.

Grab what you can? So much for blanket assignments?

The other inmates were huddled around waiting to grab a sh!tty blanket to sleep on. Once I made my way to the front of the swarm, I grabbed the first two blankets at the top of the pile and walked off to my sleeping area. All the blankets are pretty shitty and I'm still sleeping on a wooden plank.

Picking between one blood stained blanket and another isn't going to make a huge difference at this point.

I found a spot near the window over by Muhammad. His bed was ready to go. I looked around and saw that some of the other inmates seemed to be using more than two blankets?

Are you allowed to do that? I thought we only got two?

A blanket, a mattress AND a make-shift bloody pillow...how luxurious? I looked over to the right and saw the Godfather's sleeping set-up. Somehow, he managed to get hooked up with the upgraded thicker prison blankets. How did he score that?

Interesting.

I looked over at the blanket pile and there were extra blankets left on the ground? *Fu&k it, I need sleep.* I walked over as other inmates were working on getting their beds ready and nonchalantly grabbed a third blanket.

Adapt and survive.

I made my way back to my sleeping area hoping someone wouldn't scream at me through the speaker box or some prisoner wouldn't get pissed because I was breaking some unknown blanket rule. I proceeded to fold the first blue blanket over to form the thickets mattress possible. I grabbed the second blanket and rolled it up into a makeshift pillow. No one said a word. *I guess I'm good?* I removed my slippers, got up and stepped up onto the planks.

Once again, the makeshift blood-mattress did very little. You could still feel the wooden plank prying itself into your bones. There just wasn't much you could do about that. Having my own pillow was a noticeable improvement though. It wasn't particularly comfortable, but it was better than the pillow situation from the night before.

I wonder if Neil and Karl get to use extra blankets. Maybe they were still confined to two? I'm not sure if I could manage without the third blanket. Could they?

I did my best to power through the intense discomfort. With three bodies out of the cell, we had a bit more space now. Eleven bodies on this was significantly better than fourteen.

It was still cramped but I didn't have body parts draped over me or poking into my spine. We were essentially shoulder to shoulder, but the spacing was noticeably better. I could lay down flat and move about without worrying about disrupting the inmates next to me.

Maybe I would even be able to sleep?

I looked up from my area and saw two Chinese inmates walk over to the wall, grab the bright orange hats and put them on. One walked over toward the bathroom and stood there in front of the door, facing the beds. The other stayed on the opposite side of the cell by the window and did the same.

Was this some sort of sleep-watch?

They just stood there, watching over us. *This must be some type of internal monitoring program? I guess if prisoners try to harm each other when they're asleep, these guys are supposed to step up?*

There was a little two-way speaker box mounted on the wall to the left of the cell door with a bright red button on it that seemed like an emergency comms link...to the guards?

So, I guess they're in charge while we're asleep? But why these two? Is that what Muhammad was doing the other night? Do they make you do that all night? How do they select who does this? Do you have to wear the hat? Too many questions...I need sleep.

I carefully pulled my blanket up over my eyes to block out the dim sunlight that was poking through Beijing's thick smog and the cell's fluorescent lights.

I can't sleep with all that light shining in my eyes.

My brain was still trying to alert me to the constant threat of unknowns in the cell that surrounded me.

There was obvious danger involved with falling asleep in a prison cell surrounded by inmates. What crime had they committed? Were they violent? Did any of the Chinese inmates particularly hate foreigners? Did anyone in the cell particularly hate Westerners? Did anyone in the cell particularly hate Americans? If they did, a sleeping American would be a painfully easy target. Was there even recourse if something happened? If I started getting pummeled in my sleep, would the guards even notice? Would I even be able to make it to the emergency box? Would the guys on watch do anything? Would I become the next body to be harvested for China's human organ black market?

I needed sleep.

I did my best to shut my brain off and just take solace in the comfort of my stained blankets. It was a race against the clock as well. I knew that nap time had a time limit, so I had to make the most of every minute. That added pressure was yet another variable working against my ability to get any sleep. I struggled for a few minutes, tossing from one side to the next. I was still learning how to sleep on a cold and solid wooden surface. This isn't an easy overnight transition. Lying flat on my back seemed to work the best. But my brain emphatically refused to shut-off. I was trying to force my mind to understand that I needed sleep. My brain was still fighting itself, trying to keep me alive while killing me at the same time.

After about ten minutes, something clicked. Maybe it was the reassuring conversation I had with Randy. Maybe it was being able to spend some time outside of the cage for a bit today. Maybe it was the comradery of seeing Neil and Karl survive night one. My brain finally understood that it needed to recharge. *And just like that, I fell asleep.* It wasn't a deep sleep, but it would work for now. For a few minutes, at least, I was once again able to escape the physical confines of the cage.

Baaa naaa nan aa na naaaa! Fu7k, I WAS ASLEEP!!! I looked around...*where the fu&k am I!?* Oh right...I wasn't waking up from a nightmare, *I was waking up in one. I'm in a communist prison cell.*

I felt blessed by every second of sleep I managed to get. I knew I was still not nearly caught up, but I was slowly getting there.

Maybe I would eventually be able to sleep on these wooden planks like the others?

The inmates slowly rose and began to pack away their bedding. I looked up at the clock, 1:15 pm. *They certainly stuck to the schedule this time, didn't they?* I got up, grabbed my blankets and walked them over to the blanket pile. *Now what?*

A couple of the Chinese inmates walked into the bathroom to group-pee, as I walked back over to Soldier and Muhammad. Like it or not, the cell was racially segregated. Foreigners, on one side, Chinese on the other. There might have been a linguistic barrier as well, but would it have changed much if we were able to communicate?

I thought of US prisons…*probably not. Might even make things worse?* Maybe the fact that the Chinese inmates couldn't talk to Muhammad and Soldier was a positive thing and prevent any possible conflict?

After a quick bathroom run, I glanced up at the schedule. There was supposed to be another outdoor activity and some type of educational program. *Maybe this will be like the morning where the guards just forget that we're here and leave everyone locked-up? That's gotta be far easier for them.*

Once again, the schedule was ignored, and we were just left in the cell for the next two hours. It was a bit of a blessing and a curse. On one hand, it was nice to be left alone and I didn't have to worry about following orders or dealing with the guards. On the other hand, being stuck in a cell with nothing to do grinds your soul to pieces. Not only are you bored, but you're constantly affected by the very close-quarter actions of the twelve other people you're locked in a cage with. You can't run, and there's nowhere to escape.

Every sneeze. Every cough. Every laugh. Every conversation. Every fart. Every burp. Every sound. Every footstep. Every question. Every movement. You're constantly stuck in the middle of every action everyone does at all times.

I tried laying down on the cold wooden planks to catch a bit more rest before dinner. I obviously wouldn't be able to fall asleep, but maybe if I just forced my eyes shut, it would do something to relieve the grogginess? The plan kind of worked as I snuck brief fifteen to thirty minute stints of rest. You could lie down on the planks for a bit, if all the other inmates weren't doing it at the same time.

Sure, there was a camera perched on the ceiling in the corner of the room, which meant the guards were always watching us. The gist seemed to be that we weren't allowed to sleep during non-sleep hours. But it was probably hard for the guards to visibly make out whether someone was just taking a breather or dozing off and that was compounded by the sheer number of prison cells.

If there were two or three inmates lying down, they seemed to let it fly under the radar. But as soon as it caught on and more inmates started jumping in on the sleep-action…*ASOD JSOD AJSDNWO USHDWUO AJDOA!* This inaudible muffle sound flooded through the speaker instantly prompting everyone in the cell to jolt up and off the planks.

After I managed to catch a bit of sleep, we slowly began prepping for dinner. *I was starving!* I had barely eaten the day before and so far, and I was wholly unable to put down the yellow-sludge from breakfast. I needed to eat. The designated meal-prep inmate was busy washing out the bucket in the bathroom, which probably made it dirtier than anything else.

At least he was trying? Let's hope the guards don't randomly ignore scheduled meals too.

I still wasn't entirely sure of how to approach the water situation. The only option we had at our disposal was drinking Beijing's heavily polluted tap water. I never went near it in five years of living in Beijing, and for good reason. Suddenly, it was supposed to be magically keeping me alive. *Is it better to drink it and stay hydrated or limit my exposure and keep thirsty?* I wasn't sure which way to go.

The Godfather: "American," the Godfather screamed from across the room. "How was your outing today?"

Me: It was nice to be outside, for a bit.

The Godfather: A private walk with the guards?

Odd line of questioning. Was he working for the guards? Some kind of snitch? Or did he think I was?

Me: American embassy. Foreigners had to meet with our embassy representatives.

The Godfather: Lucky you! I don't have an embassy. If I am locked in your country, the Chinese embassy will be happy for a few of us criminals to die. Too many people in China. They don't have time to save us all.

Me: I think it's just protocol.

The Godfather: Was your embassy helpful?

Me: Well, I'm still in here.

He burst out laughing.

The Godfather: Did you try telling them your visa is unexpired?

Me: I told them.

The Godfather: Yes, you are in China now. The government here does not care what your government thinks.

Me: I suppose that's true.

The Godfather: You'll get out of here. The foreigners all do. Especially from the good countries. America is a good country. I wouldn't worry. The German left quickly too.

Me: The German?

The Godfather: "Yes, I saw the German inmate come and go quickly. Some countries stay longer" he said, nodding over at Muhammad and Soldier. "Other countries, they go fast. I think you'll go fast."

Me: Thank you. Ready for dinner?

The Godfather: I always eat well in here. Be sure to do the same American.

SLAM!

We heard the outer hallway door slammed shut. Outside we heard food carts being rolled up and down the hall while doors were being opened. The keys jiggled at our cell door, and the door swung open, revealing the same recognizable silver colored food cart just outside.

Once again, the food prep inmate ran over to the door with the red bucket and placed it under the square hole. The cook on the other side of the door stuck a large metal funnel through the barred door. He picked up a large metal container and waddled back over to the cell door, once again dumping the contents through the metal funnel into our communal food-bucket.

The food-prep inmate took the now-full, shiny red plastic bucket and heaved it up onto the far bed planks by the cell door. He ran back to the door, grabbing the mantou brick-sheet through the barred door, while the other inmates huddled around the bucket with their plastic containers in hand. One by one the inmates grabbed the communal container floating around in the food and scooped individual helpings into their individual plastic cups.

Please be something edible this time.

I could see the food in the plastic containers as the inmates were walking back. "Potatoes" I heard one scream in Chinese. Once the crowd slowly died down, I could see into the bucket, *it didn't look terrible.* Sure, if you offered this up on a normal day, I wouldn't touch it with a ten-foot pole. But it wasn't another helping of the yellow slop which set a hell of a low-bar, and by comparison, this was surprisingly better.

I reached in the bucket and grabbed the communal container. Surprisingly, the food looked and smelled ok, and I proceeded to scoop up a massive serving into my personal container. I grabbed a bread brick and walked back over toward the window where Soldier and Muhammad were squatting down next to their meals.

I placed my container and bread brick down on the bed and squatted down into the eating position. I examined the meal that was floating around in my plastic container, chopped bits of potatoes, some tiny balls of meat, all floating around in a light brown broth.

At least I know what it is this time. I hope…

I dug my plastic spoon into the container and lifted the food to my mouth. I proceeded to take a slow and cautious bite…*it was fu&king delicious.* No, it wasn't well seasoned. No, it wasn't properly cooked. Yes, every other unhygienic inmate's hands had been dipped into this soupy mixture as they were serving themselves…BUT *it was edible, AND I KNEW what I was eating.*

I'll gladly take that for Chinese prison food from a bucket. I started shoveling in food faster than I could breathe. I dipped the bread brick into the warm broth which softened it up making it edible too.

This was life-changing.

I looked up, not fully realizing that I had been shoveling this food into my mouth for the past few minutes. Muhammad and Soldier looked at me, somewhat suprised, and then back at each other and continued eating their meals. You could see it on their faces, *at least he's finally eating.* The fact that I was finally eating seemed to be a bit of a sigh of relief for them as well.

I finished the food in my container, got up and walked back over to the red bucket, following the other inmate's lead. I scooped up a second helping and walked back over to Muhammad and Soldier. I couldn't do more squatting, so I just stood there, shoveling more food into my mouth. I just wasn't built to squat and eat at the same time or I needed more practice. Either way, at this particular moment, I didn't really care.

Muhammad: You like it?

Me: Man, I'm starving. Better than whatever they serve in the mornings.

Soldier: Good. Eat. It will keep you strong in here. Need to stay strong.

He didn't need to tell me twice. I stood there shoveling more food into my mouth. In that brief moment, I felt happy. My mind wasn't focused on how hopelessly far away from home I was. I wasn't thinking about being locked up in a cage. I wasn't worried about what the next few weeks would bring. The hunger that overwhelmed me for much of the day was fading.

For now, a warm and edible meal would be enough to distract me from the harsh realities of communist detention.

Chapter 12:

Detention (Prison Day 1, Into the Evening)

U.S. Teacher: I Did 7 Months of Forced Labor in A Chinese Jail

"American Stuart Foster, better known as prisoner 1741, spent 7-months detained in a Chinese labor prison. Daily work in detention consisted of assembling Christmas lights for up to 10-hours a day where leaders would braid wires together and whip the inmates to drive production. A mentally disabled boy in detention was also routinely slashed across his back. Chinese guards were primarily concerned that prisoner 1741 would return to the US and tell American's about the conditions in Chinese detention."[43]

Chinese Government's official response to global letter pleading for the release of two Canadian citizens detained in China. Chinese Foreign Ministry Spokesperson Hua Chunying's press conference, January 22, 2019:

"Q: Today former diplomats and scholars from a dozen of countries sent an open letter to the Chinese side, requiring China to release the two Canadian citizens recently detained in China. What is your comment?

---

[43] Langfitt, F. (2014, May 29). U.S. teacher: I did 7 months of forced labor in a Chinese jail. Retrieved February 28, 2021, from https://www.npr.org/sections/parallels/2014/05/29/314597050/u-s-teacher-i-did-seven-months-of-forced-labor-in-a-chinese-jail#:~:text=of%20Stuart%20Foster-,South%20Carolinian%20Stuart%20Foster%20spent%20more%20than%20seven%20months%20in,his%20days%20assembling%20Christmas%20lights.

A: I have noted the letter you mentioned. It was sent by Canada and some of its allies. The former diplomats from seven countries and scholars of several countries have committed at least two mistakes.

First, they equated those who undertake research and normal exchanges between China and other countries with the two Canadians who were taken compulsory measures by the Chinese national security agencies for activities endangering China's national security. This is disrespect for people who are committed to promoting normal and friendly exchanges between China and the rest of the world.

Second, they interfered in China's judicial sovereignty. They attempted to mount pressure on China by publicly making their request to release the two Canadians who are under investigation in accordance with the law by the relevant Chinese departments. This is disrespect for China's judicial sovereignty and the spirit of the rule of law.

I want to stress once again that China welcomes all foreign citizens, including former diplomats, scholars and ordinary people, to conduct normal and friendly exchanges in China. As long as they abide by Chinese laws and regulations, there is nothing to worry about at all."

HELP

Their pain felt very real.

I couldn't peel my eyes away.

Who left this here?

I'll certainly never know. And there it was, etched into the wall. I was standing in the far corner of the room by the window, staring at this tiny bit of communist prison cell history. The walls looked like a torture room that had been designed for a horror movie. **Help** was the largest and most noticeable inscription that had been carved in the far wall by one of our cell's many forebears.

TRAPPED

Who carved this one? Did they make it out? I wonder what they used to carve this in the first place? Were they in danger? Did they make it out of here alive? Did they see anyone die here? Have people died here? Could I die here?

Would I die here?

DEATH

Maybe this is considered art?

Every last square inch of the walls were covered with inscriptions. People from all over the world had passed through this communist nightmare as plenty of languages were engraved into the walls, Arabic, Spanish, German, Russian, English, Chinese, Korean, Japanese, and other scripts I didn't recognize. Some of the inscriptions were crude, others were artistic.

Our forebears had etched faces, countdown calendars, names, dates, countries, cities, provinces, greetings, warnings, pictures, curse words; it was stunning. I'd never really seen anything like it in my life.

What had these people seen?

SUICIDE

How long had this one been here?

How long has this cell been here? How many inmates had called this nightmare home? What's the longest someone stayed locked up in here? Had there been fights? Stabbings? Had anyone killed themselves here? If so, what did they do with the body?

China is well-known for harvesting human organs.

Who had been the cell's first foreigner? How many different nationalities had passed through here? How many had not survived the experience? Had anyone ever been killed here? Was it by where I was standing? Was it where I was sleeping? How did they die?

Did anyone care?

FUCK

The words were a desperate search for meaning.

They portrayed the shared experience of others who had once been trapped in this existential nightmare. These inscriptions weren't carved because our forebears sought to convey some fundamental truth to the world.

No, the world would never see this, and the carver already knew that.

These had been produced by people who could feel their own death. There were no psychiatrists or therapists here to see you. This wasn't a treatment center where anyone was invested in your well-being. There was no voluntary process to check in or out. There were no visiting hours for friends or family. Nobody here speaks your language. No one here cares for you.

The guards probably got quarterly incentive bonuses for harvesting human organs.

This system was designed to emphasize the worthlessness of your existence. You didn't matter. Eat fecal-infested slop from a bucket you animal. How much does it take to break the human soul? No one here will miss you. Do it. We dare you.

That was the point. Once they stripped you of your humanity, you become the same as any other inanimate object.

This was either death or a chance at rebirth.

RUN

These carvings didn't originate from an assignment, fleeting passion, or a paycheck. They didn't speak in hushed gentle tones. No, they grabbed you by the throat and body slammed you through the ground; grinding your face around in gravel, kicking you in the ribs, laughing and screaming,

FU&K YOU, YOU WORTHLESS PIECE OF SH!T, WHAT THE FU&K ARE YOU GOING TO DO?! NOTHING.

You could sense the forebears inescapable pain. And all the while, there were these four walls, staring at you, and your hopeless condition. They flooded you with the torment and anguish of those who had suffered before you stepped into hell.

No, it wasn't the end of the world, but you could certainly see it from here. It was my turn to suffer. It was my turn to experience the fragility of my own existence.

I looked away and stared up at the clock. It had been about an hour and a half since dinner.

At least I wasn't hungry anymore. Tired, but not hungry. One problem solved.

I started pacing back and forth in the tiny space between the inner wall and the row of wooden planks. *Window to door. Door to window. Window to door.* Some inmates were sitting around staring at the walls while others were busy chatting. One inmate periodically stood up to pace back and forth with me. Another prisoner was catching up on sleep in the blanket pile. The Godfather was crawling around in his hunched over fashion, hopping from one group to the next. The lieutenant followed him in and out of groups, randomly slamming his hands on the planks, the wall, and the cell door. It was completely unnecessary. He thought it was hilarious.

Ignore it, I thought.

By pacing, I was trying to kill two birds with one stone. I knew I had to find a way to stay in shape because we really weren't given an opportunity to exercise. Second, pacing helped kill time. Few things in this cell were really scheduled in any meaningful way which meant you didn't really have much to do throughout the day.

Meals and sleep were about the only things that were actually scheduled so there wasn't much to ever look forward to. The passage of time largely revolved around jumping from one survival activity to the next. Everything else felt like a meaningless grey area, which compounded a painful and macro-scale question: what *was* the point? Fighting for sleep for the sake of being able to fight for more sleep? Eating for the sake of getting to your next depressing eating session?

The harsh and meaningless reality of these trends became apparent within your first day. The walls were slowly making a lot more sense.

Another compounding factor in the endlessly slow passage of time was the constant influence of every last action by the inmates surrounding you. There were annoying inmates, loud inmates, presumptively violent inmates. Everyone was crammed into this tiny space, and you weren't in control of anything.

You were relegated to a passive audience member, and every minute was a grueling test of your patience.

The "evening activity" listed on the daily schedule once again seemed to translate into, *forget the inmates exist and leave them in the cage.*

Pacing was one way to kill time, but you could only do that for so long. Eventually, that got too tiring or boring. Currently, it was only around 6:30 pm. According to the schedule there was another three and half hours of the guards pretending like we didn't exist.

Your options were limited in here.

1) Risk lying down on the wooden beds and being screamed at through the speaker.
2) Read and interpret the walls.
3) Strike up yet another conversation with Muhammad and Soldier.
4) Watch the Chinese inmates play cards.
5) Get more toxic Beijing tap water to drink.

That was essentially it.

SLAM! The outer hallway door slammed shut. Everyone jolted up and darted into place, standing or sitting along the edge of the planks. Once again, I found myself sitting next to Soldier and Muhammad, as the three of us heard the footsteps of guards approaching our cell. The guards stopped just outside of our cell as one of the guards began jingling keys around.

Great, our cell. What now?

The reinforced outer door swung open, with two guards staring in at us from the outside. One approached to unlock the inner barred door as a new Chinese inmate emerged from the hall. The guards guided him into the cell where he paused to take in his new environment. He appeared to be in his mid-thirties, not particularly tall and quite thin.

Still frozen in place, he continued to stand there staring at all of us and examining the interior of his new home. And there we were, fourteen strangers that he was about to be locked in a cage with, staring right back at him. He looked over at the closest inmate that was seated right next to the door.

You could see the discomfort on his face as he looked around at us one by one. There were the large Chinese inmates and then there were the tatted Chinese inmates with their jackets off.

Fu&K, there are foreigners here too, when he finally noticed that I was in the cell. You could see the look on his face shift when he saw me, then Soldier and Muhammad.

He saw the Godfather who was awkwardly chained and hunched over. For what appeared to be a pretty average Chinese guy, this wasn't the most pleasant environment to find yourself locked-up in.

I was seeing what I must have looked like when I entered the cell for the first time. Did I look like that?

SLAM! The guards proceeded to shut the doors behind him without so much as a word. *Poor guy. I know exactly how that sh!t feels. Baptism by fire.* He was just standing there, still frozen. Awkwardly enough, I wasn't sure what the protocol was for new prisoners. *Was it different for Chinese inmates? Would it be weird if I said something first? Was there some type of hierarchy that was supposed to be established among the Chinese inmates as new prisoners entered?*

Soldier: Another passenger.

Muhammad nodded, staring at our new cellmate.

Muhammad: Another passenger.

The first person to make a move was the Godfather. He got up into his bent over position and crawl-walked over in the direction of the new inmate with his chain clanking behind him on the floor. I felt bad, but it certainly wasn't my place to break protocol. *This poor guy looked terrified as the Godfather hobbled over toward him.* I couldn't blame him. I wasn't sure if the Godfather chain-hobbling in his direction was going to help this situation or make things worse. He stopped a few feet away and looked up at our new, terrified cellmate who stood their eyeing his approach.

The Godfather: What's your name.

Cellmate: Zhou Lin.

The Godfather: I'm the Godfather. What are you in here for?

Zhou: Fighting.

The Godfather: How long?

Zhou: A week.

Fu&k me. A week!? For a fight?! Why the Fu&k am I getting two weeks?!

The Godfather: Oh, that's nothing. I'm doing 180 days for drugs. Here, you can put your belongings over here.

The Godfather waddled over to show him an opening under one of the beds. He didn't have much of a choice, and followed the Godfather's lead, placing his bag under the bed.

Other inmates started talking to him now.

Where are you from?

What do you do?

First time in prison?

Slowly, the conversation seemed to help ease him into his new surroundings. Other inmates grew disinterested and broke away to continue their card games. Some started pacing around, while others got up to get some water. Our new inmate was still looking up uncomfortably at the me, Soldier and Muhammad who were bunched up together at the back of the cell. I could hear their conversation eventually shift to *the foreigners* as some of the other cellmates started to explain who we were.

Fu&k, back up to 14. Less sleeping space.

Muhammad: They come, and they go.

Soldier: I stay.

Me: How much more time do you think?

Soldier: Only God knows. Until then, I'm here.

Me: I'm sure you're on the way out.

Muhammad: You on watch tonight?

Me: What's that?

Soldier: The orange hats. The watch.

Muhammad: "Make sure no one kills each other" he said laughing.

Me: Oh, is that what you were doing last night?

Muhammad: Yes, if you are on watch, you must wear the hat, so the guards can monitor you.

Me: Ok, so, how does that work?

Soldier: Rotating shifts.

Muhammad: Four shifts. 10:00 to 12:00, 12:00 to 2:00, 2:00 to 4:00 and 4:00 to 6:30.

Me: What do you do?

Soldier: "You stand there for 2 hours" he said pointing to the walk space, "and you watch everyone sleep." "If something happens, you press the button on the box" pointing towards the comms box next to the door.

Me: Who decides who does which shift?

Muhammad: "We do" he said pointing at everyone. "We take turns. After you do it a few nights, you get a break and get to sleep through the night. Same thing happens during the nap hour."

I guess there was one upside to having more inmates crammed in here…fewer shifts.

Me: When do we decide for tonight?

Soldier: Depends. At some point they start talking about it. We talk it over. That's that. You'll see.

Muhammad: You're new. You'll probably be on shift. You always work your first night.

FU7K! I need sleep.

Me: Any shifts to avoid?

Soldier: They are all terrible.

Muhammad: Try and get the first or last shift so you can sleep uninterrupted.

"干嘛呢？！" (Gan Ma Ne?!) What are you doing?!

WTF?! That's different?

I looked back towards the door. *The TV works?!* Hung on the top right corner of the ceiling, opposite the camera and speaker, was what I thought was a broken and unworkable tv set from the eighties.

It was a small grey box, and I had figured that it wasn't working and someone just left it there from another era. Lo and behold, *the guards could turn it on?!* From what I could make out, they had selected some type of a Chinese soap opera, which explained the unnecessary screaming. The screen itself was hazy, and the colors were super blurred but nonetheless, *it worked.*

Me: They let us watch TV?

Soldier: Not usually, and it's only this channel. But occasionally they turn it on in the evening for an hour or two. If we have behaved.

Muhammad: Otherwise it's the educational videos.

Me: Educational videos?

Soldier: If we don't behave, they make us sit in rows on the planks and watch behavioral videos during the day.

Muhammad: Some of them are about STD's and prostitution. Others about the law in China and gambling. Always in Chinese, I don't really understand them. Propaganda.

Great. Even the TV can be weaponized against us.

A couple of the inmates gathered at the foot of the planks near the cell door, so they could hear the show over the other loud conversations.

Fu&k, it was better than staring at the walls.

I walked over and leaned up against the wall just before the bathroom door. The sound wasn't great, and the screen kept cutting in and out, but *you could generally follow what was happening.* I stood there for the next hour and a half, watching this tiny grey box from the eighties and some horrible Chinese soap opera I could barely understand or see.

Chinese dramas always seemed to revolve around the same general theme and this one was no different: family conflicts.

There was a young university girl who seemed to get in trouble with her family. She rode off with some rebellious local boys who had a motorcycle. She stayed out too late. Someone in her family ended up in a hospital from what appeared to be a stroke. She was shamed for not being at home with her family at precisely the right time.

Lesson learned. Don't have fun in China. Don't take risks. Always do as you're told. That was always a recurring theme.

I stared at that shoddy screen for as long as humanly possible.

Fu7k, it's only 8:30?! Another hour and a half?!?!

More pacing. Poison water. Repetitive conversation. Wall staring. Sitting. Standing. These were my options.

The TV blinked off a few minutes later. I guess that was our entertainment for the night? The guards had decided we had seen enough. *I wonder if there are TV's in each cell? I wonder how Karl and Neil are doing?*

I went back and sat down. *Five minutes. Ten minutes. Twenty minutes. FU&K!? Still not 9:00 pm...*

The Godfather: American!

I guess this is my new nickname.

Me: Yes?

The Godfather: You're on watch tonight. You and the new guy.

Me: Which shift?

The Godfather: Uhhh, who is on shift one?

The inmates looked around with three raising their hands...

Inmate 3: "I'm on one, you're on shift two" he said pointing at inmate 2.

Inmate 2: I just worked shift four last night, you're on shift two.

Inmate 3: "It's me and him on shift one" he said pointing to the other inmate with his hand up.

Inmate 1: "No, me and inmate two called shift one. You're on shift two."

This isn't going well.

Soldier, Muhammad and I looked around at each other watching this all unfold from the back. The inmates were tired of working shifts, that much was clear. They argued it out, pointing at each other, the clock, and the Godfather until inmate 3 finally chose to submit and take shift 2 with another inmate.

The Godfather looked over at me: "American, you and him" he said pointing at the new inmate "shift three."

Me: "Got ya, shift three" I said looking over and nodding at my new cellmate. He looked back nodding in agreement.

The Godfather: "Small black" he said in Chinese pointing at Soldier, "and lieutenant on shift four."

Soldier looked up: "No, no, no, no, no" he said, wagging his finger back and forth at the Godfather.

Oh fu&k. Not again. They can't communicate with each other.

Soldier: "Last night, I worked shift three. Night before shift 2. Tonight, I don't work. Tonight, I sleep. Make him do it," he said pointing at another Chinese inmate. "Tell him it's his turn. Boy is lazy. He never works the watch."

The Godfather stood there, hunched over, staring at me, waiting for a translation trying to figure out what the fu&k "small black" had just ranted on about in English.

Guess I'm the default translator.

None of the Chinese inmates could speak English. Muhammad and Soldier couldn't speak Chinese. *Ease tensions Steve, ease tensions. How do I word what Soldier just said, so this other dude doesn't try and punch him in the face?*

Me: He says he worked shift two and three the last two nights. He says he's sleeping tonight. Suggested another for shift 4?

Fu&k, I framed it as a question. I don't want Soldier pissed off at me either.

The Godfather: "Fine, fine." He looked back at the nameless inmate, "shift 4" then back at me, "but he'll work the nap tomorrow" he said pointing at Soldier.

Now a soldier was staring over at me with the same confused face. *The fuck did Godfather just point at me for?*

Me: He says you can sleep, but you'll have to work the nap tomorrow.

Soldier: "These Fuc7ers. That lazy ass never works. He should do both," He waved and gave the nameless inmate a thumbs up. He smiled at The Godfather signaling approval.

Soldier was running on fumes. I couldn't blame him. I was struggling, and it was still my first day. How would I feel after a week? Two? What about thirty-something days of indefinite detention?

This place was a sh1tshow and I began to see how some tiny disagreement could easily get out of hand. A bunch of tired overworked inmates, locked in a cage, battling it out for sleep. This place is a recipe for disaster.

And here I was stuck in the middle. Fu7K. I must have missed the lecture on international prison translation & conflict resolution?

Despite the initial disagreement, the night watch schedule eventually got sorted. Knowing that this same high-stress event of picking shifts had to recur every single night wasn't reassuring. The Godfather seemed to have it locked-down for now, but what would happen if he weren't here to orchestrate the process?

I looked back up at the clock, and there were thirty minutes until we were supposed to transition into "sleep" mode. Now is a great time to read through that long behavioral guide posted on the far wall. *Something new to do.* I walked over to the English version and started reading through the poorly translated sign:

> **3: Always show respect guards. Follow their instructional order.**

> **15: Inform authorities dangerous behavior. Inmates who misbehave will be punishment.**

> **21: …notify authorities if anyone commits suicide.**

Fantastic. Was it meant to be a warning or were they trying to seed ideas?

I finished the list. *There was nothing useful listed but that didn't stop me from reading it a second time.* Every second dragged by painfully slow in here. Minutes felt like hours. Time was a formidable enemy and it was always on your mind.

Not knowing how long you would be locked-up here for was a horrible feeling. That uncertainty was compounded by the fact that you had no idea what would happen next.

Would I receive the same treatment as everyone else? Would they try and tack on extra charges simply because they can? Would I end up being deported? Would I be released? What did that signed document actually say? Would I ever see my family again? Might it take months? Years?

That uncertainty and the unknowns in here are what kill you. The two worked in tandem to torment you and it worked masterfully.

Eventually, I managed to get through my first night of the ever-enjoyable "evening activity." At some point, and to my honest surprise, the clock eventually landed on 9:30 pm. My brain was shattered from exhaustion and sheer boredom. Then there were all the other adjustments like the relentless flood of noise from the other inmates. The new "food." The new "water." The new environment. The uncertainty. It was overwhelming, despite your body and mind's best efforts to adapt. Making it through evening one was a small victory, *but how many more of these would there be?*

Just as we had done in the morning, inmates began lining up against the bathroom wall to prepare for bed. I grabbed my toothbrush, toothpaste and red plastic cup and proceeded to the back of the line. When it was my turn, I walked inside, looked around at the depressing moldy tile and went to work. Pee? *Check.* Brush teeth? *Check.*

As other inmates were finishing up in the bathroom, I walked over to grab my blankets for the night. *Let's see what happens if I grab three?* I took them out of the pile and walked over to my spot near the window by Muhammad and Soldier. I rolled out my "mattress" on the wooden plank and followed that up with folding my "pillow" into place.

Me: How do we rotate in between shifts?

Muhammad: The one on watch will tap you to wake up. When you are tapped, you get up and put on the hat. Do your watch, then tap the next in line.

Soldier: Do it a minute or two early. Some of these fuc7ers are lazy. They get up slow or try and go back to bed. Don't lose sleep.

Me: Alright, good call.

It was almost 10:00 pm. I was tired. I kicked my slippers off under the metal frame and climbed up into bed. I rolled my blanket up to shield my eyes from the light.

Shift three.

Once again, I knew I wouldn't get sleep. Sure, it was time to sleep, but everyone was talking. This wasn't kindergarten nap time, it was a prison cell filled with grown adult male inmates. *No one gives a fu&k.*

At least I can control the light.

Anyone that did manage to sleep through the noise was snoring or farting. Others were laughing. What was I going to do? Yell at everyone? In a prison cell? For the time being, I was just happy to be off their radar. I wanted to keep things that way. *Racial demographics weren't tipped in my favor in here.*

At least I can control the light.

That was my victory. The one variable in my control. I don't know if the light even made a huge difference at the end of the day, but the ability to control something, once you've been stripped of everything, mattered.

At least I can control the light.

I lied there, tired yet unable to fall asleep. My saggy eyes stared into another bright blue, blood-stained blanket. The laughter. The farts. The hard plank digging into my bones. *Day one. I made it through day one. How many more of these days can I survive?*

At least I can control the light.

Six and a half hours of sleep. If I am 100% efficient, I'll get six and a half hours of sleep tonight. Would that even be enough to sustain me, given how much sleep I've already lost? How much will I realistically get? Four hours? Two hours? *What will that do to or for me?* Four hours until my shift. I'm not looking forward to standing-up from 2:00 am to 4:00 am to watch everyone else sleep.

Will I manage to get any sleep after my shift?

Once again, I tried to force my mind to shut off. I tried to will myself to sleep, even though I knew I could sense that it wasn't going to happen. My brain still sensed danger. I was sleep-deprived. My body was stressed. I didn't want to admit it, but I was *afraid*.

At least I can control the light.

At least I can control the light.

At least I can control the light…

Chapter 13:

Human Rights

Liu Xiaobo, Nobel laureate and political prisoner, dies at 61 in Chinese custody

"Peace prize winner and democracy activist dies of liver cancer, after spending almost a quarter of his life behind bars in China."[44]

Chinese Government's official response to Liu Xiaobo being awarded the Nobel Peace Prize in 2010. Chinese Foreign Ministry Spokesperson Ma Zhaoxu's remarks, October 9th, 2010:

"Q: On Oct. 8, the Norwegian Nobel committee awarded the Nobel Peace Prize for 2010 to Chinese "dissident" Liu Xiaobo. How do you comment?

A: As described in Nobel's will, the Nobel Peace Prize should be awarded to the person who "shall have done the most or the best work for fraternity between nations, the abolition or reduction of standing armies and for the holding and promotion of peace congresses". Liu Xiaobo is a criminal who broke China's laws and was convicted by Chinese judicial authorities. What he did runs in opposite directions to the purposes of the Prize. It completely violates the principles of the prize and discredits the peace prize itself for the Nobel committee to award the prize to such a person.

Q: Will the award undermine China-Norway relations?

---

[44] Liu Xiaobo, Nobel laureate and political prisoner, dies at 61 in CHINESE CUSTODY. (2017, July 13). Retrieved February 28, 2021, from https://www.theguardian.com/world/2017/jul/13/liu-xiaobo-nobel-laureate-chinese-political-prisoner-dies-61

A: Over the past years, China-Norway relations have maintained sound development, which is in the fundamental interests of both countries and peoples. The award of the Nobel Peace Prize to Liu Xiaobo by the Nobel committee not only contravenes the principles of the Nobel Peace Prize but also will damage China-Norway relations."

Growing up in California, I had never really put much thought into the concept of human rights. Sure, we *heard* about it all the time and occasionally, it would pop-up in the news or a teacher's lecture in class. Every now and then I would hear older people discuss authoritarian governments, especially growing up in a definitively immigrant family, where human rights violations were often historically referenced.

That being said, I was never personally exposed to human rights abuses in the same capacity that they occur on an international scale. For me, the concept of human rights existed in the same capacity as the civil war, electrons, and π; it was just another distant and abstract concept I learned about in school or the news.

I remember hearing people discuss Chinese, North Korean and Iranian human rights violations, and they would explain why we needed to preserve human rights in the US and why that made America such a special country. But all of this, sadly, went in one ear and out the other. These were ideas that were too advanced for my *brilliant* and *educated* mind to absorb, understand or comprehend.

I never really stopped to truly reflect, internalize and contemplate the harsh reality of human rights violations.

Why? Because I am privileged.

No, I'm not referring to the conversation about skin tone and privilege. Sure, I'm a melanin producing biracial son of Swiss and Mexican immigrants and I couldn't be more proud of that.

So, what privilege am I referring to? *The privilege of living in the United States and being an American citizen.* There is no greater privilege, irrespective of my skin-tone. That is why I never really had to stop and contemplate human rights in the same sense that people suffering at the hand's of horrific government abuse are forced to. I was privileged enough to grow up in a country where human rights are not only allowed to exist, but there is a concerted effort to embed them into the very fiber of our society and legal system.

Sure, no system is perfect but instances where human rights abuses do occur, we are lucky enough to live in a country where they make national headlines and the issue is discussed publicly.

That's the difference.

When egregious human rights violations occur in the US, the 24/7 media outlets cover these issues: newspapers, tv, radio, magazines & the internet. You literally can't escape it and these stories flood each and every last home from the East to the West Coast.

That's the difference.

In the US, you hear about those failures of the system. But it's worth emphasizing that those shortcomings are the exception, not the rule. You'll actually learn the name of the victim. You'll see a picture of their face. You'll hear what went wrong. Their family will explain their side of the case to the media. They will have their day in court and get legal representation.

That's the difference.

So, how do things work in China? Human rights violations are the rule, not the exception. That is the default standard of how law enforcement operates. Everyone there knows this, accepts it and understands that they are in no position to enact change without severe repercussions. The Chinese fear their government, and that's very much the point of how the Chinese system is designed.

That's the difference.

This is why the Chinese who land in the US think our legal system is a joke, soft, and not something that needs to be feared. "American police are more restrained than criminals", was a common phrase I heard from Chinese nationals.

Is any of this starting to make sense yet?

So what differences exist when it comes to the arrest and detention process in the US versus China? Here's a checklist of the rights you're granted in the United States if you're arrested:

+ **I was allowed to remain silent**

   One of the most important rights of a person accused of a crime is the right to remain silent. You cannot be forced to divulge information to the police. This right stems from the Fifth Amendment right against self-incrimination. In other words, you are not required to prove your case for the police. They are responsible for developing the evidence to prove you have in fact committed a crime. The right to remain silent was confirmed in the U.S. Supreme Court case of Miranda v. Arizona. If you attempted to remain silent in the face of police questioning, and were coerced or forced into speaking, your rights have been violated.

+ **I was told that anything I chose to say can be used against me**

The police must inform you that if you choose to speak, "anything you do say may be used against you in a court of law." If you were told that you had the right to remain silent but were not informed of the consequences of choosing to speak, your rights may have been violated.

+ **I was allowed to have an attorney present when I requested one**

Another absolute right of a person under arrest for a crime is the right to have an attorney present during questioning and the right to have counsel during any trial. If you requested an attorney during questioning, and the police denied you that request, your rights may have been violated.

+ **I was not asked questions while my attorney was absent:**

Once you request the assistance of an attorney, the police are prohibited from questioning you later without your attorney. In other words, you have the right to have an attorney present during the first, and any subsequent, talks with the police.

+ **I was not forced to pay for my attorney's services:**

Just as you are entitled to have an attorney, you are also entitled to a state-paid and appointed attorney if you cannot afford your own attorney per a state's or county's guidelines. If you fall within this category, you will be assigned a public defender to represent you.

+ **Although I initially didn't ask for an attorney, when I asked for one later in my questioning, questioning stopped and didn't start again until my attorney arrived:**

In many situations, criminal suspects may have false confidence that they can handle the matter on their own, without the assistance of an attorney. A criminal suspect who decides to answer police questions without an attorney present still has the right to ask for an attorney at any later point. Once a suspect asks for an attorney, all questioning must stop until the attorney arrives.

✦ I was treated humanely:

Unfortunately, police brutality and unfair treatment continue to occur in the United States. A criminal suspect is entitled to humane treatment, no matter how heinous the alleged crime. If you were not treated humanely, for instance if you were deprived of food and water or if you were beaten either during police questioning or while in a holding cell, your rights may have been violated.

✦ I was not held unfairly:

The government cannot hold you for an extended period of time without charging you with a crime. For instance, if you are placed in a holding cell under suspicion of murder, the government must officially charge you with that crime within a specified period of time. In some states, a charge must be brought within forty-eight hours; in other states the time limit is different. If you have been held without being charged for longer than the legal amount of time, your rights may have been violated.

✦ I was not treated as guilty before convicted:

Criminal suspects being held in jail awaiting trial may not be treated as guilty individuals before they have actually been convicted, no matter how strong the evidence is against them. The cornerstone of the U.S. criminal justice system is the belief that all people are innocent until proven guilty. If you were punished or treated unfairly while awaiting trial, your rights may have been violated.

✦ I was given a speedy trial:

You are also entitled to what is called a "speedy trial." In other words, once you are charged the government cannot purposefully drag its feet and wait to commence a trial against you. If it does, your rights may have been violated.

✦ I was not subjected to "cruel and unusual punishment" while imprisoned:

The Eighth Amendment to the U.S. Constitution guarantees that prisoners must be free from "cruel and unusual punishment." Once you have been convicted of a crime and incarcerated, you must be treated in a manner that does not constitute "cruel and unusual" punishment. Therefore, any punishment that can be considered inhumane treatment or which violates the basic concept of a person's dignity may be found to be cruel and unusual. For example, your rights may have been violated if you were given only dirty water to drink while incarcerated, or if the condition of your cell was unsanitary."[45]

Subtle differences compared to the arrest process in China. Sadly, many Americans don't understand these differences or how privileged they are, irrespective of skin-tone. The Chinese, on the other hand, are very much aware of these stark differences.

So, what are human rights? Well, that's one of the problems. It depends on who you ask:

"The basic rights to fair and moral treatment that every person is believed to have."[3]

Here's the UN's definition,

"Human rights are rights inherent to all human beings, regardless of race, sex, nationality, ethnicity, language, religion, or any other status. Human rights include the right to life and liberty, freedom from slavery and torture, freedom of opinion and expression, the right to work and education, and many more. Everyone is entitled to these rights, without discrimination."[4]

And the Canadian Human Rights Commission,

"Everyone in the world is entitled to the same fundamental human rights. There are 30 of them, in fact. They are the universal human rights that we, as citizens of this world, have agreed we are all entitled to. They include the right to live free from torture, the right to live free from slavery, the right to own property, and the right to equality and dignity, and to live free from all forms of discrimination."[5]

And Amnesty International,

"All human beings are born with equal and inalienable rights and fundamental freedoms. Human rights are based on dignity, equality and mutual respect – regardless of your nationality, your religion or your beliefs. Your rights are about being treated fairly and treating others fairly and having the ability to make choices about your own life. These basic human rights are: Universal They belong to all of us – everybody in the

---

[45] Find Law. 2018. Getting Arrested Checklist: Have My Rights Been Violated? *Findlaw.com*. Retrieved: March 25th, 2018, from http://civilrights.findlaw.com/other-constitutional-rights/getting-arrested-checklist-have-my-rights-been-violated.html.

world. Inalienable They cannot be taken away from us. Indivisible and interdependent Governments should not be able to pick and choose which are respected."[6]

And, of course, Urban Dictionary,

"Human Rights are rights that are ours simply because we are human. Many famous organizations have devoted their interests to these rights."[7]

On one hand, it's safe to say that there does seem to be a central theme across most definitions. The inherent idea is that these rights stem from something as basic as the fact that you exist.

Isn't that powerful? Shouldn't that be sufficient? You're here and you matter.

A Western perspective might go as far as to argue that the government's very purpose is to act as a fail-safe to ensure these *inalienable* human rights.

Whether that is true in practice is an entirely separate conversation but that overarching tone matters.

On the other hand, there is one major flaw. In 2021, there is no universal definition of human rights. The definitions that do exist are arbitrary and vague, at best.

So where did this idea of human rights emerge? From my research, it really depends on who you ask. Often, however, experts will cite what is known as the *Cyrus Cylinder.*

Often recognized as the world's first charter of human rights, the Cyrus Cylinder emerged in 539 B.C. and was inscribed on a baked-clay cylinder in the Akkadian language in cuneiform script. In that same year, Cyrus the Great (the first king of ancient Persia) conquered the city of Babylon but chose to do something entirely unprecedented, given the context of the era. After conquering the city, Cyrus decided to free all Babylonian slaves, allow people to choose which religion they wanted to follow, and enforced racial equality.

The Cyrus Cylinder has been translated into all six of the United Nations official languages and its provisions mirror the first four Articles of the Universal Declaration of Human Rights.

Granted, that's just one example. We could go through century after century, providing countless more examples of where human rights were arguably derived. For the sake of brevity, we'll skip through a lot of detailed history and fast forward to 1948.

Why?

1948 was arguably the first time that a powerful, and international (United Nations), institution drafted a document that attempted to define and establish universal parameters for human rights:

> *"The Universal Declaration of Human Rights (UDHR) is a milestone document in the history of human rights. Drafted by representatives with different legal and cultural backgrounds from all regions of the world, the Declaration was proclaimed by the United Nations General Assembly in Paris on 10 December 1948 (General Assembly resolution 217 A) as a common standard of achievements for all peoples and all nations. It sets out, for the first time, fundamental human rights to be universally protected and it has been translated into over 500 languages."*[8]

The document itself contains over 10,000 individual characters, 1,773 words, 30 articles and one preamble. How do 1948 UN standards hold up to in modern 2021 China? Let's take a brief look at some of the key articles in found in the charter:

> *"***Article 5:*** No one shall be subjected to torture or to cruel, inhuman or degrading treatment or punishment.*
>
> ***Article 6:*** *Everyone has the right to recognition everywhere as a person before the law.*
>
> ***Article 9:*** *No one shall be subjected to arbitrary arrest, detention or exile.*
>
> ***Article 10:*** *Everyone is entitled in full equality to a fair and public hearing by an independent and impartial tribunal, in the determination of his rights and obligations and of any criminal charge against him.*
>
> ***Article 11:***
>
> *(1) Everyone charged with a penal offence has the right to be presumed innocent until proven guilty according to law in a public trial at which he has had all the guarantees necessary for his defence.*
>
> *(2) No one shall be held guilty of any penal offence on account of any act or omission which did not constitute a penal offence, under national or international law, at the time when it was committed. Nor shall a heavier*

penalty be imposed than the one that was applicable at the time the penal offence was committed."[8]

The People's Republic of China must have missed the UDHR memo.

Although the UDHR was well thought out and carefully drafted, it was crafted with one painfully obvious and tragic flaw: *it's not legally binding.*

This glaringly obvious shortcoming is what plagues and undermines much of the ongoing human rights discussion to this day; *enforcement.*

In my mind, this raises several interesting questions:

Does the political and economic success of human rights abusers, like China, prove that international organizations are incapable of successfully combating human rights abuse? Are they even taking the issue seriously? Are human rights organizations capable of enacting change, or even willing to go to war over human rights violations? Is a sovereign government the only entity powerful enough to pressure human rights violators into changing their behavior?

The greatest irony of China's human rights abuses is, sadly, itself. The Chinese government works incredibly hard to point its finger at the international community, demonizing other countries for having wronged China in the past. Sure, to some degree, there is validity to the claim. Japan's incursions into China during World War Two would be the most prevalent and obvious example.

The Chinese government often references the Nanking Massacre (aka *rape of Nanjing*) as proof that foreign countries can't be trusted and that the Japanese are a fundamentally flawed and an irredeemable society. Initial reports of the death toll, including those of China's Central News Agency, in the 1930's and 40's ranged from 40,000 to 70,000 victims. Modern day Japanese historians estimate the total number to be over 100,000, which is in line with the 1945 International Military Tribunal of The Far East estimate of 155,000 victims. Western scholars in the US and Canada both agree with the figure of over 100,000 although some have asserted it to be closer to 50,000.

Remember what happened with our friend Mr. Chi and official Chinese estimates of the Tiananmen Square massacre? Well, they adjusted the numbers here too. If you go to Nanjing today and visit the war memorial, you will see a significantly different number than what was broadcast by China's Central News Agency in the 1930's: 300,000 victims.

This is the official number accepted and disseminated by the CCP domestically.

The point here is not to undermine the severity of what happened in Nanjing in the 1930's. It was an indisputable tragedy. Sure, historians might squabble about whether the final number was 40,000 or 300,000, but it underscores a more fundamental matter.

This is what China points to as the most egregious instance of foreign aggression, which it uses to validate its ongoing distrust of foreigners and ongoing demonization of the Japanese. This is what Chinese kids are indoctrinated with in school; *don't trust foreigners. ALL foreigners are bad. They killed and invaded us.*

Same logic holds for the West (eight-nation alliance).

Let's assume the 300,000 number to be accurate, for the sake of giving China the benefit of the doubt. How does China's Mao (world's largest mass murderer in history) stack up by comparison? Here are the numbers of Chinese killed by the CCP's domestic hero, Mr. Mao:

1) Mao's Campaign to Suppress Counterrevolutionaries: Low-end estimates are **712,000 Chinese executed with high-end estimates of over 2 million.**

2) Mao's Great Leap Forward: Low end estimates of death from violence are **2.5 million with an additional 1 to 3 million committing suicide. Low-end famine estimates range from 23 million to high-end estimates of 55 million.**

3) Mao's Cultural Revolution: Low-end estimates of the death toll from violence are **750,000 to high-end estimates of 3 million.**

Your initial reaction might be, wow, that's a lot of unnecessary death. Chairman Mao sure killed a lot of Chinese people! The Chinese MUST hate him. Well, not really.

Quite the opposite, in fact.

Chairman Mao died in 1976. What did the Chinese do with the body? Burn it? Bury it at sea? Shoot bullets into it? Nope!

They embalmed him and constructed a mausoleum located in the center of Tiananmen Square (oh the irony) to memorialize him!

That's right, the Chairman Mao Memorial Hall (aka *the Mausoleum of Mao Zedong*) sits in the middle of Beijing, China's capital city, where you can still go see Mao Zedong's body and pay your respects to the dear leader.

I'm not kidding.

The guy who is responsible for exponentially more Chinese deaths than the evil Japanese empire has been embalmed in China's capital city for your viewing pleasure.

Furthermore, his picture is still plastered in front of the Forbidden City in Beijing where he is regarded as a national hero. China's official stance on Mao today you might ask?

He was 70% right and 30% wrong. That's the official CCP doctrine.

Now that it's been over forty years since Chairman Mao has passed, has anything improved for Chinese people? Certainly (granted, you can only move up after murdering millions of your own people, but I digress).

How much have things improved? Has China learned from its own horrific history of slaughtering its own population? Well that's up for debate. One thing is certain, China still takes the cake for human rights abuses according to the *Human Rights Watch report on China in 2017.*

The report highlights China's most egregious forms of human rights violations, emphasizing both Xi Jinping and the Chinese government as complicit parties in what is referred to as a "broad and sustained offensive on human rights." What's worse is that these violations are all too well known by the global community, particularly Western governments, who largely choose to simply look the other way and continue conducting business with the CCP.

The report highlights key themes regarding China's human rights violations, including, freedom of expression, Hong Kong, Xinjiang, Tibet, freedom of religion, and sexual orientation and gender identity. Specific violations that are cited in the report include, censorship of social-media accounts that disagree with the State's core "socialist values", harassment of political dissidents, re-education camps for Muslim Uyghurs, authoritarian violence against Tibetans, classifying Christianity as an 'evil cult', and banning LGBT dating apps.

Welcome to the Chinese Communist Dream.

Sadly, it doesn't stop there. We've glossed over one crucial variable; the CCP's state-sanctioned executions.

According to Amnesty International's *2016 Death Sentences and Executions report*, a total of 1,032 people were executed by all governments around the world in 2016, excluding China, of course. The report clearly states that execution numbers in China are regarded as a state-secret and that official numbers are not publicly disclosed.

According to international estimates, the report cites China's official number of executions in 2016 to be in the *1,000's*. The Chinese Communist Party, alone, executes more of its own citizens every single year than the rest of the world's governments combined annual total. One Human Rights group, Dui Hua, estimated China's official number of state-sanctioned executions in 2016 to be in excess of 2,000 (over four times more than Iran, the second highest country on the list).

The truth is, these are just rough estimates, and nobody really knows how high the actual execution numbers go. The number of annual executions could, and realistically do exceed 2,000.

So, is China doing better? Unequivocally, yes, at least in comparison to 1983 when the Communist Party executed an estimated 24,000 Chinese citizens.

But by international standards they still lag far behind the rest of the world.

Old habits die hard.

On the other end of the spectrum, there is the United States. As a relative newcomer to the broader human rights discussion, one of the most surprising things to me has been the brilliance of the Declaration of Independence and the US Constitution. Remember the UN rights listed earlier? Many stem from US documents that were drafted in the 1770's and 1780's and predated the founding of the UN by around 165 years, and the UDHR by around 170 years.

Despite being written hundreds of years ago, the US set a human rights standard so painfully high, it is still the envy of the world. The sheer brilliance of these documents were so far ahead of their time, I still can't fully process and understand it. It's hard to explain to fellow Americans how privileged we are, especially in contrast to the human rights violations enveloping the Chinese population to this day.

The founding fathers were literally *hundreds*, if not *thousands* of years ahead of their time in restraining the most consistent source of human rights abuse throughout history: *government* (*look up democide*). The contribution of the first ten amendments to the US Constitution, in terms of human rights alone, is priceless. They are so valuable, that it's worth reviewing once more even if you've read them countless times before. If you ever wonder why wealthy

Chinese have flooded the US real estate market purchasing homes far in excess of their value, you don't have to look much further than the first ten US amendments to the Constitution to ensure people, not government, are in control:

"Amendment I

Congress shall make no law respecting an establishment of religion, or prohibiting the free exercise thereof; or abridging the freedom of speech, or of the press; or the right of the people peaceably to assemble, and to petition the Government for a redress of grievances.

Amendment II

A well regulated Militia, being necessary to the security of a free State, the right of the people to keep and bear Arms, shall not be infringed.

Amendment III

No Soldier shall, in time of peace be quartered in any house, without the consent of the Owner, nor in time of war, but in a manner to be prescribed by law.

Amendment IV

The right of the people to be secure in their persons, houses, papers, and effects, against unreasonable searches and seizures, shall not be violated, and no Warrants shall issue, but upon probable cause, supported by Oath or affirmation, and particularly describing the place to be searched, and the persons or things to be seized.

Amendment V

No person shall be held to answer for a capital, or otherwise infamous crime, unless on a presentment or indictment of a Grand Jury, except in cases arising in the land or naval forces, or in the Militia, when in actual service in time of War or public danger; nor shall any person be subject for the same offence to be twice put in jeopardy of life or limb; nor shall be compelled in any criminal case to be a witness against himself, nor be deprived of life, liberty, or property, without due process of law; nor shall private property be taken for public use, without just compensation.

Amendment VI

In all criminal prosecutions, the accused shall enjoy the right to a speedy and public trial, by an impartial jury of the State and district wherein the crime shall have been committed, which district shall have been previously ascertained by law, and to be informed of the nature and cause of the accusation; to be confronted with the witnesses against him; to have compulsory process for obtaining witnesses in his favor, and to have the Assistance of Counsel for his defence.

Amendment VII

In Suits at common law, where the value in controversy shall exceed twenty dollars, the right of trial by jury shall be preserved, and no fact tried by a jury, shall be otherwise re-examined in any Court of the United States, than according to the rules of the common law.

Amendment VIII

Excessive bail shall not be required, nor excessive fines imposed, nor cruel and unusual punishments inflicted.

Amendment IX

The enumeration in the Constitution, of certain rights, shall not be construed to deny or disparage others retained by the people.

Amendment X

The powers not delegated to the United States by the Constitution, nor prohibited by it to the States, are reserved to the States respectively, or to the people."[9]

Chapter 14:

Torture

Common Methods of Torture and Abuse in the People's Republic of China

"Kicks and punches, piercing of body parts, dislocation of joints, "hell shackles", sitting on a broom, hanging by feet, forced insertion of tube through nose, infusion of boiling water, "water dungeon", etc..."[46]

Chinese Government's official response to its third Universal Periodic Review (UPR) at the United Nations Human Rights Council. Chinese Foreign Ministry Spokesperson Hua Chunying's remarks, November 7, 2018:

"Q: China underwent the third Universal Periodic Review (UPR) at the United Nations Human Rights Council on November 6. Please give us more details.

A: On November 6, China underwent the third Universal Periodic Review (UPR) at the United Nations Human Rights Council in Geneva, Switzerland. The UPR mechanism aims to review how well the UN member states fulfill their duties and commitments on human rights on a regular basis. This is the third time for the UN to conduct the regular comprehensive review on the human rights conditions in China after 2009 and 2013...

The Chinese delegation took over 300 questions raised by more than 150 countries from a panoramic perspective. We have engaged in good

---

[46] Torture methods in the People's Republic of China. (2021, February 01). Retrieved February 28, 2021, from https://ishr.org/torture-methods-in-the-peoples-republic-of-china/

and constructive dialogues with all relevant parties with an open, candid, inclusive and cooperative attitude. Over 120 countries including Russia, South Africa and Ethiopia took the floor to highly commend China's development achievements, highly recognize the outlook on human rights with Chinese characteristics and speak highly of China's human rights report and the keynote speech delivered by the head of the Chinese delegation.

They said that China's experience and practices in safeguarding human rights and the right to development and eliminating poverty are worth learning and drawing upon. Meanwhile, certain western countries politicized the issue of human rights and pointed fingers at China on ethnic, religious and judicial issues. In response to this, the Chinese delegation enumerated a large number of facts and figures to forcefully refute that and make necessary clarifications, underlining that no one knows better than the Chinese people as to whether the human rights conditions in China are good or not and that no country can dictate the definitions and standards of democracy and human rights, let alone impose its own will on others.

I want to stress once again that there will always be room for improvement in human rights protection. China is willing to step up exchanges and mutual learning with all countries to pursue common progress on the basis of equality and mutual respect and with a responsible and constructive attitude. We will carefully and actively heed those sincere and constructive suggestions. Meanwhile, we firmly oppose and reject the politically-biased, malicious and unreasonable accusations made by a very small number of people."

Torture is one of the most misunderstood concepts in the world. For Western audiences, its reference elicits ruthless Hollywood scenes replete with horrifying physical abuse; electrocution, agonizing beatings, and other painful images.

To be fair, those certainly are forms of torture and horrible experiences that no human being should ever be forced to endure. Unfortunately, the realm of torture extends far beyond the spectrum of physical pain. What might that include?

Psychological torture.

As you can see from the list above, the CCP are experts at both forms of torture.

The main reason people associate physical pain with the word torture is that it is so easy to portray in film. A row of scary looking torture tools, physical violence and brutal injuries are easy to capture visually.

Psychological torture, on the other hand, is far more complex. Psychological torture is devoid of Hollywood's infamous bruises, gashes and blood. Psychological torture is obscurely hidden in the shadows and very much by design, as we will see.

How can a filmmaker adequately capture the agony of a character's internal psychological trauma? Fear? Agony? Suffering? Stress? Misery? Would something as thorough as a brain scan even begin to portray the harsh effects of psychological torture? Even when psychological torture is well captured, it's still less visually appealing to audiences than its physical counterpart.

Luckily, I never really endured physical torture at the hands of the CCP. Nonetheless, the nature of the conditions were so horrific that they still manage to break your soul within days. The mental anguish becomes so egregious that it starts to break down your physical body as well. This begged an interesting question,

Is there any significant difference between physical and psychological torture? What is psychological torture? What is torture?

A common definition of "torture" you'd likely stumble upon in a dictionary goes something like this,

> "*Torture is also the act of injuring someone or making someone suffer in an effort to force that person to do or say what you want to be done or said.*"[47]

Unfortunately, this definition does a better job of reinforcing stereotypical Hollywood scenes without directly referencing the harsh realities of psychological torture. The second definition, in my opinion, does a better job incorporating both:

> "*An injury or severe mental pain.*"[48]

---

[47] Definition of "torture" - English Dictionary. (n.d.). Retrieved: January 13, 2019, from https://dictionary.cambridge.org/us/dictionary/english/torture#dataset-cacd

[48] Definition of "torture" - English Dictionary. (n.d.). Retrieved: January 13, 2019, from https://dictionary.cambridge.org/us/dictionary/english/torture#dataset-cacd

While physical torture undoubtedly implies great mental suffering, as assumed by the first definition, the second does a better job of specifically citing *mental suffering* as a form of torture in and of itself.

Other definitions do an even better job highlighting the harsh realities of psychological torture. The Association for the Prevention of Torture (APT), founded by a Swiss banker, uses the UN's official definition.

Article 1 of the United Nations Convention against Torture and Other Cruel, Inhuman or Degrading Treatment or Punishment is the internationally agreed-on legal definition:

> *"Torture means any act by which severe pain or suffering, whether physical or mental, is intentionally inflicted on a person for such purposes as obtaining from him or a third person information or a confession, punishing him for an act he or a third person has committed or is suspected of having committed, or intimidating or coercing him or a third person, or for any reason based on discrimination of any kind, when such pain or suffering is inflicted by or at the instigation of or with the consent or acquiescence of a public official or other person acting in an official capacity. It does not include pain or suffering arising only from, inherent in or incidental to lawful sanctions."*[49]

What about here in the US? America has something called the anti-torture statute, also known as *"Title 18, Part I, Chapter 113C"* of the U.S. Code. *How is torture defined in the US?* The law consists of three sections, one of which providing the following definition:

> *"(1) "torture" means an act committed by a person acting under the color of law specifically intended to inflict severe physical or mental pain or suffering (other than pain or suffering incidental to lawful sanctions) upon another person within his custody or physical control;*
>
> (2) *"Severe mental pain or suffering" means the prolonged mental harm caused by or resulting from—*
> (A) *the intentional infliction or threatened infliction of severe physical pain or suffering;*

---

[49] Convention against Torture and Other Cruel, Inhuman or Degrading Treatment or Punishment. ohchr.org. June 26th, 1987. Retrieved January 13, 2019, from https://www.ohchr.org/en/professionalinterest/pages/cat.aspx

(B) *the administration or application, or threatened administration or application, of mind-altering substances or other procedures calculated to disrupt profoundly the senses or the personality;*

(C) *the threat of imminent death; or*

(D) *the threat that another person will imminently be subjected to death, severe physical pain or suffering, or the administration or application of mind-altering substances or other procedures calculated to disrupt profoundly the senses or personality…"*[50]

Unfortunately, torture, much like human rights, evolves greatly from definition to definition. For example, we can point to the United Nations Convention against Torture (UNCAT) which was drafted by the UN General assembly way back in 1984.

The treaty was initially signed in 1985 and went into effect in June of 1987. As of 2017 there were 162 state parties, including 83 signatories. On one hand, the UN deserves credit for at least considering torture, defining it and trying to get countries actively involved in changing their behavior. Unfortunately, the same problem we encountered earlier with human rights extends to torture, there really isn't anything legally binding as far as a mechanism for enforcement is concerned.

The punchline?

China (*Earth's Middle Kingdom*) signed UNCAT back in 1988.

But wait, it gets better.

The UN has a committee titled CAT which stands for the *Committee Against Torture*:

"*The Committee against Torture is composed of 10 independent experts who are persons of high moral character and recognized competence in the field of human rights.*

Members are elected for a term of four years by States parties in accordance with article 17 of the Convention against Torture. Members serve in their personal capacity and may be re-elected if nominated.

---

[50] 18 USC 2340: Definitions. Retrieved: January 13, 2019, from http://uscode.house.gov/view.xhtml?req=(title:18 section:2340 edition:prelim)

The 16th meeting of States parties was held in Geneva on Thursday 5 October 2017 to elect members to replace those five members whose terms expired on 31 December 2017."[51]

What does CAT do?

"The Committee Against Torture (CAT) is the body of 10 independent experts that monitors implementation of the Convention against Torture and Other Cruel, Inhuman or Degrading Treatment or Punishment by its State parties."[52]

Guess who has a seat on the committee,

"Ms. Honghong Zhang: China, 2021" [53]

Yup! The UN put China…**China**…on the Committee *AGAINST* Torture to…**MONITOR**…*TORTURE.*

This is the same China that has been caught employing horrific torture methods on domestic detainees as recently as 2015 and kills more of it's own citizens annually then the rest of the world *combined.*

That China monitors torture for the UN.

On November 26th, 2017 Mihrigul Tursun spoke publicly before the National Press Club in Washington detailing the horrific torture she endured at the hands of the Communist Chinese government. Tursun, a member of the Muslim Uyghur community in China's Xinjiang province, was detained and tortured in internment camps where Communist authorities regularly detain hundreds of thousands of fellow Muslim Uyghurs.

For three months, Tursun was detained in a cramped prison cell with sixty other women, forced to use the toilet in front of a security camera and coerced into singing songs praising China's Communist Party. Communist guards forced Tursun to take random medication causing some women to faint and others to bleed. In total, nine women in Tursun's cell died during her three-month stay.

[51] Committee Against Torture. 1996-2018. Membership. *ohchr.org*. Retrieved: March 27th, 2018, from http://www.ohchr.org/EN/HRBodies/CAT/Pages/Membership.aspx.

[52] Committee Against Torture. 1996-2018. Membership. *ohchr.org*. Retrieved: March 27th, 2018, from http://www.ohchr.org/EN/HRBodies/CAT/Pages/Membership.aspx.

[53] Committee Against Torture. 1996-2018. Membership. *ohchr.org*. Retrieved: March 27th, 2018, from http://www.ohchr.org/EN/HRBodies/CAT/Pages/Membership.aspx.

According to official transcripts of the event, Tursun was quoted saying,

> *"As if my daily life in the cell was not horrific enough, I was taken to a special room with an electrical chair, known as the tiger chair. It was the interrogation room that had one light and one chair. There were belts and whips hanging on the wall. I was placed in a high chair that clicked to lock my arms and legs in place and tightened when they press a button. The authorities put a helmet-like thing on my head. Each time I was electrocuted, my whole body would shake violently and I could feel the pain in my veins…*
>
> *I felt a huge sense of guilt and worthlessness. I cried and begged them to kill me. I don't remember the rest. White foams came out of my mouth and I began losing my conscious. The last words I remember them saying was, "You being an Uyghur is a crime" and I fainted."*

Once Tursun was detained, her three babies were stripped from her by Chinese authorities. After three months of detention, the government decided to put her on parole because she was informed that her children had become "sick." The day following her release, Chinese authorities handed her the body of a dead baby at the hospital, her eldest son, saying that they were unable to save his life.

On three separate occasions, she was prevented from boarding a plane in Beijing to fly to Egypt. On her fourth attempt, she managed to escape to Cairo where Tursun contacted U.S. authorities and, in 2018, was granted permission to settle in Virginia.

How did CCP officials respond to Turnsun's allegations of torture and infanticide? Here are the public remarks of China's Foreign Ministry Spokesperson, Hua Chunying, January 21st, 2019:

> *"Q: Last weekend, CNN carried a Xinjiang-related report, citing the "personal experience" of a Uyghur woman named Mihrigul Tursun. She also talked about similar "experience" as a witness at a hearing of the US Congressional-Executive Commission on China on November 28, 2018. Recently, Rubio and other US Senators re-proposed the Uyghur Human Rights Policy Act at the Congress. What is your comment?*
>
> *A: Second, on April 21, 2017, Mihrigul was taken into custody by the public security bureau of Qiemo County on suspicion of inciting ethnic hatred and discrimination. During this period, she was found to have infectious disease. Out of humanitarian consideration, the public security*

bureau of Qiemo County terminated the compulsory measures against her on May 10, 2017. Apart from the twenty days' criminal detention, Mihrigul was totally free during her stay in China…

In a nutshell, Mihrigul has never been detained by police in Urumqi. Neither has she been jailed or received penitentiary education in any vocational education and training center. I don't know on what basis she went as far as to claim that she witnessed the death of nine women during her detention and she was detained by the police in a cell with over 50 women in the interview with CNN and at the hearing of the US Congress!

Third, according to our verification, Muezi, one of Mihrigul's sons, because of pneumonia, hydrocephalus and right-side indirect inguinal hernia, was taken by Mihrigul and her family to Urumqi's Children's Hospital for hospitalization on January 14-19, May 6-12 and November 4-8 respectively in 2016…

Second, on November 28, 2018, Mihrigul talked about her so-called "experience" at a hearing of the US Congressional-Executive Commission on China in the capacity of a witness, which became an important basis for Senator Rubio and others to propose and promote the Uyghur Human Rights Policy Act. The US congressmen levied unwarranted accusations on and defamed the Chinese government and China's ethnic policies based on a liar's made-up story. We can by no means accept that. We urge the relevant US congressmen to respect the basic facts, abandon ideological bias and the Cold War mentality, and stop maliciously slandering and smearing China's policies on religion and the governance of Xinjiang. As to such kind of farce, once is enough, otherwise it will further chip away at the credibility of these congressmen and the US."

I'll leave you to draw your own conclusions.

So now that we've defined torture, how do we adequately discuss *psychological torture?* I wanted to find out if there was any research on psychological torture that could provide context on the nightmare that I was living through in Chinese detention. I was wondering if anyone had even attempted to create a universal definition of the term?

To my surprise, the answer is a resounding yes:

"Defining psychological torture

The term "psychological torture" can relate to two different aspects of the same entity. On the one hand, it can designate methods – that is in this case the use of "non-physical" methods. While "physical methods" of torture can be more or less self-evident, such as thumbscrews, flogging, application of electric current to the body and other similar techniques, "non-physical" means a method that does not hurt, maim or even touch the body, but touches the mind instead. Just as readily recognizable as methods of torture in this category are prolonged sleep deprivation, total sensory deprivation or having to witness the torture of family members, to cite only three examples.

It has been stated that it can be difficult to define torture in general. It is even harder to define "psychological torture". As has been seen, the definition of torture is firmly based on "severe pain and suffering". The fact that this notion is qualified as being both "physical and mental" is a recognition that both aspects go together. Physical torture produces both physical and mental suffering; the same applies to psychological torture. It therefore becomes difficult to isolate psychological torture per se as a separate entity and define its different features.

A report by Physicians for Human Rights (PHR) in 2005 broke new ground by providing a definition of the term "psychological torture", based on the interpretation formulated in the United States Code (USC) – the codification of the general and permanent laws of the United States – of the prohibition of torture. The Code's interpretation refers to "severe mental pain or suffering" caused by the threat of, or actual, administration of "procedures calculated to disrupt profoundly the senses or personality."[54]

What would you have to do to another human being to elicit such severe levels of mental anguish and human suffering? Is there an official list of prohibited actions that constitute psychological torture? Surprisingly, yes. Here are a few of those items, including some that I personally experienced:

"Phobias used during interrogation.
Solitary confinement.
Sleep deprivation.
Constant taunting.
Repeated annoyances petty in themselves but magnified out of proportion by the context.

---

[54] Kramer, Daniel. "The Effects of Psychological Torture." International Human Rights Law Clinic. Berkeley Law. June 2010. Retrieved: March 27th.

Food and drink deprivation.
Stripping detainees naked.

Finally, two additional factors need to be considered here, as they are of direct relevance to the discussion on methods of interrogation and torture and certainly have a bearing on the use of cumulative methods. They are the roles of uncontrollable and unpredictable stress in torture. It has been found that these factors, which have been studied extensively, always come into play in any situation involving stress. In the case of detainees held in custody and interrogated by "aggressive measures", they will obviously influence the overall situation."[55]

Although more comprehensive lists exist, this does a good job of providing some general examples and tying them into the experience of incarceration. Once you are detained, your entire environment and existence is instantaneously controlled by strangers.

You eat when you are told to eat, and you sleep when you are told to sleep. That complete lack of control over seemingly trivial things coupled with the unpredictability of your new environment elevate stress levels compounding things that could normally be written off as mere *annoyances.*

Another painful form of psychological torture is being detained *incommunicado,* as I had been:

> *"'Incommunicado detention' means that the detainee cannot communicate with anyone other than his or her captors and perhaps his co-detainees. In other words, an incommunicado detainee is permitted no contact with the world outside the place of detention or incarceration."*[56]

Chinese guards explicitly refused to allow foreign inmates to contact their embassies, make a phone call, or communicate with the outside world in any way.

Well, that can't be so bad. At least you're not being physically tortured...right?

According a recent study from Kings College in London, 300 survivors of psychological torture from the former Yugoslavia described suffering an equal amount of mental anguish as those who were physically beaten. Subjects who

---

[55] Kramer, Daniel. "The Effects of Psychological Torture." International Human Rights Law Clinic. Berkeley Law. June 2010. Retrieved: March 27th.

[56] Hayes, Lindsay M. "National Study of Jail Suicide: 20 Years Later." National Institute of Corrections, National Institute of Corrections, 13 Dec. 2017, nicic.gov/national-study-jail-suicide-20-years-later.

endured psychological torture developed equal levels of PTSD and rated their suffering to be on par with those who had been physically tortured.

The lead author of the study described psychological torture as being just as bad as physical torture. He emphasized that neither form of torture should be employed given the severity of the ensuing trauma.

Before experiencing these conditions, I too, was very much in the common "physical torture must be worse than psychological torture" camp. Unbeknownst to me, and as the research indicates, the two exist on a level playing field. And therein lies the brilliance of psychological torture; it is masterfully hidden.

You can cause indescribable levels of horrific suffering without the easily recognized gashes or scars left by physical torture. How does one adequately assess the mental scars of psychological torture? For these reasons, the CCP loves employing psychological torture as it syncs with their MO; operate in the shadows.

Unless you find yourself locked up in these conditions, the mental trauma associated with CCP detention is truly indescribable. Each individual element, while seemingly trivial on its own, compounds the others. The cumulative effect of these variables, *including time*, cause a great deal of agony:

> *"Psychological torture is a very real thing. It should not be minimized under the pretext that pain and suffering must be physical in order to be real. Indeed, some psychological methods on their own constitute torture, such as solitary confinement and sleep deprivation.*
>
> *It has been argued that the concept of the use of non-physical methods also applies to use of the many other methods which undoubtedly do not constitute torture on their own if merely considered in isolation. These so-called "minor" methods are, however, part and parcel of the torture process and constitute a "background environment" of harassment and duress for detainees under interrogation who are subjected to them for prolonged periods. Their combined use and cumulative effects over time must therefore be considered as part of a system of psychological torture.*
>
> *What is arguably merely "malevolent" and possibly humiliating if inflicted for 24 hours has to be considered very differently if applied for 24 days…[Torture] may be committed in one single act or can result from a combination or accumulation of several acts, which, taken individually and out of context, may seem harmless … The period of time,*

the repetition and various forms of mistreatment and severity should be assessed as a whole."[57]

Here we begin to see the introduction of time as yet another compounding variable in the broader conversation regarding psychological torture. A minor annoyance over the course of an hour becomes a fundamentally different reality for those without control of their environment who are forced to endure it for days or weeks on end.

These individual variables create a horrific experience that words are simply unable to capture. So, what happens to inmates who survive these conditions? Is there any long-term damage left behind after you are released? Unfortunately, there is. Research has found that the trauma of psychological torture can persist long after inmates are released,

> *"As bad as physical torture is, psychological torture can in the long run be much worse," stated Dr. Frank Summers, a psychologist specializing in the effects of severe emotional disturbance. "Because if somebody breaks your leg or breaks your arm, that can heal. But if somebody breaks down your mind, you may never get it back.*
>
> *Common chronic health effects of psychological torture include post-traumatic stress disorder (PTSD), anxiety, and depression. Going one step further and explaining the severe threat that high stress levels pose to the autonomic nervous system and basic gastrointestinal and circulatory system functioning, Dr. Rona M. Fields, a psychologist with expertise in violence and terrorism, wrote: "There is no longer any basis for arguing" that the use of such techniques "neither does organ damage nor endangers life itself.*
>
> *Finally, neurobiologists have documented that psychological torture techniques affect the biology of the human brain. These so-called "non-injurious" techniques can result in a loss of brain mass by inhibiting the regeneration of brain cells. They can also produce abnormal slow wave activity in the brain, which indicates brain pathology and dysfunctional neural tissue. Researchers have also documented that such techniques can cause impairment of the hippocampus (a component of the brain) which plays an important role in spatial navigation and long-term memory."*[58]

---

[57] Kramer, Daniel. "The Effects of Psychological Torture." International Human Rights Law Clinic. Berkeley Law. June 2010. Retrieved: March 27th.

[58] Kramer, D. (2010, June). The Effects of Psychological Torture. Retrieved from https://www.law.berkeley.edu/files/EffectsofPsychologicalTorturepaper%28Final%2911June10.pdf

As we can see, psychological torture can be so harmful it elicits a wide-array of very negative and long-term health complications. What about the actual process of detaining a human being? How does the average person handle the transition from their normal life into the harsh confines of a prison cell?

Not very well.

There's another ugly variable that appears when humans are forcefully incarcerated…*suicide,*

> *"There are several reasons for the higher rate of suicide in jail. Jail environments are conducive to suicidal behavior and an individual entering a jail is at increased risk of facing a crisis situation. From an inmate's perspective, certain features of the jail environment may enhance suicidal behavior: fear of the unknown, distrust of an authoritarian environment, perceived lack of control over the future, isolation from family and significant others, the shame of being incarcerated, and the perceived dehumanizing aspects of incarceration…Some inmates simply are (or become) ill equipped to handle the common stresses of confinement.*
>
> *Suicide continues to be a leading cause of death in jails across the country; the rate of suicide in county jails is estimated to be several times greater than that in the general population.*
>
> *The study identified 696 jail suicides in 2005 and 2006, with 612 deaths occurring in detention facilities and 84 in holding facilities.*
>
> *Twenty-three percent occurred within the first 24 hours, 27 percent between 2 and 14 days, and 20 percent between 1 and 4 months."*[59]

Again, it's worth emphasizing that this data reflects people who are detained in a system and country that they intrinsically understand. There are no linguistic barriers, the arrest experience is likely understood, and legal recourse exists.

Despite all of this, suicide numbers still spike drastically under these conditions. Imagine, then also having all these variables, like language, simultaneously stripped from you. Imagine instead that you are detained half-way around the world in an undisclosed prison complex where nobody speaks your language.

---

[59] Hayes, Lindsay M. "National Study of Jail Suicide: 20 Years Later." National Institute of Corrections, National Institute of Corrections, 13 Dec. 2017, nicic.gov/national-study-jail-suicide-20-years-later.

Psychological torture is very, very real. Understanding the severity of psychological torture allows us to understand why my prison cell was plastered with suicide warnings.

Chapter 15:

Prison Day 7 (Lost in Translation)

China's hi-tech 'death van' where criminals are executed and then their organs are sold on black market

"Ambulances in China take on a different role than what we are generally accustomed to in the West. These vehicles are often refitted into 'mobile execution vans', responsible for carrying out the thousands of executions ordered by the Chinese government every single year. These vans have largely replaced China's traditional method of execution, firing squads. The Chinese government says that this more humane method of mobile lethal injection in refitted ambulances is proof of its improving human rights record. These mobile execution ambulances have been directly linked to the Chinese government's ongoing human organ harvesting operations."[60]

Chinese Government's official remarks regarding Canadian National Robert Lloyd Schellenberg's death sentence. Chinese Foreign Ministry Spokesperson Hua Chunying's remarks, January 15, 2019:

"Q: Yesterday, the Canadian defendant Robert Lloyd Schellenberg was sentenced to be executed for drug smuggling. Canada's Prime Minister Justin Trudeau said that it is of extreme concern to Canada that China has chosen to arbitrarily apply the death penalty. What is your comment?

---

[60] 1. Andrew Malone for the Daily Mail. (2009, March 27). China's hi-tech 'death van' where criminals are executed and then their organs are sold on black market. Retrieved February 28, 2021, from https://www.dailymail.co.uk/news/article-1165416/Chinas-hi-tech-death-van-criminals-executed-organs-sold-black-market.html

A: *The Canadian side accused China of "arbitrarily" applying the death penalty, and this could not be further from the truth. Before saying these words, has he read through the information released by the Dalian Intermediate People's Court on this case? Has he studied relevant Chinese laws?*

The Dalian Intermediate People's Court made it very clear in the information it released. The defendant Schellenberg was involved in organized international drug trafficking and conspired with others to smuggle 222.035 kg of methamphetamine. His actions constitute drug smuggling. The prosecutors made all his criminal facts clear with concrete and adequate evidence.

We all know that drug-related crime is considered a felony by the international community because of the serious social damage it could incur. It is cracked down in all countries with the strictest punishment, as is the same case in China. The true spirit of the rule of law implies that everyone is equal before the law. The remarks by the relevant person in Canada show not the slightest respect of the rule of law. We are strongly dissatisfied with that and urge the Canadian side to respect the rule of law, respect China's judicial sovereignty, correct its mistakes, and stop making irresponsible remarks."

BAaAa NA na NA nAAAA!

That fu&king music.

Again.

Fu&k. Day seven. Fu7k.

This isn't a nightmare you eventually wake up from. No, this is a very real and permanent condition. That was the first thing that flashed into my mind every single morning.

Fu&k, I'm still here. What day is it? How many days has it been? I hadn't lost count, had I? This is day 7. Or maybe it's not. Maybe this is day 8? Did day one even count? Maybe I'm counting all wrong? Nobody tells you anything in here. What's the date again?

I'm not sure what I was even doing at this point. I was just standing there, in the middle of the pacing area, staring at the carvings in the wall. All around me, I could see other inmates slowly waking up and climbing out of bed. Some were busy folding up their blankets, while new inmates were busy trying to process what the morning routine was.

Fu&k.

Another one of the newer Chinese inmates folded their blanket up the wrong way. The guards instantly screamed at us when that happened through the speaker. I hopped up on the wooden planks and fixed it. The Chinese inmate stood there watching me as I pointed out what was wrong. He was new, and I didn't mind helping; *it gave me something to do.* I pointed at the blanket and he nodded in agreement understanding that he had messed up.

It happens.

I was already done with the bathroom. I had brushed my teeth, taken a squat shit, and stashed away my toiletries. It was 6:30 am.

Time for another day of existing.

That was what your day was reduced to. *Existing.* That was the positive way of looking at it. The negative way? *Another day of not dying.* Another day of meaningless nothing. Another day of surviving, to get to yet another day of... more survival, to then do the same thing, again and again and again and again and again and again...

This is how you felt after just seven days here. The irony?

I was doing better than most. I was still eating.

Deep down, there was still some optimism. *Try and treat it as a break from work. Think about what I would normally be doing during a routine day in Beijing? Think of people you know. What time is it in their country? What are they doing today? What is happening in the outside world? What's on the news? I wonder if anyone knows I'm here?*

BANG! I looked over at the door. The lieutenant once again slammed the door with both hands for no reason. *That Fu7ker. I wanted to punch him right in the middle of his angry little face. Back to reality. Fu&k shift 4.* I walked back toward the window and hung my orange hat on the wall.

That was the worst one yet. Two and a half hours of standing and watching people sleep while you're sleep deprived. *This really fuc&s with you mentally after a while.* I hadn't once slept through the night. *Not many people do.* The extra thirty minutes tacked on to the 2-hour watch made shift four that much more unbearable than the other three.

I could see other inmates' eyes glazing over into a lifeless gaze from the sleep deprivation. You can physically see the look on people's faces fading by the day. After only a week in these conditions, you feel yourself becoming a different person as you slowly become a product of your new torturous environment. I could literally feel that my brain was not functioning properly.

My mental acuity had slowed dramatically, as if there was some type of thick fog obstructing my brain's normal flow of traffic.

Is it the bucket food? Is it sleep deprivation? Is it the toxic water? Is it the violent and mentally unstable inmates? Is it all of the above?

The cloudy thinking made it progressively harder and harder to focus and problem solve the impossible situations you routinely encounter in a prison cell. My thought process was becoming more fight or flight and less rational by the minute. In here you just *are*, and everyone shares the same increasingly meaningless goal of not dying.

It was like being in a prison cell full of half-zombies that had failed to properly transition to full-zombie. Occasionally, you catch them just staring, at nothing. They're alive, they're breathing, but their mind is slowly shutting-off and it's readily apartment through their actions. Their spirit, their life-energy, their soul…whatever you want to call it… was slowly flickering-off.

They see it in you too.

Me: You feeling better brother?

Raheem: Man, I still feel sick.

Me: Need to puke again?

Raheem: Nah. Just not feeling 100%.

I don't think he was sick. I think he was scared. Who could blame him?

Me: Grab some of the warm water. Soothes the soul.

Raheem: They have warm water?

Me: Yea, only in the mornings. Go quick, before they shut it off.

Raheem grabbed his cup and walked off.

Raheem was thrown in our cell last night. Unlike me, he was rounded up and taken there alone.

Going through the arrest and processing phase in isolation must have been a thoroughly shit$y experience.

Raheem was born and raised in Baghdad, Iraq. He ultimately moved to China for education where he became employed as an engineer. He got married in Beijing to a local Chinese woman.

Raheem was around Neil's age, somewhere in his mid-30's. He arrived in our cell at around 11:30 pm last night. You could sense that he was mentally in a bad place from the second he entered our room. Hearing a cell-door in a CCP prison complex shut behind you while a room full of foreign prisoner's stare at you isn't a particularly warm feeling.

Upon entering he looked around, walked over to the bathroom and vomited.

Understandable.

The rest of us looked around at each other unsure of what to do.

Some people ignored Raheem's vomit and tried to go back to sleep. *Also, understandable.* Muhammad and I stood and walked over to the bathroom door to check on him.

I'm not sure if this initially helped the situation or freaked him out more. He had no idea who we were or why we were approaching.

We talked to Raheem, explained what was going on and managed to help him get to bed. He complained extensively about the wooden planks and pretty much every other shitty condition. He couldn't mentally grasp the reality of his new environment. *Yea, we know,* I thought to myself. *It's a sh!thole.*

He was complaining as if there was something Muhammad or I would be able to do. It was almost as if he was trying to plead. *It is what it is,* I told him. *We're all in here together.* He wasn't handling the transition well, but he managed to get through the first night.

Muhammad: How's he doing.

Me: Figuring it out. You?

Muhammad: Another day. Another passenger.

Soldier: Another passenger.

Me: Another passenger.

The medical team came through to do their morning check. As usual, they didn't give a shit. They hated the prisoners. They hated having to deal with us. They were educated and superior so *why bother with a lower form of humanity?*

We were pests to them or worse and inmates were treated as such.

Once yellow-piss breakfast was finally poured through the funnel and into the bucket, I walked over with my container. *Time for more fecal-contaminated porridge.* I dunked the central container into the bucket and took out a huge helping, pouring the yellow liquid glop into my personal feeding dish. I grabbed a hunk of brick bread and made my way over to my squatting meal area by the window.

Raheem was sitting there with his warm water staring at us in shock.

Raheem: How can you eat this filth?

Me: You just do after a while.

Muhammad: You should eat. Need to stay strong in here.

Raheem: I can't eat this. What is it supposed to be? Is this what they always give us for breakfast.

Me: Porridge. It's warm. Takes your mind off a bit.

Soldier: Occasionally you get an egg too.

Raheem: I can't.

Me: I don't blame you. I didn't eat this for a few days either. Eventually you just get hungry enough.

Raheem: Is this all they serve?

Muhammad: No. Lunch is potatoes sometimes. Dinner is usually re-boiled cabbage. Depends on the day and time.

Raheem: Oh God. Does everyone touch the communal container and the bucket?

Me: Yea, I guess so.

Raheem: You can get diseases in here. This isn't sanitary. This is very dangerous.

I know. We all fuc&ing know. This place could kill you a million different ways. It's unsanitary. It's not safe. They're playing with people's lives. No here gives a flying fu&k about you. Let me eat my warm piss-porridge.

You start to realize people handle detention in very different ways. Some can't wrap their minds around the conditions, or the overall situation, even after they've arrived. They're still trying to bargain. They're still in denial.

We made our way through breakfast. Raheem sat there in silence sipping on his water staring at the wall in front of him in disbelief with a look on his face…*where the fuck am I?!*

To be honest, I wasn't really sure either. Hell, probably. This has to be pretty fu&king similar.

As we made our way through roll call, and then releases, we found out more of Raheem's story. He initially graduated from university as an engineer and went on to study at a Beijing university, ultimately landing a Chinese engineering degree. He was working in Beijing, with a legal work permit and held a Chinese marriage visa. For a foreigner in Beijing, from a Chinese legal standpoint, you can't do much better than that.

Furthermore, Raheem spoke great Mandarin, English and was clearly well-educated. His crime? Despite having a good income, he and his wife were busy saving up money to do some travelling. He decided to take on a part-time English teaching job on the weekends and save up some extra money.

And why not? Not only was he married to a local Beijing woman, but he was a Chinese trained engineer who had also acquired his English training certificate. What Raheem had discovered about China is, if they need a foreigner to arrest, they will arrest anyone for any reason at any time.

Same story. Police raid on the education center. Sham interrogation, accusation, arrest, processing, prison cell. No judge. No lawyer. Nothing.

No matter what you do, you're never accepted in China. You're always an outsider. Regardless of how much you believe you're part of the team, you're not. You're expendable. You're not wanted.

It was around 10:15 am and I was waiting to speak with the guards. Soldier had asked me to inquire about trying to make contact with his embassy. It was around day 40 for Soldier now and he still hadn't heard from anyone in the outside world in over a month. He had not been allowed to contact his family, any of his contacts or even his embassy. Even though Chinese inmates were allowed to make calls on a public phone just beyond the outer hall, foreigners were expressly forbidden from doing so.

Understandably, this was all taking a heavy toll on him and I had become his only outlet for translation. He didn't speak any Chinese and spoke very limited English. I was arguably the only person that could try to get answers for him; I routinely defaulted to the translator.

Soldier gave me a list of questions to ask the guard when they came around. It's not that the guards cared, and we already knew that they wouldn't do anything to help. We knew they barely spoke to us and that they were annoyed by our presence. But trying, yet again, was something to look forward to on another empty day of nothingness.

SLAM! We heard the outer hall door shut.

Guards approaching.

People jumped into position, sat up straight and waited curiously. I looked up at the clock. *Odd.* They don't usually make rounds at this hour?

New inmate?

I was positioned in the back of the cell's pacing area staring straight ahead at the metal door. The guards opened our cell's heavy outer door. One of the guards approached looking in at the inmates until his eyes landed on me. He raised his finger at me,

"*American. Come.*"

I looked up at him, a bit surprised, and the other inmates were equally confused. We didn't really trust people who spoke to the guards in private, so my cellmates were understandably wondering why I was being randomly called out of our cell.

But fu7k it, anything to get a few minutes out of this nightmare.

I approached the door, and the guards escorted me out into the hallway slamming the door on the prisoners behind us. I recognized the lead guard. He was the only respectable guy that worked our cell block.

Guard: We have an African inmate who stopped eating several days ago.

Me: Again?

This was the second time in seven days that I had been pulled out of my cell to translate for an inmate who had stopped eating.

The first time caught me by surprise.

Isn't there a mental health professional that is supposed to do this? Oh right, stupid me...hell doesn't have those.

Why would you defer to a depressed inmate, with no mental health training or experience, to translate for someone who has stopped eating? Then again, TIC (This is China).

Why spend money on trivial things like mental health?

Guard: Yes. I'll walk you to his cell so the two of you can chat.

I didn't have a choice. On one hand, it was nice being out of the cell. *On the other, what the FU%K do you say to someone that is so depressed they've stopped eating?!* There's no rulebook for this.

Translating for Foreign Inmates on Hunger Strike in Chinese Prisons 101. Which university hosted that lecture series again?

But here I was, approaching another cell-door to talk to another person who had stopped eating. *I guess this was my job now.* Shouldn't the prison hire someone to do that?

Nope. China is far too practical to waste money on such trivial things.

The cell was positioned right next door to Karl's cell. *I wonder how he's holding up? I wonder how Neil is doing?* I hadn't really seen either one since the embassy encounter on day two.

The guards began unlocking the cell door. I had a little bit of experience with this as I had just done the same thing for a Nigerian inmate a couple days ago.

Hopefully this time I'll sound like less of an idiot. Practice makes perfect.

The outer door swung open, producing a mirrored copy of my cell. Same depressing interior. Same carvings etched into the wall. Same room full of glossed over inmate faces. The guards called what appeared to be the only black inmate in the cell over to the door. They stepped back and pointed at me to approach the door as if they were pointing at a broken tv that I was expected to troubleshoot.

You could see the anguish on this poor guy's face from miles away. *He was suffering.* He didn't want to be here. You could just look into his eyes and understand everything you would ever need to know without ever having to exchange a single word.

He appeared to be in his late twenties, had a naturally strong build and was a bit taller than I was. He probably had no idea why the guards grabbed a random American inmate from another cell to chat with him, so I decided to try and break the ice…

Me: Hello, what's your name.

Inmate: John.

Me: Nice to meet you John. My name is Steve. How long have you been here?

I wonder if he saw the same decaying look on my face?

John: "Seven days now."

That's when it all started spilling out.

John: "I have no idea why I am here. They ripped up my visa and randomly said I'm here illegally. I haven't been allowed to contact my embassy. I can't contact my family. They won't let me call anyone. We are eating junk out of a bucket. There is one squatter toilet. These conditions are dangerous, it's dirty. I'm the only black inmate here, I'm sick of the ridicule from the Chinese. Asking about my skin, or hair. I'm…"

He went on. This was his moment and he needed to be heard. I was all this poor guy had and right now it was my job to listen. He felt alone. He clearly didn't have anyone to talk to. He was worried. He had been ridiculed. He was being held incommunicado. He was afraid. The night watches. The sleep deprivation. The fecal-infested piss-porridge. There was a lot to get off his chest and this was his moment. He was desperate.

We all were.

I waited patiently until he finished, looking him directly in the eye the entire time to try and ensure that he knew he was being heard. As he went on, he slowly came to the realization that I too, was just another inmate, trying my best to hear him out.

Most of the conversations with foreigners who were locked up were painfully similar. This was no exception. There was a detailed account of their innocence, the horrific conditions and the maltreatment. If you cut through all the words, the recurring and fundamental theme was always the same: *Will I die in here? How long can I survive this? I see the suicide signs too.*

That's all anyone wanted to say. But of course, nobody ever said it that way. It was a dance. No one wanted to admit what they were actually thinking. Nobody wanted to say it. Who wants to honestly discuss how much longer you think you can stay alive? That's not a pleasant conversation.

Me: Yea, I understand. You're absolutely right, these conditions are terrible. It's the same in my cell too. I'm also eating out of the bucket. John, where are you from?

John: South Africa.

Me: Very cool man, I've never been. Always wanted to go.

John: It's better than this. You?

Me: U.S. California.

John: Damn, I've never been there. I hope I can visit someday. They sure got a lot of people in here don't they?

Me: That they do. Look, here's what I can tell you. You might be here for a while, but everyone gets out of eventually. *You will get out of here eventually.* I have a Chinese cell mate with a 180-day sentence, and he has seen a ton of foreigners come and go. *We all go. You will go too.* Are you doing ok besides the conditions?

John: "I stopped eating a few days ago to protest. Nobody listens to me. Nobody is talking to me. They don't speak English. I don't speak Chinese. I'm trying to contact my embassy." He seemed to be reliving his initial shock.

It's the indefinite, in indefinite detention that kills you.

Me: I understand. I didn't eat that porridge shit for a few days. Look, you're going to get out of here. How long is your sentence?

John: Two weeks. But it's already been a week and I've heard nothing.

Me: I'm in the same boat man. I have a two-week charge and I still have no idea how long I'll be here for. I haven't heard anything definitive either. Here's what I can say. My cellmate from Ghana has been here for a month, *every foreigner he's seen has come and gone.* Same thing with my Chinese cellmate…every foreigner comes and goes. *Same for you. You came, and you will go.* Until you go, you need to eat. You need to stay strong here. The food will keep you strong.

John: I can't eat it man.

Me: You have to. And in the meantime, I will talk to the guards about getting you into a different cell.

John: Yea I know you're right. It's just these conditions man. Can't treat people this way.

Me: I hear you man. I'm a couple cells down. But look, I've heard you and I'll explain this to the guards. For the time being…please eat. Lunch and dinner are alright. Stay strong. And remember, you will get out of here. We all do.

Do we? Did he buy it? Did I buy it? One severely depressed inmate trying to convince another to eat. Is there a more tragic punchline on the planet?

We chatted for as long as possible, said our goodbyes and he slowly retreated into the depths of his cell. The guards pulled me away from the door and shut it.

Had I done a good job? Did I forget to say anything? Should I have worded any of the sentences differently? I don't know. I don't fuc&ing know anything anymore.

The guard broke the silence.

Guard: Will he eat?

It was that black and white for the guards. They didn't understand that these conditions weren't normal. They couldn't comprehend that these conditions were inhumane. They didn't know much beyond this sick prison world. They found it odd that people wouldn't eat. No gratitude for translating for another inmate on hunger strike. The only pertinent information, in their mind, was…is the tv functional now?

But this was their dance. Here, you unfortunately had to adapt to their world in order to communicate with them. I could sit here and scream and shout about American standards and human rights, but they would have no point of reference. They wouldn't understand it. It would be as if I were screaming at them in French, even if I used Mandarin. They would probably just end up punishing me. So, I played by their rules as best I could.

Me: "I think so. But…" I paused for dramatic effect. "He can't speak in Chinese, so he can't communicate with anyone in his cell. Also, he is the only black inmate there. Can he be put into a cell with other foreigners?"

Guard: I see, I think this is possible when we free up some space later. More blacks will come.

What did that actually mean? I didn't fuc&ing know. Did they care? Would they move him? Was all of this simply ceremonial? Probably.

As they escorted me back to my cell, I brought up the Soldier's situation. The guards nodded but said that they would return to discuss it later. *I knew they wouldn't.* But at least I could tell Soldier that I had brought it to their attention.

Simply being heard went a long way in here.

I made my way back into the cell realizing how fortunate I was to be locked up with three other foreign inmates. We didn't have much in common beyond surviving this horrific situation together. But at the very least, we could do our best to talk each other through this hellish nightmare.

That alone was nothing short of a miracle.

Raheem, Muhammad, and Soldier asked about where I had gone. I explained that there was another inmate on hunger strike and that I had been asked to translate for him. Raheem was once again staring at me in disbelief, as he heard me share yet another absurd story. I let Soldier know that I had explained his situation to the guards and that they would return later to discuss it.

It seemed to lift his spirits a bit.

We spent the next few hours walking Raheem through life in the cell. *He had a lot of questions.* We did our best to answer based on our individual experiences. We described the stories of other inmates we had seen released, our respective interactions with our embassies, how we had been arrested and of course, prison conditions.

He was still trying to internalize everything. Fortunately for Raheem, he was as close to a Chinese national as you could get. Instead of a fourteen day sentence for *working illegally*, he was given ten days. As he was being processed his wife seemed to be able to negotiate authorities away from deportation and assured them that Raheem would simply be released after his tenth day.

Would they follow through for Raheem? Was this just another lie? Would he end up being deported?

We would have to wait and see.

We made our way through lunch time and the scheduled afternoon nap. Luckily, I worked the dreaded fourth shift last night which meant I wouldn't realistically have to work another shift until the following day. Usually, inmates would work two or three night shifts back to back before getting the coveted and well deserved night off.

You never really had enough sleep in here, so you were constantly trying to play catch up. There was a bit of relief on your *off* days because you had one less distraction. You could finally focus on sleep, even though you already knew it would never be enough.

To my surprise, the guards returned shortly before dinner, at around 3:30 pm. They weren't here for the foreigners, but I figured this would be a good time to follow up on Soldier's request to speak with his embassy.

The guards were busy talking to another Chinese inmate. I walked up to the door and stood behind them, waiting for their conversation to die down. Once it did, a new guard looked over at me,

Guard: What?

Me: "This guy" I said pointing back at Soldier. "He needs to contact his embassy."

Guard: No, he can't.

Me: There's a public phone outside the hall that the Chinese inmates are allowed to use, and he's been in here for over forty days now. His sentence is two-weeks and he hasn't seen his embassy since the first week. He wants to call them.

Guard: That's illegal. You can't contact your embassy.

Me: Yes, he can. He's a foreign national from Ghana. He is not a Chinese national and has a right to contact his embassy. His two-week sentence is over.

Guard: He can't contact the embassy. Immigration must collect him.

If I could reach through the cell door and punch this as$hole in the face, I would.

Me: Ok when does immigration arrive?

Guard: We don't know, we're not immigration.

Me: Ok, so he wants to contact his embassy or the immigration office to find out.

Guard: They don't have telephones.

Me: His embassy has telephones.

Guard: That's illegal.

Me: Keeping him for over forty days on a two week charge is illegal. He's a foreign national and there are international laws you must follow.

The guard didn't give a sh!t. He wasn't paid to. That's how China works.

Guard: "Look, what country are you from?" the guard asked abruptly in an angry tone.

Me: Me? I'm American.

He repositioned himself, squared straight up and stared me straight in the eye through the barred cell door.

Guard: You're lucky American. You'll be out of here a couple days after your sentence. All you big countries...American, Germany, Japan; your embassies care. Your embassies look after you. Your embassies get their people out of here fast. These smaller African countries don't care about their people. Their embassies are slow and irresponsible. This is why their countries are this way. He'll get out eventually, I'm not sure when. Be happy that you're American. You're lucky. Your embassy cares about its people. Be very happy that you have an American passport.

SLAM! He shut the outer cell door in my face and disappeared.

I was speechless. I just stood there, staring at the heavy metal door that had just been slammed in my face. I turned around looking at a silent prison cell that had stopped to listen to my conversation with the guard. At the end of the cell I saw Soldier staring at me with a blank look across his face trying to figure out what we had just said in Mandarin. I was his only hope. I was his only medium for communication.

Once again, I failed.

Once again, I didn't know what to say. I didn't know what to do. How many more of these conversations could I be thrown into in a single day? Had I helped at all? Had I made everything worse? I don't fuc&ing know anymore.

I gathered my thoughts, turned around, and started walking toward Soldier while I stared at the ground.

I can't tell him what the guard just said.

I have about four seconds.

What the fu&k do I say to him now…

Chapter 16:

Malnutrition & Toxic Water

All Five of Beijing's Major Water Systems Seriously Polluted

"Studies have found that about a third of industrial waste water and over 90 percent of household sewage is released back into Chinese lakes and rivers without being treated. As a result, an estimated 500 million Chinese citizens in rural areas are forced to rely on these polluted systems for daily use. According to certain metrics, water scarcity is defined as fresh-water resources falling below 500 cubic meters per person per year.

In Beijing specifically, that number stood at 145 cubic meters of fresh-water per person in 2014. In addition to the ongoing water scarcity issues, forty percent of Beijing's water systems have been found to be too polluted for use. As a result of these (and other) stressed resources, Beijing's government recently implemented a population cap, ensuring the municipality's population not exceed 23,000,000 people."[61]

Official Beijing Municipal Public Water Supply Management Legislation (2010 revision):

"Chapter II water supply, water management

Article 4 Water supply enterprises must abide by the following regulations:

---

[61] 2021, C., Politics, N., Pacific, A., Soccer, & Europe. (2013, August 18). All five of Beijing's major water systems seriously polluted. Retrieved February 28, 2021, from https://www.theepochtimes.com/all-five-of-beijings-major-water-systems-seriously-polluted_251030.html

(1) *Ensure that the water quality of the water supply meets the national sanitary standards for drinking water.*

(5) *Accepting the supervision and inspection of the competent authorities of the city's public water supply work and the relevant administrative agencies such as health, quality and technical supervision, and price.*

Article 17 prohibits the following acts:

(6) *Digging, removing soil, planting trees, embedding rods, and dumping waste liquid in the safe space on the ground and on both sides of the public water supply facilities;*

(8) *Other acts that endanger the safety of public water supply facilities.*

Article 19 The municipal public water supply authority shall impose penalties on other acts in violation of these Measures in accordance with the following provisions:

(5) *Digging, removing soil, planting trees, burying rods, or dumping waste slag in the safety ground on the ground and on both sides of the public water supply facilities shall be ordered to correct and restore the original condition, and the responsible unit shall be fined 3,000 yuan or less.*

(7) *If the construction causes damage to the public water supply facilities or water supply accidents, the responsible unit shall compensate the losses according to law."*[62]

Aside from the psychological torture of being arbitrarily arrested without charges, held incommunicado, indefinitely detained on blood-soaked blankets and sleep deprived; there's Beijing's notorious food and water pollution problems too.

For Beijing residents, water pollution is a constant, pressing, and serious issue. To some degree, there were steps that you could take to mitigate these problems if you were willing to do some research. For example, residents often researched water sources, the quality of local bottled-water companies, and purchased water filters. While it was impossible to eliminate the water pollution issues outright, there was a lot that could be done to mitigate the negative effects.

Those options, unfortunately, don't exist in CCP prison compounds.

---

[62] Laws of the Beijing Province. (n.d.). Retrieved February 27, 2021, from http://www.asianlii.org/cn/legis/bj/laws/mobmowc533/

After arriving in my prison cell, one of the most pressing concerns was discovering that we were being forced to drink Beijing's notorious toxic tap water. It's universally understood by Beijing locals that you don't drink water straight from the tap. I was very worried about what the short-term health-effects might be.

Would it make me sick while I was detained? Could I contract any serious diseases?

These conditions were bad enough without having to worry about diarrhea and vomiting. Furthermore, the "medical" staff didn't give two fu&ks about our health. If you were sick, you were entirely on your own.

But even if I did manage to get through here alive, would there be any long-term damage from consuming Beijing's notoriously polluted tap water?

According to a 2016 study led by the Chinese Academy of Sciences, *Deep Challenges for China's War on Water Pollution*, over half of China's groundwater is heavily contaminated when measured against domestic Chinese standards,

> "*Groundwater accounts for one-third of total water usage across the domestic, agricultural and industrial sectors in China, and approximately two-thirds of cities utilize groundwater as a major water supply. According to the latest Bulletin of Land and Resources of China (2014), groundwater from 61.5% of 4896 monitoring wells in 202 cities across China was characterized as poor (IV class) or very poor (V class) (Fig. 1b) (Ministry of Land and Resources, 2014).*
>
> *Additionally, according to a recently published monthly groundwater status report of the Ministry of Water Resources, 80% of groundwater samples taken from more than 2000 shallow groundwater monitoring wells in China's northern basins falls into classes IV and V (Ministry of Water Resources, 2016).*
>
> *According to the national groundwater quality standard (GB/T 14848-93), water at or below Class IV is unfit for domestic or agricultural uses. The main pollutants above safe levels in these assessments, and which therefore determine the water quality classes, are the three types of nitrogen (NO_3N, NO_2N, NH_4N), phenol, heavy metals and COD.*"[63]

---

[63] Han, Dongmei. Deep challenges for China's war on water pollution. (2016, September 06). Retrieved, February 9th, 2019 from https://www.sciencedirect.com/science/article/pii/S0269749116310363

It's worth repeating that this report found that 60 to 80% of China's ground-water was unfit for domestic or agricultural use. Bear in mind that this was benchmarked against Chinese standards, which are notoriously lower than international standards.

This raised an interesting question, how might this data stack up against Western scientific standards that aren't beholden to CCP propaganda or arbitrary Chinese standards? And what about the quality of Beijing's water specifically? After all, that's where I was being detained. Maybe the CCP held Beijing to a higher standard?

According to a 2016 study in the Journal of Environmental Informatics, water from the Danjiangkou reservoir, which is a major source of Beijing's drinking water, contained levels of lead 20 times higher than the approved safety levels set by the World Health Organization. The lead contamination in the Danjiangkou reservoir exceeded 200 micrograms per liter which stood in stark contrast to the WHO's upper threshold for lead levels in drinking water of 10 micrograms per liter.

Chinese researchers involved in the study declined to interview or answer questions related to the report.

Glossing over Beijing's rampant water contamination for a moment, it's fascinating to simply compare and contrast the *safety* levels for lead established by these respective environmental organizations,

> *WHO: 10 micrograms/liter*
> *US EPA: 15 micrograms/liter*
> *Chinese Government: 50 micrograms/liter*
> *Beijing's actual water supply: 200+ micrograms/liter*

During my latter years in East Asia, China's rampant cancer epidemic began popping up on everyone's radar. The polluted underbelly of China's economic miracle was readily catching up to its unsuspecting population. Although there were several factors that researchers had pointed to over the years, tainted water was a key contributing factor. That research stems directly from one of China's elite universities in Beijing,

> *"China's tap water contains a dangerous amount of a known carcinogen, according to a study released this weekend out of Tsinghua University.*
>
> *The carcinogen known as nitrosodimethylamine (NDMA) is a byproduct of the chlorination process to make water safe for consumption.*

What Tsinghua professor Chen Chao discovered after spending three years testing water across 23 provinces and 155 sites was China's NDMA levels reaching 3.6 times those in U.S. and even more compared to Western Europe."[64]

Sadly, these reports don't even begin to scratch the surface of China's water pollution issues. The key takeaway here is simple, *the water is toxic and deadly.*

So, what short-term health risks might people might encounter from drinking polluted tap water,

"Around the world, water contamination diseases lead to widespread illness and death on a regular basis. While not every disease caused by water contamination is fatal, a huge number of them are. Unfortunately, many of the countries that face these diseases are also developing, which means they don't have access to good quality health care and treatment options. These types of illnesses affect people on a global scale, however, and geography has little to do with it.

Bacterial Diseases

Bacterial diseases are some of the most common when it comes to water contamination, but just because they're common doesn't mean they're any easier to treat. Unfortunately, these diseases can very easily become fatal in the wrong circumstances, and they continue to take lives around the world, and even in the United States.

Shigellosis

Diarrhea, stomach pain, and high fever are the most common symptoms of a shigellosis infection. In rare instances, the disease may spread through the body and infect and blood stream. Severe diarrhea may lead to weakness, fatigue and dehydration.

E. coli

Watery or bloody diarrhea, stomach pain and cramps, and nausea and vomiting are the most common symptoms of Ecoli infection. Bloody diarrhea is a sign that you need to seek medical attention.

---

[64] Cendrowski, Scott. October 17th, 2016. China's Tap Water Is Scaring People After Study Finds a Known Carcinogen. *fortune.com*. Retrieved: March 31st, 2018, from http://fortune.com/2016/10/17/china-tap-water-scaring-people-study-dangerous-carcinogen/.

Gastroenteritis

Symptoms include diarrhea and vomiting, both of which may be mild to severe. Patients may also have stomach cramps and dizziness as well as a high fever.

Hepatitis A

Symptoms include fever and fatigue, diarrhea, vomiting, loss of appetite, and jaundice. Liver failure may occur in serious cases.

Meningitis

Symptoms include a stiff neck, severe headaches, nausea and vomiting

Hookworm

Stomach pain and cramping, fever, loss of appetite, rash, and bloody stool are all signs of hookworm infection."[65]

Chinese prison cells are so deadly, the water is yet another variable that is trying to kill you too. The water toxicity issue was a very real concern for all of us, but we didn't have any other options. Unfortunately, the risks didn't stop there. Even if you survived in the short-term, the consumption of polluted water can also have devastating long-term health effects:

"Heavy metals can leach into drinking water from household plumbing and service lines, mining operations, petroleum refineries, electronics manufacturers, municipal waste disposal, cement plants, and natural mineral deposits. Heavy metals include: arsenic, antimony, cadmium, chromium, copper, lead, selenium and many more. Heavy metals can contaminate private wells through groundwater movement and surface water seepage and run-off. People that consume high levels of heavy metals risk acute and chronic toxicity, liver, kidney, and intestinal damage, anemia, and cancer.

Organic chemicals are found in many house-hold products and are used widely in agriculture and industry. They can be found in inks, dyes, pesticides, paints, pharmaceuticals, solvents, petroleum products, sealants, and disinfectants. Organic chemicals can enter ground water and contaminate private wells through waste disposal, spills, and surface

---

[65] All About Water Filters. 2018. 13 Fatal Diseases Caused by Water Contamination (and How To Know if You've Got One). *all-about-water-filters.com*. Retrieved: April 1st, 2018, from http://all-about-water-filters.com/fatal-diseases-caused-by-water-contamination/.

water run-off. People that consume high levels of organic chemicals may suffer from damage to their kidneys, liver, circulatory system, nervous system, and reproductive system.

Radionuclides are radioactive forms of elements such as uranium and radium. They are harmful to humans and can be released into the environment from uranium mining and milling, coal mining, and nuclear power production. Radionuclides may also be naturally present in ground water in some areas. Radionuclides can contaminate private wells through groundwater flow, waste water seepage and flooding. Drinking water with radionuclides can cause toxic kidney effects and increase the risk of cancer."[66]

Despite the extensive research and data detailing these obvious health-risks, the Chinese government has labeled Beijing's water safe for consumption.

But don't take my word for it, I'll let the Beijing Water Authority speak for itself:

"All tap water in Beijing is drinkable according to standards set by the World Health Organization. You can definitely drink the water. If you are afraid of germs, just boil it. There is no reason to worry."[67]

It gets better.

From time to time the water in our cell would simply shut off without warning. *Yup, they even managed to torture us with the absence of Beijing's toxic water.* Someone would walk to the bathroom to fill up their cup, open the faucet and; nothing would happen.

"Water is off again" someone would randomly scream at the cell.

What the FU*K, the waters gone?!?!?!

Were you thirsty? Had you had a drink recently? No? Well, now there's no water. Do we sit down and wait it out? Would the water turn back on? Would you get water in the next hour? Would you get water that day? Would you get water again?

---

[66] Environmental Protection Agency. February 23rd, 2018. Potential Well Water Contaminants and Their Impacts. *epa.gov.* Retrieved: April 1st, 2018, from https://www.epa.gov/privatewells/potential-well-water-contaminants-and-their-impacts.

[67] Lung, Jessica. December 20th, 2016. Is the tap water safe to drink in China? *medium. com.* Retrieved: March 31st, 2018, from https://medium.com/foreign-accent/is-the-tap-water-safe-to-drink-in-china-8f1ce638fd3d.

Nobody knew.

Bear in mind, this was the water that you relied on for survival. Sometimes it would shut off in the morning, other times they turned it off at night. It also meant the entire bathroom wasn't receiving any water, including the one squatter toilet 16 inmates were sharing.

Guess what that looked like?

Inmates still need to, and do, use the bathroom when the squatter toilet isn't flushing.

Bear in mind, there's nowhere to go when this happens. You're still locked inside the cage, indefinitely.

How long can you deal with those conditions? What if the food stopped coming too? What if they just left you in here? How long until the inmates started to turn on each other?

No one would ever know how you died.

Many of these pollution issues arise in China's food as well. Hygiene, by Chinese admission, is not a well-defined process domestically, so you can imagine the impact on food-prep. This issue becomes exponentially more serious when you consider that most of the people preparing your food aren't well educated, again, *by Chinese standards.*

Education, in China, is seen as the only medium in which people would learn about things like hygiene.

We could tell that a lot of the food we were eating had been recycled for days on end and the nutritional content was also seriously lacking. The Chinese inmates would often say that the detention facility was realistically only using twenty percent of the funds allocated for our food, on food. The rest was likely just pocketed. That is how the Chinese inmates explained the sub-par "meals" we were being served.

That being said, where do China's food pollution issues originate? The obvious answer is that the contaminated water supply feeds into everything they produce and export to the world. But a great place to better understand this reality is to start at Chinese farms,

> "A fifth of China's farmland is polluted, according to an official report based on the results of an extensive survey.

Soil pollution has long been a concern in China due to the country's rapid industrialisation and the report carried on the website of the Ministry of Environmental Protection confirms the extent of the problem. The report states that pollutants in more than 16% of Chinese soil exceeds national standards and that figure rises to 20% for arable land.

It describes the situation as "not optimistic" and said that the quality of farmland is worrying while deserted industrial and mining land is seriously polluted. The main causes of soil pollution are industry and agriculture, according to the report. Cadmium, nickel and arsenic are the top three pollutants found.

The survey was carried out over seven years, ending in December 2013 and covered around 630 square kilometers of land across the country. According to state media, the survey took around 100,000 samples. Almost 70% of the samples were found to be "lightly polluted" with pollution levels twice the national standard. Around 7% were found to be "heavily polluted" with levels more than five times the national standard."[68]

Farmland and soil pollution are national security concerns that the CCP takes very seriously. A reliable and safe food supply is a fundamental concern when you house the world's largest population. And therein lies a fundamental problem for the CCP. In order to maintain complete economic, societal and political control over their population, they need to ensure and maintain sustained economic growth for their people. At the same time, this record-setting industrialization is what has simultaneously wreaked havoc on Chinese agriculture,

2015:

"As it stands, China's arable land per-capita numbers are below half of the global average. Those ratios are dwindling from both ends, as China's population is booming while land pollution has been increasing. After years of rapid industrial expansion, China has finally begun to crack down with stricter standards on the industry's cadmium, arsenic and lead levels that are rendering surrounding farmlands essentially unusable.

The problem is: soil clean-up is notoriously difficult — and with a food crisis potentially looming around the corner, China may have to find

---

[68] Duggan, Jennifer. April 18th, 2014. One fifth of China's farmland polluted. *theguardian. com*. Retrieved: March 31st, 2018, from https://www.theguardian.com/environment/ chinas-choice/2014/apr/18/china-one-fifth-farmland-soil-pollution.

a balance between investing in food factories (while drastically cutting the pollution output) and investing in the much-needed remediation of its lands."[69]

The upside to Guanxi (bribery) is that you can skirt regulations by knowing the right people and maintaining the right network. The downside to this is that corruption becomes rampant and standards simply fly out the window in place of maintaining relationships. In the broader food pollution conversation, the reality of this corruption becomes readily apparent in China's F&B industry,

2016:

"China, rocked in recent years by a series of food safety scandals, uncovered as many as half a million illegal food safety violations in the first three quarters of the year, an official said.

Chinese officials have unearthed a series of recent food health scandals, including rice contaminated with heavy metals, the use of recycled "gutter oil" in restaurants as well as the sale of baby formula containing lethal amounts of the industrial chemical melamine in 2008.

According to a transcript of Bi's report published on the official website of the National People's Congress, Chinese food safety departments conducted more than 15 million individual inspections in the first three quarters of the year and found more than 500,000 incidents of illegal behavior, he said.

Among the offences were false advertising, the use of counterfeit products and ingredients and the sale of contaminated food products, Bi said."[70]

Unfortunately, this contaminated food supply doesn't start and stop inside of China. It directly impacts the food the rest of the world consumes on a daily basis. China is one of the West's largest trading partners and food is an integral two-way element of that import-export relationship. That's right, this polluted Chinese food lands on your family's dinner table too,

---

[69] Wade, Chris. April 4th, 2015. Under The Surface: China's Soil Contamination Crisis. *enfos.com*. Retrieved: April 1st, 2018, from http://www.enfos.com/blog/2015/04/04/under-the-surface-chinas-soil-contamination-crisis/.

[70] Stanway, David. April 1st, 2018. China uncovers 500,000 food safety violations in nine months. *reuters.com*. Retrieved: April 1st, 2018, from https://www.reuters.com/article/us-china-food-safety/china-uncovers-500000-food-safety-violations-in-nine-months-idUSKBN14D046.

2017:

"The first known shipment of cooked chicken from China reached the United States last week, following a much-touted trade deal between the Trump administration and the Chinese government.

But consumer groups and former food-safety officials are warning that the chicken could pose a public health risk, arguing that China has made only minor progress in overhauling a food safety regime that produced melamine-laced infant formula and deadly dog biscuits.

Chicken from China will not be labeled, and a representative from Qingdao Nine-Alliance Group, the first exporter, did not specify the name brand it's being sold under. The privately owned chicken company, one of the largest in China, already supplies markets in Asia, the Middle East and Europe.

China has experienced repeated episodes of both avian influenza and food contamination — a situation that the country's own food safety chief admitted in December, when he told China's National People's Congress that there were still "deep-seated problems" in the Chinese food system.

Among China's biggest issues is the presence of several highly lethal and contagious strains of avian influenza, which has killed more than 270 people and closed a number of poultry markets since October. The risk of bird flu is what prevents China from exporting raw chicken.

Four in 10 of the several thousand Chinese facilities Asia Inspection audited last year failed their safety checks, Breteau said. Separately, China's food safety chief, Bi Jingquan, reported that his agency found 500,000 instances of illegal food safety violations in the first three quarters of 2016."[71]

I guess we're all in the prison cell together.

Again, there were steps Beijing residents can take to mitigate these risks. But once again we weren't granted those options once you were incarcerated. For a moment, we'll ignore the fact that nobody prepping the food bucket in my cell ever washed their hands. Ever. Even if by some miracle you got the bucket-prep guy to do it in our soapless prison cell, the other inmates would refuse.

---

[71] Dewey, Caitlin. July 7th, 2017. The dark side of Trump's much-hyped China trade deal: It could literally make you sick. *washingtonpost.com*. Retrieved: April 1st, 2018, from https://www.washingtonpost.com/news/wonk/wp/2017/07/07/the-dark-side-of-trumps-much-hyped-china-trade-deal-it-could-literally-make-you-sick/?utm_term=.988685176df1.

Why does that matter? We all use the same communal container to scoop food out of the bucket and it's left floating around in there when everyone is done. And even if by some miracle we managed to get all the inmates to wash up, you have no control over the food prep people in the kitchen who, realistically, don't care. Additionally, we'll gloss over the fact that all the food we're eating is heavily polluted with harmful compounds.

Then there's malnutrition.

As mentioned, a lot of the food was recycled and re-cooked, and there was almost no protein present. On certain days, beef and fish balls were tossed into the soup, but the other inmates would literally scavenge through the bucket to pick these out. Occasionally, they would throw in a hardboiled egg with breakfast.

The recycled food options become painfully repetitive. Dinner would routinely be the same re-boiled cabbage from the night before. As a result, even if you're still managing to eat, you start immediately losing weight. In other words, you become malnourished,

> *"Malnutrition refers to deficiencies...imbalances in a person's intake of energy and/or nutrients. The term malnutrition covers 2 broad groups of conditions. One is 'undernutrition'—which includes stunting (low height for age), wasting (low weight for height), underweight (low weight for age) and micronutrient deficiencies or insufficiencies (a lack of important vitamins and minerals)."[72]*

> How do you know if you're malnourished?
> *"Weight loss, indicated by loose clothes, belts, jewellery and even dentures*
> *Being tired and less energetic*
> *Not being as capable at performing usual tasks*
> *Being less physically active, not being able to walk as far or as quickly as before*
> *Changes in mood, such as becoming depressed and lethargic*
> *Loss of appetite and not being interested in food and drinks*
> *Poor concentration, for example, the person may need more time to understand questions and reply to them"[73]*

---

[72] World Health Organization. July 8th, 2016. What is malnutrition? *who.int.* Retrieved: April 1st, 2018, from http://www.who.int/features/qa/malnutrition/en/.

[73] WebMD. 2018. Malnutrition. *webmd.boots.com.* Retrieved: April 1st, 2018, from https://www.webmd.boots.com/healthy-eating/guide/malnutrition.

After a few days of consuming this "food", you can tick every box on that list.

But it gets even worse, as you get to a point where you mentally no longer want to consume more of this liquid slop. Normally, a good meal is a part of the day you look forward to. Whether you love to cook or simply enjoy a certain cuisine, food carries an important psychological reward system that keeps you mentally and physically healthy.

In CCP detention, both the psychological and nutritional benefits of food are categorically stripped from you. You're forced to eat whatever is provided. Not only is that food toxic, unsanitary and recycled, it lacks any basic nutritional value. Eating, in and of itself, becomes the worst part of your day.

Not only do you realize that the food you are eating is unsafe, but that horrific meal is keeping you partially alive, so you can enjoy more, detention, sleep deprivation, violent behavior, and malnutrition.

At some point, the logical thing to do is to stop eating.

Eating, ironically, becomes what tortures you. This toxic food is keeping you partially alive, so you can stay trapped in this dreadful nightmare; for longer.

Why not just stop eating, your brain asks.

Not eating becomes one of your only options to exert control in an environment in which you are otherwise powerless. It becomes a way to stop the nightmare. Why bother with survival when you can just wither away?

At least you're finally in control of something again.

After about ten or twelve days, I had to literally force myself to eat. Often, I would just stare at the food for a few minutes before I could even think about consuming it. Eating, ironically, became the worst part of your day.

I dreaded it. Eating scared me.

Often, I would consider not eating as well. It was the most confusing feelings imaginable. On one hand, you felt very hungry and your body was craving food. On the other, this food prolonged your suffering. It's one of the most genuinely baffling and incomprehensible mental paradoxes I have ever experienced.

Having to force yourself to eat when you're hungry, spoonful after painful spoonful, is one of the most egregious forms of torture you could imagine. Every last spoonful is a forced action. You have to force yourself to chew.

It was horrible.

I completely understood why other grown men in detention chose to stop eating within four or five days.

Then again China is the expert on using food and malnutrition to torture detainees,

> *"At some [Chinese] prisons, requests for health checkups and medicine are refused, human rights experts and former prisoners say. At others, ill prisoners suffer physical abuse and malnutrition. In some cases, chronic ailments and serious diseases are left untreated, or medical care is repeatedly delayed.*
>
> *Chinese prisons, which house more than 1.6 million inmates, are notoriously grueling institutions, plagued by torture, forced labor and malnutrition. Political dissidents battling illnesses while in detention face additional threats to their well-being, activists say.*
>
> *Torture and other abusive practices in prisons have exacerbated the health problems of many inmates. Malnutrition is common in some jails because of the poor quality of meals. Sleep deprivation has also been used as a tactic against dissidents, rights activists say."*[74]

As bad as the conditions were that I had to endure, Chinese nationals who end up in detention are often forced to survive far worse. They don't have the luxury of foreign governments going to bat for them over human rights violations or advocating on their behalf. That doesn't exist in China, it isn't allowed to,

> *"Prominent Chinese dissident and human rights lawyer Gao Zhisheng has broken his silence to describe how he was allegedly tortured and kept in solitary confinement while in detention.*
>
> *The 51-year-old lawyer was released from prison in August 2014.*
>
> *At the time, his lawyer described Mr. Gao, a Nobel Peace Prize nominee, as emotionless, "basically unintelligible" and missing teeth due to malnutrition.*

---

[74] Hernandez, Javier C. July 10th, 2017. Ailing Dissident's Case Fits a Pattern in Chinese Prisons, Critics Say. *nytimes.com.* Retrieved: April 1st, 2018, from https://www.nytimes.com/2017/07/10/world/asia/liu-xiaobo-medical-care-dissidents.html.

Mr. Gao was speaking to AP, in his first interview in five years."[75]

And China isn't one to discriminate. Whether you are a Nobel Peace Prize winner or a human rights advocate protesting the Chinese practice of forced abortion, you'll likely end up in the same place,

> "*After repeated beatings and malnutrition suffered in house detention, blind pro-life activist Chen Guangcheng's health is deteriorating quickly. Now, human rights organizations are pushing harder than ever for his freedom.*
>
> '*Chen's wife sounded the alarm in a letter recently smuggled out of China,' says Reggie Littlejohn, president of Women's Rights Without Frontiers. 'She said that Chen's health is very fragile and worsening every day because of beatings, malnutrition and an intestinal illness. She is worried about his survival. Chen sacrificed everything to tell the world the brutal truth about forced abortion in China. He is a warrior for women's rights. Now it's our turn to sacrifice on behalf of Chen by fighting for his freedom.'"*[76]

Welcome to the Middle Kingdom's *peaceful* rise.

---

[75] BBC. September 24th, 2015. Gao Zhisheng: Chinese lawyer describes 'torture'. *bbc.com*. Retrieved: April 1st, 2018, from http://www.bbc.com/news/world-asia-china-34341069.

[76] Charisma Staff. July 17th, 2011. China Activist Chen Suffers Malnutrition in Detention. *charismanews.com*. Retrieved: April 1st, 2018, from https://www.charismanews.com/world/31501.

Chapter 17:

Sleep Deprivation

A Brief History of Sleep Deprivation and Torture

Sleep deprivation is one of the most misunderstood concepts in the world. Sleep deprivation is often mistakenly associated with pulling an all-nighter for work or school. The main issue here is that you are still able to exert some degree of control in relation to your sleep. For example, you can likely still decide where you will sleep, whether you can turn the lights off, surrounding conditions (bed, blanket, etc), and who you fall asleep around (if anyone at all). When all sleep-related variables are forcefully removed from your control through coercive measures, eliminating sleep indefinitely, you are being sleep deprived.

Severe Sleep Deprivation Causes Hallucinations and a Gradual Progression Toward Psychosis with Increasing Time Awake. Frontiers in Psychiatry. 2018; 9: 303.

"Results: A total of 476 articles were identified. Of these, 21 were eligible for inclusion. Duration of sleep loss ranged between 24 h and 11 nights (total 760 participants; average 72–92 h without sleep). All studies except one reported perceptual changes, including visual distortions (i.e., metamorphopsias), illusions, somatosensory changes and, in some cases, frank hallucinations. The visual modality was the most consistently affected (in 90% of the studies), followed by the somatosensory (52%) and auditory (33%) modalities. Symptoms rapidly developed after one night without sleep, progressing in an almost fixed time-dependent way.

Perceptual distortions, anxiety, irritability, depersonalization, and temporal disorientation started within 24–48 h of sleep loss, followed by complex hallucinations and disordered thinking after 48–90 h, and delusions after 72 h, after which time the clinical picture resembled that of acute psychosis or toxic delirium. By the third day without sleep, hallucinations in all three sensory modalities were reported. A period of normal sleep served to resolve psychotic symptoms in many—although not all—cases."[77]

Sleep deprivation is a cruel form of torture.

After a few days of forced sleep deprivation, I could feel myself almost transforming into an entirely different person. For example, I felt a severe decline in my overall cognitive ability and I was becoming increasingly hostile. Once you've experienced genuine sleep deprivation, the mere thought of the experience makes you want to vomit.

Repeatedly working the night watch, in addition to was already an unhealthy sleep environment rips the fabric of your mind apart. Not only is a consistent sleep cycle nonexistent, but you're already sleep deprived on top of it. As much as it was a blessing to occasionally have fewer inmates in the cell during the day, it also meant that we now had to compensate by working more night shifts.

That random increase in the frequency of 2-hour standing shifts gradually took its toll, night, after night, after night, after night. Some night shifts were also more coveted than others which meant that sleep deprived inmates often argued with each other to decide how shifts were allocated.

It was a tinderbox in the middle of a forest fire that could go off at any moment.

Well so what, you might think? I've pulled an all-nighter before or maybe my baby wakes me up every night. Hell, you've stayed up on little to no sleep for days on end because of a tough work schedule. No big deal!

Same here. This is fundamentally different from sleep deprivation.

Unfortunately, these situations are incomparable, which is what makes them so fundamentally different. It's one thing to willfully keep yourself awake to perform a task. It's one thing to stay up for midterms or power through a hectic week at work. I founded a company, in Beijing, and worked through countless sleepless nights. I also have a STEM degree and routinely stayed up for 24 hour stretches during midterms and finals.

---

[77] JD;, W. (n.d.). Severe sleep deprivation causes hallucinations and a gradual progression toward psychosis with increasing time awake. Retrieved February 28, 2021, from https://pubmed.ncbi.nlm.nih.gov/30042701/

These situations don't even begin to compare with sleep deprivation.

Coerced sleep deprivation is far worse for a variety of reasons. Most notably, you're not in control. Instead of thinking about it as a lack of sleep, focus instead on the moment after that when you've reclaimed control of sleep.

For example, imagine yourself having just worked another long shift or staying up super late studying. *Finally*, you retire to your home, put on your comfy clothes, tuck yourself into bed, turn off the lights and start to doze off. *BAM!* That's when it happens. Something, at that point in time, prevents you from getting to sleep, over and over and over again. That moment when you're supposed to be sleeping, or catching up on sleep, is precisely when you are prevented from doing so.

That is when sleep deprivation starts.

Whether it's the guards, your cellmates, the bright lights that never shut-off or the inadequate sleep schedule; you quickly realize that you aren't in control of your environment. The entire process is so unpredictable, that that single variable, unpredictability, wreaks havoc on your sleep schedule.

First, you're trying to sleep in a completely foreign environment, a prison cell that you're locked inside of. Second, you're surrounded by completely foreign, often violent and mentally unstable inmates. Third, there's the noise factor. Whether it's farting, burping, talking, or laughing, their sounds don't stop. Other times, the guards randomly scream something through the speaker at an inmate for any number of reasons.

Your environment owns you.

And then there's the schedule. Under normal conditions, you *can* access sleep whenever *you* want. If you decide to pull out of the library at 3 am instead of 4 am, you are in charge of making that decision. In a prison cell, you're at the mercy of the schedule. You either sleep during the allotted sleeping hours or you don't. This introduces a second variable; pressure.

If I arbitrarily command you to sleep at some random hour, can you? Maybe you're one of those people that can.

I certainly can't.

So, what happens if you can't sleep on command and miss those vital sleep allocated hours? Sleep deprivation.

But let's, for a moment, assume you can sleep on command and you can compensate for a chaotic and uncontrolled environment.

There's a third variable, the conditions.

You're not retiring to a comfortable bed with a nice mattress and a cushy pillow. You're sleeping on a wooden plank that digs into your bones. You're sleeping with blood stained blankets, body parts digging into or hanging over you, cramped space, and bright flood lights that never shut off. It's painful, uncomfortable, harsh and unforgiving.

Is this starting to make sense? You're not meant to sleep here.

Let's say you magically overcome all those conditions. You manage to block out the environment, you align to the schedule and you grow accustomed to the unforgiving wooden planks.

You still have to work the night watch.

There you are, finally managing to doze off, comfortably resting under your bloody blanket. You manage to sneak a few hours in there but hey, it's your night to work watch three. At 2:00 am, some inmate starts repeatedly tapping your head until you wake up. It's your turn to stand up for 2-hours and he wants to sleep. You instantly get up otherwise you're cutting into his sleep schedule and he will certainly inform you of this right away. If you mess up the watch, you're reporting to CCP guards that hate entitled foreigners with sovereign governments that protect human rights.

You're dead tired but you get out of bed anyway and watch the other guy retire into your sleeping space. He hands you the bright orange hat, you put it on and take your standing position against the wall. For the next two hours, you stand there, watching everyone sleep and sulk further into sleep deprivation. If something happens, like a group of inmates physically assaulting another, you're responsible for pressing the little red button on the speaker. If you shut your eyes while on watch, the guards scream at you through the speaker, waking up everyone else on the planks.

Good luck!

It's worth mentioning that we are glossing over other variables as well. Suppose you have an issue with one of the violent inmates in the cell? This inmate also works the watch and stands over you while you are supposed to be sleeping. But I digress, I think I've introduced enough variables for now. So, all this goes on night, after night, after night, after night.

As you feel your mind fading, you start to wonder, how long can you survive sleep deprivation? Do you get to a certain point where you are no longer able to recover? Can you literally go insane after you lose enough sleep?

To properly understand sleep deprivation as a form of torture, we need to first understand what it is. Is there a universal definition? Well, it depends on who you ask. Here's the CIA,

> *"The CIA authorized sleep deprivation "for up to 180 hours." In January 2003, the Office of the Director of Central Intelligence produced interrogation guidelines, which classified sleep deprivation for more than 72 hours as an "enhanced" interrogation technique while sleep deprivation for less than 72 hours was considered a "standard" technique.*
>
> *On January 10, 2004, following a November 2003 email entitled "Al-Hawsawi Incident" from CIA General Counsel Scott Muller suggesting reducing the threshold to 48 hours, 'CIA headquarters informed CIA detention sites...that sleep deprivation over 48 hours would now be considered an 'enhanced' interrogation technique.'"*[78]

There are other definitions as well. Appendix M of the US Army Field Manual also attempts to explain sleep deprivation by other means. They simply define the constraints or limitations of the practice,

> *"...must not preclude the detainee getting four hours of continuous sleep every 24 hours."*[79]

Now that we have a point of reference from the military, can we qualify sleep deprivation as a form of torture?

> *"I do know that the methods of sleep deprivation reportedly used are clearly acts of torture. In fact, prolonged sleep deprivation is an especially insidious form of torture because it attacks the deep biological functions at the core of a person's mental and physical health.*
>
> *Why is this? Start with the fact that sleep is a basic biological necessity for all humans, indeed for all creatures on the planet. There is some natural variability and flexibility in the sleep cycle, hence people can go 24 or more*

---

[78] Human Rights First. Senate Report on CIA Torture. *humanrightsfirst.org*. Retrieved: April 1st, 2018, from https://www.humanrightsfirst.org/senate-report-cia-torture/sleep-deprivation.

[79] Pilkington, Ed. November 28th, 2014. UN torture report condemns sleep deprivation among US detainees. *theguardian.com*. Retrieved: April 2nd, 2018, from https://www.theguardian.com/law/2014/nov/28/un-condemns-sleep-deprivation-among-us-detainees.

hours without sleep in the right circumstances, without any lasting harm other than additional "rebound" sleep the next time they are able to sleep normally. However, if a person is deprived of sleep for longer than that, several mental and physical problems begin to develop."[80]

These descriptions sync with the definitions of psychological torture outlined in earlier chapters. This begs an interesting question, why is sleep deprivation such an effective form of torture?

"Sleep deprivation may sound quite tame in comparison with other forms of torture, but in the hands of an expert interrogator, it quickly renders someone open to suggestion, whilst reducing resistance to physical pain and psychological enquiry.

It leaves no scars, at least physical ones, and in recent years it has become one of the the preferred methods of "torture lite" by regimes who claim to respect international law and human rights."[81]

That lack of a lasting and visible physical injury makes sleep deprivation a highly effective weapon that syncs into the CCPs MO. They can torture people indefinitely without having to worry about the consequences of international outcry.

So, what does sleep deprivation actually do to you? Well, we've all likely been kept up for a long stretch for one reason or another. You obviously feel tired after a while. But what starts to happen when your mind and body are prevented from accessing sleep beyond that,

"After Twenty-Four Hours

Concentration is impaired, decision making ability is reduced, the memory deteriorates and there will be a degree of cognitive impairment, similar to that which is caused by alcohol intake. Physically, hand-eye coordination and hearing are also affected adversely.

---

[80] Bulkeley, Kelly. December 15th, 2014. Why Sleep Deprivation Is Torture. *psychologytoday. com*. Retrieved: April 2nd, 2018, from https://www.psychologytoday.com/us/blog/dreaming-in-the-digital-age/201412/why-sleep-deprivation-is-torture.

[81] Editor. May 4th, 2017. Timeline: The Effects of Sleep Deprivation. *hacktosleep.com*. Retrieved: April 3rd, 2018, from https://hacktosleep.com/timeline-the-effects-of-sleep-deprivation/.

After Thirty-Six Hours

> *After a period of thirty six hours the physiological effects of sleep deprivation become more serious…You are also likely to suffer an increase in blood pressure and a reduction in your body's ability to fight infections. You will find yourself nodding off for periods of "micro sleep" and are likely generally to be irritable and short tempered.*

After Forty-Eight Hours

> *After two sleepless days and nights, the body will start to shut down, with the periods of "micro sleep" becoming more frequent and uncontrollable. Mental functioning will be severely impaired. The ability to concentrate will be much reduced and you are likely to suffer from mood swings, short and long-term memory impairment and problems in making decisions.*

After Seventy-Two Hours

> *After a prolonged period of sleep deprivation, the psychological and physical effects become even more debilitating. The mind will deteriorate and there is a likelihood of hallucinations. Paranoid and/or schizophrenic delusions may occur in addition to wild mood swings, where the subject switches between uncontrollable laughter and tears. The impact on the body's internal systems also becomes more marked.*

After Ninety-Six Hours

> *The implications of sleep deprivation for periods in excess of four days are likely to be dramatic. There will be a critical reduction in the efficiency of the body's immune system, resulting in the buildup of toxins that the body normally deals with during sleeping hours. The body's ability to regulate its hormones is also adversely affected. Blood pressure and heart rate will rise and there will be metabolic and digestive problems. The risk of stroke, heart attack and Type 2 diabetes will also increase.*"[82]

This seemingly innocuous method of torture produces well documented and severe health complications. The first few days of sleep deprivation are painful, but to some degree it's tolerable. At a certain point, however, it starts to cause underlying biological damage that is beyond your ability to control. You feel your body and mind start to shutter in different ways as you are unable to

---

[82] Editor. May 4th, 2017. Timeline: The Effects of Sleep Deprivation. *hacktosleep.com*. Retrieved: April 3rd, 2018, from https://hacktosleep.com/timeline-the-effects-of-sleep-deprivation/.

adjust to this brutal new reality. You need sleep, but you are constantly prevented from getting any,

> *"Medical science has demonstrated over and over that there is serious physical and mental harm caused by sleep deprivation. As a report on the effects of psychological torture notes, short and long-term effects can include 'memory impairment, reduced capacity to concentrate, somatic complaints such as headache and back pain, hyperarousal, avoidance, irritability, severe depression with vegetative symptoms, nightmares, feelings of shame and humiliation, and post-traumatic stress disorder … incoherent speech, disorientation, hallucination, irritability, anger, delusions, and sometimes paranoia.'"*[83]

After a while you feel your mind slipping and you don't recognize yourself any longer. A different part of your brain takes over clicking you into something that I can only describe as survival mode. It's like your phone going into battery saving mode where only the basic functions are still operational. After a while, sleep deprivation starts disrupting basic cognition,

> *"The most pronounced impact of total sleep deprivation is cognitive impairment, which can include "impairments in memory, learning, logical reasoning, arithmetic skills, complex verbal processing, and decision making." Sleep-deprived individuals take longer to respond to stimuli, and sleep loss causes "attention deficits, decreases in short-term memory, speech impairments, perseveration, and inflexible thinking." These symptoms may appear after one night of total sleep deprivation, after only a few nights of sleep restriction (5 hours of sleep per night). Sleep restriction also can result in hypertension and other cardiovascular disease. One study correlates sleep deprivation with decreased pain tolerance, which has significant implications for torture and other situations in which sleep restrictions are implemented in tandem with other torture techniques."*[84]

There is an extensive body of research on what happens to a sleep deprived brain. I wanted to figure out what the neurobiological effects of sleep deprivation were on my mind throughout this experience.

---

[83] Carvin, Stephanie. July 14th, 2017. Yes, sleep deprivation is torture. *macleans.ca*. Retrieved: April 3rd, 2018, from http://www.macleans.ca/opinion/yes-sleep-deprivation-is-torture/.

[84] Borchelt, Gretchen. May 2005. Break Them Down Systematic Use of Psychological Torture by US Forces. Physicians for Human Rights. Retrieved: April 3rd, 2018, from http://physiciansforhumanrights.org/library/reports/us-torture-break-them-down-2005.html.

Why was I unable to think clearly? Why was it becoming harder to make rational decisions? Why did I feel my mind becoming increasingly hostile? Was I even still the same person that had initially entered into the cell?

2014:

> *"Veasey and her colleagues studied mice who were submitted to a sleep schedule similar to that of shift workers. They slept for short periods during inconsistent hours. The researchers found that sleeping for only brief periods of time caused massive brain damage: the mice lost 25 percent of the neurons in their locus coeruleus, the section of their brain associated with alertness and cognitive function.*
>
> *'This is the first report that sleep loss can actually result in a loss of neurons,' Veasey said in a statement on the University of Pennsylvania website. The team plans to study the brains of deceased shift workers next to see if they show similar brain damage."*[85]

"Short and inconsistent" sleep hours makes your brain literally start to atrophy. Surprisingly, this paper wasn't even trying to explore prison or torture conditions. They were simply trying to understand what happens to workers that sleep irregular hours. We're off to a great start, my brain was likely starting to atrophy. Anything else?

2015:

> *"The study, published in Nature Neuroscience, found that beta-amyloid—a protein that has long been suspected of being a catalyst in Alzheimer's— aggregates in higher concentrations in the brains of people who suffer from consistently poor sleep. As deposits of beta-amyloid grow, the protein further hampers one's ability to sleep, which feeds into a miserable cycle that may lead to dementia.*
>
> *UC Berkeley neuroscience professor Bryce Mander co-led the study with Alzheimer's expert William Jagust, a professor at Berkeley with a joint appointment at Lawrence Berkeley National Lab. They and their colleagues were intrigued by recent animal research that suggested a reciprocal relationship between lack of sleep and the beta-amyloid pathology.*

---

[85] Dockterman, Eliana. March 19th, 2014. Study: Sleep Loss Can Cause Brain Damage. *time.com*. Retrieved: April 4th, 2018, from http://time.com/30238/ study-sleep-loss-can-cause-brain-damage/.

The results from the scans revealed that individuals with the highest concentration of beta-amyloid in their brains experienced the worst sleep during the study and performed poorly on the word pair test. According to Mander, this indicated that beta-amyloid has a direct impact on memory by ruining the sleep required for building memories."[86]

"Higher concentrations of beta-amyloids in the brains of people who suffer from consistently poor sleep." Great. The sleep deprivation likely undermined the little sleep I did get while also impairing my cognition. Anything else?

2016:

"In a study published on Tuesday, researchers show for the first time that sleep resets the steady build-up of connectivity in the human brain which takes place in our waking hours. The process appears to be crucial for our brains to remember and learn so we can adapt to the world around us.

The loss of a single night's sleep was enough to block the brain's natural reset mechanism, the scientists found. Deprived of rest, the brain's neurons seemingly became over-connected and so muddled with electrical activity that new memories could not be properly laid down.

Nissen next turned to another form of brain stimulation to mimic the way neurons fire when memories are laid down. He found it harder to get the neurons to respond in sleep-deprived people, a sign that the process of writing memories was impaired by sleep loss."[87]

Lovely, memory damage. Yes, the CCP is well aware of what these conditions were doing to us. No, they don't care and yes, this behavior will continue unabated as governments around the world continue to sign billion dollar trade agreements with them. Welcome to the Middle Kingdom. Brain atrophy, cognitive impairment, and memory damage. Anything else I should know about?

---

[86] Wolfe, Eli. June 2nd, 2015. Lack of Sleep May Lead to Dementia: New Research Finds It Makes Brain Vulnerable. alumni.berkeley.edu. Retrieved: April 4th, 2018, from https://alumni.berkeley.edu/california-magazine/just-in/2015-06-02/lack-sleep-may-lead-dementia-new-research-finds-it-makes.

[87] Sample, Ian. August 23rd, 2016. Sleep 'resets' brain connections crucial for memory and learning, study reveals. *Theguardian.com*. Retrieved: April 4th, 2018, from https://www.theguardian.com/science/2016/aug/23/sleep-resets-brain-connections-crucial-for-memory-and-learning-study-reveals.

2017:

> "*A lack of sleep can cause parts of the brain's synapses to be 'eaten' by other brain cells, according to a new study by researchers at the Marche Polytechnic University in Italy.*
>
> *Astrocytes are a cell in the brain that clean out worn-out cells and debris. Scientists studying the brains of mice found these cells were more active when the animals had been deprived of sleep, breaking down more of the brain's connections.*
>
> "*We show for the first time that portions of synapses are literally eaten by astrocytes because of sleep loss," research leader Michele Bellesi told New Scientist.*"[88]

Another mechanism causing my brain to atrophy. What was the full extent of the long-term damage here? I may never actually find out. But this is what makes sleep deprivation the CCP's operative form of torture. How do I show people what I suffered through?

I don't have a scar from the CCPs torture that I can point to for the world to see and understand.

Checkmate; CCP. All of this translates to a story that tortured inmates have a very difficult time conveying to the world. But again, Chinese nationals are forced to endure far worse than anything I survived,

> "*All those interviewed by Human Rights Watch, except for a former procurator, said that shuanggui detainees are subjected to various forms of physical and psychological abuse, which include beatings, solitary confinement, prolonged sleep deprivation, extended periods in stress positions, exposure to extreme temperatures, deprivation of adequate food and water, and threats to their families. Lawyer He Gang told Human Rights Watch:*
>
> "*They didn't let me sleep. I had a total of 10 days without closing my eyes.*"
>
> —*Yang Zeyu, former shuanggui detainee, December 2015*

---

[88] Boult, Adam. May 26th, 2017. Sleep deprivation can cause brain to start 'eating' itself. *telegraph. co.uk*. Retrieved: April 4th, 2018, from https://www.telegraph.co.uk/science/2017/05/26/sleep-deprivation-can-cause-brain-start-eating/.

Sleep deprivation appears to be one of the most common means of torture for detainees in shuanggui, according to lawyers we interviewed. One, Huang Xinyao, said:

"All my clients were mistreated, mostly in the form of sleep deprivation."

In some cases shuanggui detainees were not allowed to sleep at all for days. Others were allowed very little sleep. Ren Zhiqing said:

"In the first eight or nine days, they required that I sit in certain ways and I wasn't allowed to move... I began to hallucinate, as if I had split into several people at once. This was because I was tired: sitting all day from 6 a.m. to 11 p.m., then being interrogated at 11 p.m., and only after that do they let you sleep."

According to former detainee Lu Yicheng:

"The CDI officers used all kinds of methods to disturb my basic sleep...it was very hot, stuffy, and humid, and I was detained in a room without windows. [They] shined dozens of 1,000 watt lights on me at all times, and didn't turn them off at night so I [often] couldn't sleep at all. Even if they let me sleep, before I slept they made me drink large amounts of water before I could lie down, so that as soon as I closed my eyes I felt I had to urinate, so I couldn't sleep in peace. But when I was so extremely tired... and closed my eyes they'd shake my bed with a great force, pulled my mattress, or clapped their hands loudly on top of my head, so I couldn't sleep."

Forced standing or sitting is often is used in conjunction with sleep deprivation. Lawyer Du Qing told Human Rights Watch:

'I had a case, the client said for the first eight days he could only sleep for an hour [each day]. For the remaining 23 hours he was forced to stand, and that he had to hold a book on his head without it falling. He stood for eight days and couldn't stand it, and confessed to everything and to whatever they said. After he said it, he was allowed two hours of sleep every day. At that point his feet were swollen like an elephant's, and he could no longer urinate.'

The former President of Nanchang University spoke about his torture in court, according to a press report:

During shuanggui, he was forced to stand 10 days and 10 nights, "his feet became swollen like winter melon, and the blisters on his legs were as big

*as ducks' eggs." He was 'deprived of sleep for seven days and seven nights"
and subjected to "non-stop interrogations for five days and five nights."*[89]

Sleep deprivation, even when compounded by all the other horrible conditions, is tolerable for a few days. Beyond that, you mentally start to break down and the damage spirals beyond your control.

Even though my experience was not as horrific as the accounts of these Chinese nationals, prolonged sleep deprivation is something that leaves a painful mental scar. Simply writing about the experience makes me feel physically uncomfortable...almost nauseous. After about two weeks of being sleep deprived, I started developing a weird twitch in my eyelids when I tried falling asleep. It wasn't a light twitch but a deep and heavy prod.

It concerned me because I recognized it as something symptomatic of an underlying physical ailment being caused by sleep deprivation. Furthermore, and it's hard to explain, but there was a part of my brain that physically hurt. It was as if I could feel it pumping away in agony. Nope, it wasn't a headache, it was something far worse.

I kept thinking, if this is happening now, *what happens next? And how long can I survive whatever comes next?*

I have no history of illness and I have never experienced any type of spontaneous or prolonged muscle twitch in the past, and certainly not on my face.

No, this was the direct result of that CCP prison cell. This developed after countless nights of doing the watch. This developed after countless nights of broken sleep. This developed after being forced to sleep on wooden planks under blood stained blankets with heavy flood lights beaming down on your face.

To this day, the same twitch on my eye emerges anytime I feel excessively stressed or tired.

I guess that's my CCP scar.

---

[89] Human Rights Watch. December 6th, 2016. 'Special Measures' Detention and Torture in the Chinese Communist Party's Shuanggui System. *hrw.org*. Retrieved: April 4th, 2018, from https://www.hrw.org/report/2016/12/06/special-measures/detention-and-torture-chinese-communist-partys-shuanggui-system.

Chapter 18:

Death & Violence

Chinese Hackers Accused of Breaching US military, Government Systems in Global Campaign Linked to Beijing Government

List of US organizations and entities targeted by Chinese cyber espionage: U.S. Navy, Apple, C.I.A., Amazon, Marriott, U.S. Department of Defense, Westinghouse, SolarWorld, U.S. Steel, Sandia National Laboratories, U.S. State Department's East Asia Bureau, U.S. House Foreign Affairs Committee, Arizona Counter Terrorism Information Center, New York Times, U.S. Satellite systems, Google, Nortel, US Chamber of Commerce, The Pentagon, U.S. Naval War College, Campaigns of then Senators Barack Obama and John McCain, Lockheed Martin's F-35 fighter program, etc.

Chinese Government's official remarks regarding Canadian National Robert Lloyd Schellenberg's death sentence. Chinese Foreign Ministry Spokesperson Hua Chunying's remarks, January 15, 2019:

"Q: The US Department of Justice indicted two Chinese nationals on charges including conspiracy to commit computer intrusions, conspiracy to commit wire fraud, and aggravated identity theft, accusing China of undermining the US cyber-security for a long time. What is your comment?

A: In response to the erroneous words and actions made by the US side on the cyber-security issue, China has made clear its stern position at the earliest time possible.

The US side fabricated stories out of nothing and made unwarranted accusations against China on the cyber-security issue. It "indicted" two Chinese nationals on the grounds of the so-called "cyber stealing". This move, with its egregious nature, has gravely violated the basic norms governing international relations and seriously damaged China-US cooperation. The Chinese side strongly opposes this and has lodged stern representations with the US side.

The Chinese government holds a consistent and clear position on the cyber-security issue. China is a staunch defender of cyber-security and has been firmly opposing and cracking down on all forms of cyber espionage. The Chinese government has never participated in or supported others in stealing commercial secrets in any form.

...We urge the US side to immediately correct its wrongdoings, stop defaming and discrediting China on the cyber-security issue, and withdraw its so-called indictment against the Chinese nationals so as to avoid seriously damaging bilateral relations and cooperation in relevant fields. China will take necessary measures to resolutely safeguard its cyber-security and interests.

...The US is the world's No.1 superpower. But it is filled with arrogance and selfishness. It has been leaving no stones unturned to suppress other countries' legitimate development rights because of its narrow-mindedness and zero-sum mindset in order to preserve its hegemony. It has gone so far to fabricate stories out of nothing. This is not what a superpower is supposed to do. A US like this augurs badly for world peace and development. In a long-term view, it is not helping its own interests."

Often, I thought death was a very realistic outcome here.

It's a weird thing to think about and a painfully strange reality to experience if you haven't before. Weeks earlier, I had been eating at upscale Beijing restaurants, attending business meetings and traveling around China. Now I was locked in a prison cell, contemplating death.

Fu&kin surreal.

While in detention, on two separate occasions, I encountered situations where a violent death became a highly probable outcome. Even if I was fortunate enough to avoid death in these instances, I could have just as easily been exposed to long-term and permanent injury.

To better understand how incarceration influences violence, we'll explore the effects of the detention process. More fundamentally, what is it to be imprisoned and locked in a cage? Let's explore a definition,

Imprison: *"Put or keep in prison or a place like a prison."*[90]

What then, is the intended outcome of incarceration? Rehabilitation? Suffering? Regardless of the intended outcome of incarceration, there are some well documented long-term psychological effects on detainees,

> *"People become more institutionalized if they have to spend hours of enforced idleness. The Chief Inspector of Prisons stated, "There is nothing worse for the mental well-being of those who find it difficult to cope with life in prison than being idle"* (HMCIP, 1999: 62)

> *In a study by Jo Nurse, Paul Woodcock, and Jim Ormsby, prisoners and staff emphasised the negative effects on prisoners' mental health of 23 hour bang up. Extended periods of inactivity lead to frustration, anxiety and a temptation to use drugs. Some prisoners explained the emotional impact of enforced idleness:*

> *'...not letting me get to education, not giving me a chance to work, not giving me a chance to do anything. You build up anger, you know what I mean. It's going to release one day. It's just building up inside you and got to hold it down, hold it down, hold it down.'* (Ormsby, Nurse, 2003)

A compelling description of institutionalization comes from a report published in 1971:

> *'Imprisonment ... denies autonomy, degrades dignity, impairs or destroys self-reliance, inculcates authoritarian values, minimizes the likelihood of beneficial interaction with one's peers, fractures family ties, destroys the family's economic stability, and prejudices the prisoner's future prospects for any improvement in ... economic and social status.'* (AFSC, 33)

In her evidence to the Joint Committee on Human Rights, the Policy Director of MIND, Sophie Cortlett, stated:

> *"From the evidence it appears that [people with serious mental health problems] become more ill and it would appear that people who have less severe mental health problems in prison develop more severe mental*

---

[90] Oxford Dictionaries. 2018. Imprison. *oxforddictionaries.com*. Retrieved: April 7th, 2018, from https://en.oxforddictionaries.com/definition/imprison.

health problems. Prison appears to be a good greenhouse for developing mental health problems." (JCHR, 2004: 31)

The Joint Committee on Human Rights concluded:

"The evidence we have gathered suggests that prison actually leads to an acute worsening of mental health problems. By sending people with a history of attempted suicide and mental health problems to prison for minor offences the state is placing them in an environment that is proven to be dangerous to their health and well-being. (JCHR, 2004: 32)"[91]

Whether detention serves as an effective form of punishment goes a bit beyond the scope of this book. Nonetheless, it's an important topic and one I would certainly ask you to think about as you read on. My goal in sharing this information, however, is to provide context regarding the psychological impact of that process.

Given this information, how does the average person respond to detention conditions? What happens if we changed a few of the parameters from my experience of being incarcerated in China?

Let's say we create a simulated prison environment for the sake of this experiment that was voluntary? You're not in a foreign country, everyone speaks your language and it's not a real prison. In fact, you're in your own city, at a known location and you're not being held indefinitely. You are able to communicate with everyone throughout the experience because there's no language barrier and you've been psychologically screened beforehand to ensure that you, and everyone involved, are mentally stable. Seems easy enough right?

So how do people perform in this safe, controlled and simulated prison environment?

Not well.

Stanford infamously ran this exact experiment back in August of 1971,

"To study the roles people play in prison situations, Zimbardo converted a basement of the Stanford University psychology building into a mock prison. He advertised asking for volunteers to participate in a study of the psychological effects of prison life...

---

[91] Prison Reform Trust. 2016. Prisons Can Seriously Damage Your Mental Health. *yumpu.com.* Retrieved: April 7th, 2018, from https://www.yumpu.com/en/document/view/50015984/prisons-can-seriously-damage-your-mental-health-prison-reform-.

More than 70 applicants answered the ad and were given diagnostic interviews and personality tests to eliminate candidates with psychological problems, medical disabilities, or a history of crime or drug abuse. The study comprised 24 male college students (chosen from 75 volunteers) who were paid $15 per day to take part in the experiment.

Participants were randomly assigned to either the role of prisoner or guard in a simulated prison environment. There were two reserves, and one dropped out, finally leaving ten prisoners and 11 guards. The guards worked in sets of three (being replaced after an 8-hour shift), and the prisoners were housed three to a room. There was also a solitary confinement cell for prisoners who 'misbehaved.' The prison simulation was kept as "real life" as possible."[92]

Even under these conditions, things took a turn for the worse almost immediately. Bear in mind, this was a *simulated environment,*

"The First Prisoner Released:

Less than 36 hours into the experiment, Prisoner #8612 began suffering from acute emotional disturbance, disorganized thinking, uncontrollable crying, and rage. In spite of all of this, we had already come to think so much like prison authorities that we thought he was trying to "con" us – to fool us into releasing him.

When our primary prison consultant interviewed Prisoner #8612, the consultant chided him for being so weak, and told him what kind of abuse he could expect from the guards and the prisoners if he were in San Quentin Prison. #8612 was then given the offer of becoming an informant in exchange for no further guard harassment. He was told to think it over.

During the next count, Prisoner #8612 told other prisoners, "You can't leave. You can't quit." That sent a chilling message and heightened their sense of really being imprisoned. #8612 then began to act "crazy," to scream, to curse, to go into a rage that seemed out of control. It took quite a while before we became convinced that he was really suffering and that we had to release him."

---

[92] McLeod, Saul. 2017. Stanford Prison Experiment. *simplypsychology.org*. Retrieved: April 7th, 2018, from https://www.simplypsychology.org/zimbardo.html.

It is worth emphasizing that this all happened less than 36-hours in a completely safe environment that simply mimiced existing prison conditions in the US. But of course, the experiment went on,

"#819

> The only prisoner who did not want to speak to the priest was Prisoner #819, who was feeling sick, had refused to eat, and wanted to see a doctor rather than a priest. Eventually he was persuaded to come out of his cell and talk to the priest and superintendent, so we could see what kind of a doctor he needed. While talking to us, he broke down and began to cry hysterically, just as had the other two boys we released earlier. I took the chain off his foot, the cap off his head, and told him to go and rest in a room that was adjacent to the prison yard. I said that I would get him some food and then take him to see a doctor.
>
> While I was doing this, one of the guards lined up the other prisoners and had them chant aloud: "Prisoner #819 is a bad prisoner. Because of what Prisoner #819 did, my cell is a mess, Mr. Correctional Officer." They shouted this statement in unison a dozen times.
>
> As soon as I realized that #819 could hear the chanting, I raced back to the room where I had left him, and what I found was a boy sobbing uncontrollably while in the background his fellow prisoners were yelling that he was a bad prisoner...
>
> I suggested we leave, but he refused. Through his tears, he said he could not leave because the others had labeled him a bad prisoner. Even though he was feeling sick, he wanted to go back and prove he was not a bad prisoner.
>
> At that point I said, "Listen, you are not #819. You are [his name], and my name is Dr. Zimbardo. I am a psychologist, not a prison superintendent, and this is not a real prison. This is just an experiment, and those are students, not prisoners, just like you. Let's go."
>
> He stopped crying suddenly, looked up at me like a small child awakened from a nightmare, and replied, "Okay, let's go."[93]

The human brain is not built to cope with these conditions. Had I not spent a lifetime in sports that pushed me far beyond my mental and physical limits, I'm not sure that I would have survived. Again, I'm not trying to brag, but it's

[93] Zimbardo, Philip G. 1999-2018. Stanford Prison Experiment. *prisonexp.org*. Retrieved: April 7th, 2018, from http://www.prisonexp.org/escape.

hard to emphasize how horrific these conditions were. There's a reason grown men from around the world stop eating after a few days of CCP detention.

For your average person who has not spent years being pushed to their absolute limits, these conditions are deadly. But before that happens, this environment will make you incredibly hostile and angry. It breaks you mentally, spiritually and pushes you to extremes you didn't know existed.

If this happens to people who are psychologically screened, what do these conditions do to people that are not?

What happens in a country where there is no history or culture of mental health evaluation, like China? What happens when you throw anyone who has broken any law into a single prison cell without regard for mental health? What do these conditions do to someone who is mentally unstable? Someone who is prone to aggression? What about someone with a history of violence and aggression?

Day 5:

It was bedtime and I had been lying on the plank trying to sleep. I was tasked with working shift three that night and I wanted to try and get as much sleep as possible. Another inmate and the lieutenant were tasked with working shift one.

The lieutenant wouldn't shut the fu*k up.

He was far and away my biggest point of frustration and irritation in the cell. The lieutenant was loud and obnoxious and being locked in a room with him was absolute hell. He was also mentally unstable. During the day he would punch the cell door to try and show off how tough he was. As he paced around, he would slap the walls and the wood beds and he liked to scream at people from the other side of the cell.

Screaming seemed to be his preferred medium for casual conversation.

He was also prone to violence. My guess was that he had been abused in his youth and acting out was his way of overcompensating for whatever had scarred him. He was the kind of person that had no filter but that in and of itself is an understatement. On one hand I felt bad for him. He needed professional help. On the other, his erratic behavior made everyone want to bash his head through the wall.

This is the last type of person you want to be locked in a prison cell with.

He was a form of torture all his own.

Luckily, I was significantly bigger than he was. Despite his rash behavior, he wasn't super strong and was small enough to where you knew you could handle him if things got messy. But his erratic behavior was still discomforting. You couldn't calculate what he would do next and he lived for the attention. If he didn't get attention, it caused him to act out even more. This was the lieutenant's process.

I wasn't myself at this point, nor was I thinking rationally. Every single outburst made me want to punch him straight in his smug little face. Unfortunately, the Chinese inmates generally outnumbered me about twelve or more to one. It was a nonstop struggle to stay off of their radar. If I had a physical outburst, how many would respond violently to the lone American in the cell?

Those weren't odds I wanted to test or go up against. So, I did my best to ignore it.

His behavior became significantly more pronounced during the scheduled sleep hours. The rules didn't seem to apply to him and he would continue being loud and obnoxious during my coveted sleep time.

By night five, I couldn't tolerate him any longer. I guess everyone has a breaking point and the lieutenant helped me discover mine.

It was bedtime and for the fifth night in a row, the wooden plank below my body was digging into my bones. I was sleep deprived, running on fumes and still hadn't fully adapted to my new prison environment. I had been listening to this fu&ker scream and slap sh!t for the last five days. It was nighttime, and the lieutenant was standing up in the pacing area wearing his bright orange hat. He was farting, poking prisoners who were trying to sleep and *clonking* around with his annoying and heavy footsteps.

Unsurprisingly, I wasn't the only person who was frustrated by his behavior.

The biggest guy in the cell was a Chinese inmate and he was massive. It wasn't that he was particularly muscular or the kind of guy that seemed to hit the gym, not that he needed to, but he was just naturally strong. He stood somewhere around 6'6" tall and could likely handle anyone in the cell if he needed to.

Luckily, he was also incredibly peaceful and quiet.

For no reason, the lieutenant had walked up to him and tickled his chin as he was trying to sleep. *Bad move.* The friendly giant opened his eyes and rolled over onto his stomach staring him straight in the eye as a predator would with cornered prey. The lieutenant froze as the friendly giant delivered a painfully terrifying look that silently screamed, "stop that sh!t right now or I'll snap your arm off." I was scared, and I was on the opposite side of the room. The whole room seemed to freeze as the angry giant proceeded to roll back over and go back to sleep.

Message delivered.

The lieutenant backed up slowly and walked over to my side of the room. Fortunately, this was one of the few things that the lieutenant understood; fear. But even the giant's terrifying gaze could only do so much. I could see the lieutenant's facial expression as he tried to process what had just happened. He recognized, maybe from experience, that he now needed to stay away from the giant, which he did. But it also seemed as if he failed to fully connect the giant's undesirable response to a specific action of his.

What his brain failed to process was that this behavior was annoying everyone in the cell and that it needed to stop, period. He quieted down for a few minutes processing what had just happened. Other inmates, including myself, tried to move past it and go back to sleep.

Unfortunately for the lieutenant, he failed to process the message the giant tried to deliver.

Once again, I heard his loud, obnoxious footsteps clamouring his way over to another inmate next to me. I desperately needed sleep and this idiot was preventing me from that. It was around 10:30 pm at this point and he had now cut into 30 minutes of my designated sleep time.

Not ok.

I looked up with a painfully angry expression plastered across my face. As he approached the other inmate, he looked over at me and began to smile, as he proceeded to look back down at the other Chinese prisoner. Once again, he tried to poke the sleeping inmate in the face thinking it would be funny.

The other inmate, who was partially asleep at the time, woke up trying to figure out what the fu&k was going on. He looked up annoyed at the lieutenant and shot him a disapproving look. Right then and there, something happened and I'm still not sure what that was. I guess this is what it feels like when fight mode clicks on in the fight or flight response. I guess 5 nights of this bullshit was my breaking point.

It was literally an involuntary survival response.

I shot straight up out of bed almost flying into a vertical position from my wooden plank and began shouting at him in Chinese:

Me: "What time is it?!" *I bellowed pointing at the clock on the wall.*

I didn't even have time to process what I was doing. I didn't realize that I was now standing on the wooden planks, towering over everyone else. I didn't realize that I was shouting. I didn't realize that every inmate in the cell was now awake and staring at me. I didn't realize that the guards were probably watching all of this unfold through the cell camera. I didn't realize what I was doing. It was just happening, as if it wwere part of a well-rehearsed script.

This is what it feels like to snap? Maybe it's a survival mechanism where some evolutionary part of your brain takes over? *And on I went...*

Me: "It's 10:30 pm! We were supposed to be asleep 30 minutes ago! Look at the fucking sign!" I screamed pointing at the large schedule posted on the wall in Chinese and English.

Me: 10:00 fuc&ing pm! I'm working shift three tonight, I need to fuc&ing sleep!

It wasn't until I stopped shouting that I finally processed what I had just done. My sleep deprived brain had finally caught up to the fact that I had just snapped. My brain needed something done and my body simply responded in what seemed to be the most efficient way possible. Once my body had completed the task, my mind came back online and seemed to catch up to the present.

The lieutenant just stood there in utter silence. I looked around, the entire room was just staring at me, unsure of what to do.

Oh fu&k. What did I just do?

Silence. Gradually, a couple of the prisoners rolled over and went to sleep. The lieutenant just stood there, staring at me in silence. He looked away and glared straight ahead at the wall in front of him as if he were in a trance. Other inmates looked up at him and shot each other confused looks. I didn't know what to do next. I walked back over to my sleeping place laid back down.

What the fu&k just happened? What the fu&k did I just do?! What the fu&k happens now?!

I was supposed to sleep now, five feet away from where the mentally unstable lieutenant would be fuc&ing standing for the night watch. For the next hour and a half, he would stand mere feet away and watch me sleep.

Fu&k.

He could easily get the jump on me and kick my head in.

Does he have a weapon? Can he access one? Can he make a shank and slit my neck while I'm sleeping? Does that happen in Chinese prisons? Does he have a little posse in here? Will they team up while I'm asleep tonight? Tomorrow? Eventually? Strap me down and punch me in the face until I'm unconscious. Kill me?

Fu&k

I'm in the Middle Kingdom, where the government harvests human organs and sells them on the black market.

Is that the goal? Is he a mole? Is he even a real prisoner? Do they just send mentally unstable guys into the cells to fu&k with foreigners? Hope that they commit suicide, so the bodies can be used for testing? Human organ harvesting?

Fu&k.

I rolled the blanket over my eyes to make it look like I was going back to sleep. I turned in his direction with the blanket drawn in such a way that I could see his legs and monitor his movement. Sleep had entirely disappeared from my radar.

Fu&k.

All I could think about were the many ways he could attack or kill me. I was desperately tired, but I felt my body produce a hardcore kick of adrenaline that was now pumping through my veins. My brain had never been on a higher state of alert. I was monitoring every single one of his movements and listening for anything happening in the cell that he may be orchestrating.

Under the blanket my eyes were wide open. *I had never been more scared in my life.* There was no way out here if something went wrong. And I just did a whole lot of wrong in the span of thirty seconds.

Time wasn't even moving slow now. It had completely frozen and I didn't know what the fu&k to do. I just stared straight into the blanket.

Fu&k, fu&k, fu&k, fu&k, fu&k! Do I die here? Is this it? In a prison cell in Beijing? No one will ever know what happened. I can't stop all of them. I guess this is how I go out.

Death felt very, very real. It was like watching someone get killed in a movie, but you were watching it happen to yourself. I don't know how long I laid there for, completely alert and frozen in place. I went on for as long as humanly possible, expecting anything to happen at any moment.

To my complete and utter shock, nothing did. I heard him pace back and forth a few times but for the most part, he just stood there in silence.

None of the other prisoners did anything either.

Did they agree with me? Did they want to sleep too? Were they also annoyed? Was I the one guy in the classroom asking the question, or screaming, what everyone else had been thinking? Maybe they actually supported my outburst? Maybe they were actually happy that things were now quiet?

Eventually, my brain gave in. I was already tired, but I could only go on for so long like this. Slowly, sleep, surprisingly, overpowered me. As I was falling asleep, I heard the lieutenant wake up whoever was on shift two and trade places.

My brain registered that someone else was on watch and that he would now be sleeping.

Thank God.

I dozed off. I made the most of the two hours of sleep I could get before I would be awoken to work shift three.

Day 11

The Tank.

That's what I thought when I saw him. He looked like a tank.

I had never seen a Chinese guy built like this before, and I had spent five years traveling up and down the country. This guy looked like he was created in some type of Chinese military genetic experiment, and somehow, he landed in my prison cell.

I don't think he had blood, just pure testosterone flowing through those arteries. He could have easily been cast as the villain in any action movie, and he would have fit right in. The guy was built like one of those orcs you see in movies, just a larger and stronger frame than humans had. He had a thick neck, oversized muscles, and massive traps that were surprisingly visible through the thick prison jacket we wore.

This isn't the build that you get from a gym. This guy was just born this way. I've worked with some strong Chinese guys and seen some built Chinese men in the gym, but this dude was on a whole different level.

He looked like he had worked in coal mines from the time he was an infant and was raised on a diet of oak and raw earth metals. If he felt inclined to, he could simply punch a hole in the wall and walk out of the cell if he didn't feel like staying any longer.

I'm not necessarily small, but I'm certainly not the biggest guy you'll encounter. I stand around 6'1" and that alone usually gives me the height advantage on people. It's not everything, but it's usually enough to intimidate someone or make them think twice about a physical altercation. Given that the average male height in China is around 5'5" and 5'10" in the US, it's an advantage that usually works in my favor.

None of that mattered here. Not only was this guy built like an ox, he stood around 6'3" or 6'4" tall.

He was fu&king terrifying.

He was also just as violent and mentally unstable, if not worse, than the lieutenant. He had a dumb look on his face that screamed Neanderthal. He was engineered to rip lesser men to shreds on a battlefield.

And here I was, locked in a cage with him. Fu&k.

He punched the wall from time to time like it was a pillow. He did the same with the metal barred doors. He didn't like being in the prison cell. It was his third or fourth time here.

He would randomly start doing push-ups when he was bored. People lost count after a while because he could just go on indefinitely. He also knew he was in control of the cell, by default. Even the giant, who was a big guy, older and significantly taller, looked like he was afraid of this dude.

The Tank didn't care. The main problem was that he was young and super immature. The first time I met him, he asked where I was from. America, I told him. Instantly, he started listing off the name of every male actor in the Expendables movies. He knew every one of them by heart and talked about them like they were his heroes. He looked up to them and tried to act like them.

His crass behavior and impulsive outbursts annoyed everyone in the cell. But he wasn't the lieutenant. He was five lieutenants wrapped into one terrifying force of nature.

And I was stupid enough to piss him off.

He had been in the cell for around five days at this point, serving a 10-day sentence. I could barely handle another day with him. He would go up to you and talk right into your face, for as long as he wanted. It didn't matter if you were paying attention or not, he would just go up to you and say sh!t. On and on he would ramble.

He was loud, obnoxious, annoying, and deadly. And there we were on day eleven, getting ready for nap time. For some reason, I assume it was the expendables being an American movie, he really wanted to be my friend. But again, in these conditions, you're not in your right state of mind to handle someone this aggressive and unstable. The smallest thing that you could normally tolerate in the outside world could throw you into a tailspin. Being nice to this guy was survival but he had no filter, and constantly pestered everyone.

I did everything humanly possible to tolerate him, because I knew that he could body slam me to death on a whim.

It was almost 12:00 pm and we were trying to figure out who would be on watch for the afternoon nap. I knew I would be on this rotation because I didn't work last night's watch.

At this point, most of the other detainees already had their beds made and were settling in for the nap hour. Tank saw that I had volunteered for the shift and asked the Godfather to join me in working this watch.

I had been putting up with a lot of his bullsh!t over the past few days and for whatever reason something in my mind just snapped.

I was tired of him nagging Muhammad and Soldier about their black skin and their hair. I was tired of this guy going right up to me and talking random sh!t into my face. I was tired of this guy punching things. I was tired of this guy screaming. I was tired of this guy bullying the smaller inmates. I was tired of this guy being loud and obnoxious thinking everything he said was hilarious. I was tired of him being loud during his working shifts, clonking around and messing with sleeping detainees. I was tired of letting him think that he was God.

He was standing on the wooden planks looking down at everyone.

Tank: I'm not tired, I'll work the shift with the American.

Fu&k. I can't handle that. He's just going to annoy me for the one hour of silence that I can use to get away from him. He's going to try and talk to me, and I won't be able to stop the conversation. It's going to annoy all the inmates trying to sleep. It's going to annoy me. I just want to stand here in silence and do my job…in peace. It's the one break I'll get all day long. This is my escape and he's ruining it.

Me: "I think he volunteered" I said, pointing to another random inmate who wasn't in bed yet.

T: "No, we're working this shift" he said pointing to me.

Something snapped, and I said something I shouldn't have.

Me: No man, you're too loud.

I might as well have just walked up to him and spit in his face.

He turned away from the Godfather, and started walking in my direction, looking me dead center in the eye. His posture straightened, and his chest was fully puffed out. He stopped about six feet away, towering over me from the wooden planks.

He looked like he was ready to charge into a battlefield and shred people. The entire prison cell was watching, equally terrified at whatever he would do next. I just pissed off arguably one of the biggest, scariest, strongest and unstable guys I had ever encountered. And I'm locked in a cage with him. FUUUUUUUUUUUUUU&K. There's nothing I can do.

Tank: What? Say that again.

I froze.

We both knew he could kill me right then and there. I don't care how strong you are or how good you are at fighting, this guy just had raw power and looked like he was born to kill. I've been in fights, I'm not a tiny guy but there was just nothing I could do to a guy like this.

I didn't know what to do. There's no protocol here. This is raw, unfiltered survival. I just stood there staring up at him from the pacing area. If he charged, he'd be at me in less than a second, and attacking from the high ground.

There were no odds in my favor. He had no reason not to demolish me. No reason for me to survive the encounter.

We stood there for a good 10 or 15 seconds, in this odd stare down. It felt like a month had passed.

Me: "Ok, my bad. We'll work the shift" I said slowly.

He didn't say anything. He just stood there staring at me. You could see the absolute rage and terror in his eyes. This guy wasn't human, he was an absolute animal. I stood there, not budging, still staring at him.

I die here today. That was the only thought flooding through my mind. I die here today, all alone, in a prison cell far away from home.

I had already lost weight due to the food and detention conditions. I was probably operating somewhere around 70% of my normal physical and mental capacity. I couldn't give this guy a run for his money if I was in peak health, but in my current condition, I was a broke man's punching bag.

Me: "Ok, my bad" I said once more.

He didn't budge. He just stood there, staring at me. Like a predator eyeing its prey before it leapt in for the kill.

Fu&k. How the fu*k do I talk this guy down? Is there a lecture somewhere for talking down a killing machine in a prison cell using Mandarin.

Everyone was frozen in place, just watching, including the Godfather.

I tried again.

Me: My bad, we'll work the shift together.

He just stood there, staring at me. I was out of options now. I had used all of my tricks. He was testing me. What would I do? Would I run to the box and press the button for help? Would I plead and beg for mercy? He wanted to see how this foreigner would respond to death.

In a last-ditch effort, I looked over at the Godfather who was on the far side of the cell. He had initially been orchestrating the nap watch.

Me: "Godfather, we'll work the shift together" I said pointing at Tank.

The Godfather could tell I was trying to diffuse the situation. He looked over at Tank.

Godfather: Just work the shift together, let's get to bed.

Somehow, the Godfather's words did something. Ever so slowly, Tank backed up and dropped his posture. His chest dropped down, and he gazed up at the clock.

He knew he was in control of the cell. Maybe he was using this as an opportunity to send a message to every other cell member: don't fu&k with me or I'll eat your face and snap your legs off. The American is big, and if I can make him shut the fuck up, I can break any of you.

Me: I'm sorry. Let's work the shift.

Tank: Ok.

Message delivered for him. Lesson learned for me. The Godfather probably just saved my life.

Ever so slowly, he calmed down. He moved over towards the bathroom, dropping down off the planks into the pacing area. He snatched the other orange hat and put it on. I moved over to my side of the pacing area wearing my stupid bright orange hat, terrified out of my mind.

I felt as if I had just high fived the grim reaper.

I didn't want to go near him. I looked over one last time mouthing the words, "my bad" in Chinese.

He shot me a very subtle nod, signaling that I had been heard and proceeded to look away.

I was still terrified that he would rush me while the other inmates were asleep. We weren't more than ten or fifteen feet apart. I just stood straight ahead at the wall in front of me, standing in position.

The situation seemed diffused for now, but would he randomly snap later on? Tomorrow? One punch from this guy would be deadly.

Lesson learned: When you're locked in a prison cell with an angry orc, don't be the idiot that pisses him off. He can and will kill you. He knows this. You know this. The cell block and the guards know this. Learn your place and be happy that the angry killing machine is simply trying to talk to you about the Expendables movies.

Lesson learned, communist prison survival 101.

Chapter 19:

Prison Day 14, Hope & Despair

American Universities Are Welcoming China's Trojan Horse

A growing number of Confucius Institutes are importing Chinese censorship into U.S. campuses.

"Open Hearing on Worldwide Threats. Hearing Before The Select Committee On Intelligence Of The United States Senate. One Hundred Fifteenth Congress, Second Session: Tuesday, February 13, 2018:

Senator Rubio (R-FL): In that vein, last week I wrote a letter to five higher education institutions in Florida about the Confucius Institutes, which are funded by Chinese government dollars, at U.S. schools. It is my view that they're complicit in these efforts to covertly influence public opinion and to teach half-truths designed to present Chinese history, government, or official policy in the most favorable light. Do you share concerns about Confucius Institutes as a tool of that whole of society effort and as a way to exploit the sort of naive view among some in the academic circles about what the purpose of these institutes could be?

Director Wray (8th Director of the Federal Bureau of Investigation): We do share concerns about the Confucius Institutes. We've been watching that development for a while. It's just one of many tools that they take advantage of. We have seen some decrease recently in their own enthusiasm and commitment to that particular program, but it is something that we are watching warily and in certain instances have developed appropriate investigative steps."[94]

Chinese Government's official remarks regarding the threat of Confucius Institutes against US universities. Chinese Foreign Ministry Spokesperson Hua Chunying's remarks, March 22, 2018:

"*Q: Three US Republican lawmakers have proposed that the Confucius Institutes operating in the United States should be registered as "foreign agents". I assume the Chinese government would be extremely unhappy to see this happening. Do you have comments on this?*

A: The Confucius Institutes in the US are set up at the voluntary request of US universities by Confucius Institute Headquarters, Chinese universities and local universities with the principle of mutual respect, friendly consultation, equality and mutual benefit upon formal agreement. The purpose of Confucius Institutes is strengthening educational and cultural exchange and cooperation between China and other countries and enhancing mutual understanding and friendship between their peoples. In fact, we have seen that Confucius Institutes are warmly welcomed in many countries and they have played an important role in promoting the mutual understanding, friendship and cooperation between China and relevant countries.

I noted that recently certain American individuals have made noises from time to time, which actually comes down to the way they view the world and China's development or the question whether they are really able to discard the cold-war mentality, zero-sum game mindset and the outdated either-or concept and pursue mutually beneficial and win-win cooperation with other countries..."

I just stood there, staring at the grey sky. I couldn't see a thing. I wasn't even looking for anything. I was just standing there...staring...at nothing.

How long have I been standing here?

I wasn't even thinking about the time anymore. It didn't matter. I was just there, in a meaningless state of existence. Psychologically, I had never felt like

---

[94] Peterson, R. (2017, May 09). American universities are Welcoming CHINA'S trojan horse. Retrieved February 28, 2021, from https://foreignpolicy.com/2017/05/09/american-universities-are-welcoming-chinas-trojan-horse-confucius-institutes/

this before. I was no longer me. I didn't feel much different from one of the walls or wooden planks. We were all just, there…existing. You didn't really feel human at this point.

None of us did.

Muhammad: You ok man?

Me: Yea, yea…I'm good.

Muhammad: Ok.

He walked back to the wooden planks and sat next to Solider. I could hear them talking to each other, but I wasn't really paying attention. They probably thought that I had lost my mind.

I probably had by now.

I had been standing next to the window, just staring out through the bars. It was probably the most depressing day imaginable. There was nothing outside of the window. Just a deep and thick grey smog. That's all I could see.

It mirrored the way my mind felt.

I suppose I was broken already, psychologically. *Well, now I know: 14 days. That was my limit.*

There I stood, just staring into nothing. This was my new hobby. You could only pace and sit for so long. One day they surprised us by handing our cell a copy of the sports section from a Chinese newspaper. I probably re-read each story 15 times until I couldn't mentally stand reading it for a sixteenth.

Nonetheless, it was a welcome reminder that there was still a world beyond these walls.

It was day fourteen. I was supposed to be released today. This was supposed to be my day. I had served my sentence, and yet, the guards came and went. They called the released prisoner's names in my cell, removed them, and that was that. I was still here.

This was supposed to be the end of my stay. And here I was, slowly edging my way into day 15.

Does that mean I'm being deported? Am I in immigrations hands now? How long will they keep me here until that happens? I still haven't seen any foreigners released in my cell. Raheem was still here, day 7. Soldier was still here, day 50. Muhammad was still here, day 17. We had a new Indian inmate named Aarav. He had been here for 3 days. He hadn't eaten any food aside from the bread brick since his arrival.

The fleeting nature of your own existence was readily apparent here. The carvings on the wall made complete sense at this point. This was some obscure form of conscious life-support. Here we were, mindlessly wandering around in our little torture box. How little can they provide to prevent us from dying? Did they have an objective beyond that?

I had no idea when or if I would be released.

So, there I stood, watching…nothing. On the nicer days there wouldn't be any smog and you could see the clouds go by. That was lovely. I could literally stand there for hours, just watching the clouds hover in the sky. They weren't locked in a cage like me. I daydreamed about what it would be like to sit on the cloud and float around the world. What a beautiful view it must be from up there, sailing around on top of a cloud.

The fact that that wasn't remotely possible didn't even matter. I wanted to feel free like the clouds. Maybe they were staring back down at me? Could they see me from way up there? Maybe they were mocking me? Stupid human, who ends up locked in cage? Look at us, we're not locked in a cage, you fool!

These were some of the thoughts going through my mind as I stood there…staring at clouds…again. I felt sad when they floated off beyond the range of my view. I would say goodbye to each one as they slowly drifted off on their journey.

This hardcore depression was compounded by my cellmates. I could visibly see them breaking down, day by day. They literally looked different over this two-week stretch than they had on day one. Their eyes were just lifeless and their faces looked as if they had aged.

The water. The watch. The food. The stress. The noise. The lack of information. The sleep deprivation.

We had all been stripped from our families without explanation. We were barred from contacting our embassies. No one knew where we were. All we had was each other.

Their depressed faces made you feel surprisingly more depressed. Your depressed face made them feel the same way. Everything in here was desperately trying to break you.

The contaminated water. The piss porridge. The violence. The anger. The walls. The lack of sleep. The assho!e guards. The "medical" staff. Everything.

One of the younger Chinese inmates had been asking us weird questions for a few days now. Do you use drugs? Do you do this? Have you ever done that?

What. The. Fu&k?!

Who asks those things in CCP detention? *To just the foreign inmates?* Sh!t was getting weird in here. Maybe we were paranoid, but you had to have your guard up in here. There are no rules in a country that harvests human organs from conscious detainees.

Maybe he was a mole that had been sent in by the police? Were they trying to make up more charges to extend our detention?

We, the foreign inmates, had already alerted each other and stopped talking to him.

The paranoia makes you become further isolated. You want to talk less and less. I wanted to fade into one of the walls and just disappear. Maybe then, the world would just leave you alone.

Even though I was still forcing myself to eat, I had lost a ton of weight by now. I looked decrepit, hadn't shaved in weeks and I could feel my beard had grown out significantly. I showered in the evenings when they occasionally had hot water during the wash hour. Some days there was warm water, most days it wasn't.

Like everything else in here, you just never knew how or when or why.

When I would strip down to go shower, I would hear the new Chinese inmates speaking in Mandarin, "Look how skinny he has become."

They were right. I could see my muscle mass withering away.

I still had a couple shampoo packets left, but I was out of toilet paper by now. One of the outgoing Chinese inmates who was serving a shorter three-day sentence was nice enough to hand over his remaining toilet paper roll and toothpaste.

SLAM! The hall door shut. Everyone raced into place. I just stood there, staring out at the grey.

I didn't fu&king care. Fuc* the guards. Pieces of sh!t.

Behind me, I heard the guards unlocking our cell door. I turned around, slowly, just staring at the cell bars. One of the guards looked up around the cell, until his eyes landed on me.

Guard: American! Come!

Fu*k, what now? I was baffled.

Was I being released? *No, that's impossible.* They already made it painfully clear that there was an immigration process.

Guard: Embassy.

Once again, I was completely perplexed. I thought protocol was that they could only visit us once? Was this another trick?

I slowly made my way out the cell-door and stood against the wall. I was used to this spot. This is where we generally stripped down naked during their random cell-inspections. The guards slammed the door shut and continued down to other cells. I looked down to my left and saw Neil stood against the same wall. Another set of guards had let him out as they continued making their way down to other cells.

It was a relief to see that he was doing ok. It was a sign that there was still a world beyond my cell. I wasn't in this alone.

There weren't as many foreigners this time around, just four or five of us. The guards walked Neil and the other foreign detainees down toward us. We stood in a row facing the cell doors.

Guard: "Clothes! 1, 2, 3"

Fu*k me, not again.

Neil and I shot each other a frustrated look and proceeded to start undressing. First, jackets off and on the ground, and then we dropped our pants. And there we stood, lined up, and naked.

I guess this was some type of safety thing to make sure we didn't have any contraband on us?

The guards looked at us, assessed that we weren't a threat and then instructed us to put our clothes back on.

That was necessary.

Once we had our uniforms back on, they marched us toward the main hall door and out towards the stairwell. Neil was marching right behind me.

Neil: Embassy?

Me: Yea, same. How are you doing?

Neil: It's shit, but there are a couple good guys in my cell, so we're making do. You?

Me: Same. Shitty, but I'm lucky to have the guys in my cell that I do. They're absolute heroes. I'm not sure where I would be if it weren't for them. Any word from Karl?

Neil: I saw him a couple days ago on a walk. His cell seems pretty fucked. I don't think he's making it through as well.

Me: What happened?

Neil: I think it's just really wearing him down mentally. Some foreigner went crazy in there. I guess he had been kept for around two months and just snapped. Stripped down naked one night and just started peeing everywhere and trying to hump everyone while he was peeing. The guards had to drag him out of the cell apparently.

Me: Fu&k. I can't say I'm surprised. I'll probably be there in a week or two.

Neil: Yea, apparently, he doesn't really have anyone else to talk to. He's just kind of in there by himself which isn't helping. And the tv in his cell is broken.

Me: That really sucks. When do you think we're out of here?

Neil: I'm hoping the embassy will know. But it should be fast, we've already been here for 14 days.

Me: Yea, I hope so.

The guards marched us back into the same building next to the main entrance that we had entered during our first visit with our embassy consular officers. Once again, we were greeted by the same large black sofas, wall art and other décor meant to give the consulate officers a completely false impression of what the conditions in here were like.

To our surprise, the consulate officers were already there when we entered. Once again, the various embassies were present and spread out around the room. Sat there on the couch closest to the door was the man himself, Randy.

It was a relief to see him again. Please have some good news. Please have some good news. Please have some good news.

He stood up, looked me up and down and shook my hand.

Across our table was a Chinese officer of some type wearing a different, all black uniform. Once again, he had a video camera on his vest and a second one sat on the meeting room table with the red record lights flashed on.

I didn't care.

US CO: We're actually waiting for one more but uh, how are you doing Mr. Schaerer?

Me: "This place is a fu7king nightmare" I said staring straight into the video camera on the table.

I don't even know if I was angry. I wasn't trying to get revenge, it was just brutal honesty that was flowing out at this point. Although Randy's seemed to agree with me, he was a hardcore professional. He knew I would say what was on my mind. He had probably seen a lot worse.

Me: "It's fuc7king dangerous and it's unsanitary. I want to be let out of here tomorrow, I've done my 14 days and today is day 14" I said pointing straight at the officer across the table and looking him dead in the eye.

You could see the concern building on Randy's face, he wanted to keep things civil.

US CO: Ok, ok. Hold on now. This gentleman is the Chinese immigration officer. There's good news and bad news.

Me: What's the bad news?

US CO: Well, you're gonna be deported.

Me: "HAHAHAHAHAHAHAH!"

I literally couldn't stop laughing out loud.

Randy and the immigration officer just sat there in silence, staring at me.

Me: Hahaha, I said the bad news…not the good news!

I was still laughing out loud. I couldn't stop.

The immigration officer didn't seem pleased with that and he could clearly speak English. Randy, sensing the tension did his best to preserve the peace and keep the conversation professional.

I didn't care anymore, they are playing with people's lives here. Fu7k this government and every single fu&ker that works for them. Fu&k anyone that willfully puts human beings into these conditions.

US CO: Ok, so the good news is your flight costs are covered. Now we just need to pick the city that you're going to fly back home to in the US. By law, it must be a nonstop flight to a city in one of America's 50 states. Where would you like to fly?

Me: Well, San Francisco, California is home. So that makes the most sense.

US CO: "Ok, San Francisco…" he said as he jotted down the words on paper. He looked over at the Chinese immigration official.

US CO: San Francisco, did you get that?

Immigration: Yes, San Francisco, California. Got it.

Just then our second guest arrived through the door. She looked dazed and frail. The female guard sat her down next to me. Female inmates were held in the same compound, but on the floor below our cell block.

Female inmate: You're both American?

US CO & I: Yes.

She grabbed my arm and started crying.

Randy and I tried to console her but there was a lot of emotion bottled up that had to come out. She had clearly been holding it in for a while and this was her moment to deal with the pain.

I didn't even have to ask, I could just see the look on her face. Her frail physique. The sound in her voice. It was the same as every foreigner in my cell, and me.

These conditions had broken her.

She was terrified. So was I. This was her first opportunity to show the emotion that had been bottled up during her stay, and to connect with someone that would understand her. *Someone from her country. Someone who spoke her language with a shared culture. What had she experienced in her cell? What had she seen? What had she survived?*

Randy and I did our best to console her, but her raw emotion told the entire story. We didn't even need to bother with questions. Her name was Lucinda and she looked to be in her mid to late 40's, with dark brown hair and hazel eyes. She described how she had been receiving the wrong medications and how the Chinese inmates explained that the medicine was most likely fake or supposed to treat an entirely different illness altogether.

She described how the "medical" staff would shout at the younger foreign girls who sought medical attention. She explained how women struggled to get by on their periods and how she worked to be strong for younger foreign girls in detention. As one of the older women in the cell, she worked hard to look after them, but it had taken a severe psychological toll on her at this point.

Once she had said what she needed to, she asked me if the conditions were the same in the male prison cells. She was a bit more relieved knowing that one of us understood what she had survived for the past week. We discussed eating out of the bucket, sharing a single squatter toilet with 15 other inmates, the food, everything. We talked about how the water would randomly turn off in our cells and the sleep deprivation.

I'm sure Randy had heard this a million times before, but it was therapeutic for us to get everything off our chests.

Randy, being the absolute gentleman that he was, simply sat there and listened to us as we vented our anger. Eventually, he regained control of the conversation,

US CO: Well, the good news is you're both going home.

For the first time since she had entered the room, a huge smile spread across her face.

Lucinda: I guess that means we're being deported?

US CO: Yes, that is correct. According to the law, you must pick a destination within the US.

Her smile quickly faded.

Lucinda: Only the US?

US CO: Yes, that is correct. Any American city.

Lucinda: I haven't lived in the US for over 15 years. My entire family left years ago. I don't have anywhere to go in the US.

US CO: Do you have any family members, or friends anywhere in the US?

Lucinda: Not at all. I mean, I was born and raised in Arizona but that was decades ago. I don't have anyone there any longer.

Randy and I looked at each other. He looked over at the immigration officer asking if it was possible to send her to another country where her family was located. The immigration officer shook his head saying that that would not be possible as she was a US citizen here on a US passport. She had to fly back to an American city.

Me: What about friends? Any friends back in the US that you can get in contact with?

Lucinda: Not that I can think of. We picked up and left so long ago. I mean I know people, but I wouldn't have any way of finding them. Even if I did, I…I haven't seen them in ages.

Once again, she was nervous and scared. You could see the frustration on her face as she was desperately trying to think of solutions.

US CO: Well, if we send you back to Arizona, would you be able to find your way around?

Lucinda: No, it has been so long. I know where things are, but I wouldn't know anyone to go to. I don't have money to just travel around.

We were perplexed.

There wasn't a solution. Randy was sitting there staring down at the floor. Lucinda looked worried, and the Chinese official just sat there with a blank glare on his face impatiently waiting for her to make a decision.

That's when it hit me. I have no idea where it came from, but it was something. Sure, it was a dumb idea, but it was better than nothing. Was it at all possible to turn this into a positive experience for her?

I looked up at Randy:

Me: Anywhere in the US, right?

262

Randy looked up and asked the immigration officer,

US CO: Any city in America?

The immigration official nodded his head saying yes.

Me: Well, is there anywhere that you would just enjoy going?

Lucinda looked up at me, confused by the question.

Me: I mean, it's a free one-way ticket to any American city. Is there any place that you've always wanted to visit? What if you thought of it as winning a free vacation?

Lucinda started to understand where I was going with this. Once again, the guard didn't look pleased.

He can go fu&k himself.

Me: Like have you been to Miami before?

Lucinda: Well, I've always wanted to go to Hawaii.

Me: Well, this might be God's way of opening that door for you.

I looked around at everyone. I could see them trying to think this through. Lucinda paused for a moment and looked up at us with a smile.

Lucinda: Can I fly to Hawaii? I mean, I've never been, and I've always wanted to go.

Randy understood what I was trying to do. He looked over at the immigration officer,

US CO: Can she fly to Hawaii?

Immigration: Which city?

Randy looked back over at Lucinda,

Lucinda: How about Honolulu? I've always wanted to go.

US CO: You know you'll be an island, right?

Lucinda: All I can see are the beaches right now Randy.

Me: I think it's a fantastic choice Lucinda.

Randy looked back over at the immigration official,

Immigration: Yea, I mean, it's American right?

US CO: Yea, it sure is.

Lucinda: "Ok, then, it's settled. I'll fly to Honolulu" she said with the biggest smile imaginable.

She was absolutely beaming from ear to ear.

I started smiling too. Her smile was absolutely infectious, and it immediately spread to Randy and I. This poor woman had been thrown into the depths of hell and she was battling to survive. Just a few minutes ago she was overcome with despair and now, she couldn't stop smiling.

Victory for team USA.

With a little bit of creative thinking, we managed to work together and turn a horrific scenario into a positive opportunity.

Me: I think that's a fantastic choice.

As with the previous embassy visit, we dragged the conversation on for as long as humanly possible. Lucinda and I had one obvious objective, stay out of our prison cells for as long as humanly possible. It didn't even have to be said, we were all just on the same page there. This time around, I was far better prepared than last. I had spent the past few weeks doing nothing else but thinking about all the questions I should have asked the first time.

This was my opportunity.

It was a Friday and Randy mentioned that an immigration official should be visiting us today. He explained that those visits do happen beyond the standard 9 to 5 working hours. Whenever this immigration officer would arrive, he would have us sign a few documents and specify a release date.

I repeatedly asked both Randy and the immigration officer when we would expect to be deported. The concrete answer I managed to nail down was apparently the following Wednesday, *at the latest, apparently*. I wasn't betting on it. At this point I was mentally preparing myself to be in here for at least another month, if not longer.

Everyone lies here.

Eventually, the guards had finally decided that our conversations with the embassy needed to end. Randy passed a few messages along from my family, whom he said he had been in touch with every single day. He even had emails from my relatives that he passed along to me.

That was probably the only thing that gave me the strength to carry on.

I knew there were people counting on me to get through this. I would have to carry on through this hell no matter what came my way. It wasn't even about me at this point; I had to do it for them.

My sister, Dalia Vazquez, passed away unexpectedly when I was 9 years old. I'm the last child left in the family. I wasn't going to die in this fuc*king prison cell. I owed her and my family that much. I knew she had my back. She got me this far. I could handle the rest.

I thanked Randy for all he had done. He told me that I would be out of here soon and to just hold on a little bit longer.

I didn't want to let him down either.

The guards took the embassy officials to one end of the building and brought us to ours. Neil and I exchanged tidbits of information over the course of our short march back to the prison cell. He had also been told that we would be deported on Wednesday at the latest. Although it gave me some hope, I still felt conflicted.

What if Wednesday came and went without a word?

I was trying to be hopeful, but I also didn't want to be let down again. I wasn't sure what to think. Once I was thrown back into my cell, the waiting game for immigration began.

Should I even bother waiting? I looked over at Soldier who was sitting in a corner mumbling hymns to himself. How long until I become Soldier number 2? Endlessly held in this nightmare waiting for immigration to arrive?

What if immigration doesn't come today? Do they work weekends? Maybe they work Sundays but not Saturdays? Maybe it was the other way around? Are they in the office on Monday? What time?

Who the fu&k knows?!

I tried to stop thinking about it. Lunch came and went. Nap time came and went. More Sitting. Pacing. Sitting. Dinner. Standing. Shower. 90's box tv with Chinese soaps. Sitting. No immigration officers.

Maybe he's coming tomorrow? But it's Saturday tomorrow. They don't work on Saturdays?

8:00 pm. 9:00 pm. 10:00 pm, bedtime. *Nothing. Fu&k those liars.* The immigration officer probably just lied in front of the embassy officials to peddle more bullshit. Everything was a lie just like the expensive art in the embassy room. The comfy black sofas. The entire building for embassy official visits was *one big fu*king lie.*

Deception and lies. TIC

I buried myself into bed. I wasn't working tonight. At least I can sleep. At least for one night I can escape this fuc&king nightmare.

I was pissed. I'm not a violent person, but if someone bumped into me, I'd probably try and rip their limbs off. If for nothing else than it would have been something new to do. Worst case scenario, I get my ass kicked. At least it's something fu&king different. A day here felt like a month. It was as if the Chinese had perfected time distortion as a form of punishment.

This prison cell had changed me. I was something different now. I had adapted to my surroundings to survive. But what had I become? Would this become permanent?

I put my head down trying to doze off.

At least I got some time outside of the cell today, I thought to myself. *At least I heard from my family. At least I saw Randy. At least Lucinda will be going to Hawaii. At least they know I'm in here. At least…*

SLAM!

The outer cell door in the hall slammed and we heard commotion as guards approached our cell.

Great…another fu&king inmate. We're already cramped as it is. Fu&k these wooden boards. I didn't give a fu&k.

I just wanted to sleep. *Don't fu&k with my sleep. Not tonight.* I didn't care so I just pretended to be asleep and looked away from the door, I didn't want to have to move and give up any extra sleeping space.

I heard the keys unlocking the door as it proceeded to swing wide open.

Guard: American!

You've got to be fuc&ing kidding me. If this is a joke, I'm going to throat punch the next person I see.

I turned around and looked at the door. The guard was staring at me, waiting. Stood next to him was another guard in a, *black uniform?! IMMIGRATION?! At 10:30 PM?!*

I practically jumped out of bed, almost kicking an inmate's face next to me. I threw on my shoes and went for the door. Same outfit as the immigration official earlier today. I stepped out into the hall and they shut the door behind me. I stood up against the wall and looked to my left seeing Neil and Karl stood outside of their cells as well.

Thank God.

Karl looked like a mess, but he was standing, which was good. The two were marched in my direction and we paused momentarily to greet each other. Under normal circumstances, we would have taken the opportunity to chat and figure out how everyone was doing.

This time, we practically ignored each other. All we could focus on was the immigration official and trying to figure out what the fu&k was going on as we were being marched downstairs to the lobby.

Immigration: Hello everyone, my name is Frank. I'm with immigration and we will be processing you tonight for deportation.

He was pleasant and spoke great English. Thank God. Get me the fu&k out of this sh!thole country.

Karl: Ok, so what's going on?

Immigration: A couple of things. First, we have to process a few documents. You are being deported from China, and you need to sign the papers confirming this process. Furthermore, as a result of your criminal activity in China, you are being banned from the country as well.

Banned?!

Immigration: Normally, you would be banned for five years. Seeing as you have been well behaved in detention and the severity of your crimes is not great, this ban has been reduced to three years.

Karl, Neil and I looked around at each other in confusion. Fuc& it. Whatever.

Immigration: Once the documents have been signed, you will be allowed to retrieve your phones and make calls to your family members.

Neil: Do you know which day we will be deported?

Immigration: Next week definitely, Wednesday at the latest.

Frank was carrying three different massive bags. He had a backpack on, a satchel for documents and what appeared to be an old-school camcorder bag full of electronic equipment.

Me: Do you have anything for us to charge our phones?

Immigration: "Yes, we do" he said pointing at the camcorder bag.

He brought us through the lobby and through a back door leading into a brightly lit hall. Inside, there were more cell doors, which were being used as makeshift offices. We sat down in the first one.

He tossed the satchel on the desk and pulled out a stack of documents. He had all our passports, personal information, everything. He pointed at random documents and instructed us to sign here and there. Date this and initial that. We simply followed his cues and tried to make sure we didn't mess anything up. First was the deportation document which he explained. Next came the document explaining the charge against us, "illegal employment" and our three-year ban.

Just get us the hell out of here. Throw me on a raft and I'll fuc%ing take my chances paddling across the Pacific at this point.

Once all our T's were crossed and I's were dotted, he collected the documents. With the guards, we were marched back into the room where we had stashed all our personal belongings on night one. We dug through our stuff to find our cell phones. Once we had them in hand, we put our bags back on the shelf and were marched back out into the lobby.

To the camcorder bag.

Frank opened it up and pulled out a giant mess of electronic equipment. He had handfuls of every conceivable charger you could imagine. He handed the first one off to Neil, then to me. Our phones had died long ago, so we had to find outlets around the lobby to charge our phones.

It was late, and we probably didn't have a lot of time. Frank probably wanted to get home. Who knew how long he had been working today? Here he was still running around at 11:00 pm on a Friday night collecting deportation signatures.

I wanted to make the most of my phone time.

Neil got lucky. He found an outlet by the desk and was able to stand to make his phone call. Me? Not so much. The only other available outlet I could see was around knee height. I had to sit on the ground to charge. That was fine. I just wanted to talk to my family and let them know I was ok.

I plugged my phone into the outlet and watched my phone slowly blink to life.

Thank God.

Once it finally booted up, I just stared at it. The screen was so bright, and the display looked so new and crisp. It almost felt as if I were using a phone for the very first time. I remember staring at the display as my finger swiped through the screen. It's hard to describe but it felt like I was using alien technology. It was such a weird phenomenon.

It had only been two weeks, so why did everything feel so foreign? My brain struggled to re-adjust to something as simple as using my own phone.

What an odd experience. What happened to me in that cell?!

I looked over at Neil who was already on the phone yapping away in German. Karl had finally managed to find the right charger, but it was a very short cable that wasn't meant to be used for speaking and charging simultaneously.

He was hastily pacing around the massive lobby, unable to find a third outlet. As I got re-acquainted to my phone, I opened the app I generally used for international calls.

First call, mom and dad.

Don't fail me now. I pressed the call button…ring…ring…ring…

Good. It's working.

Ring:

Dad: Hello?

I didn't even stop to think about what time it was in California. I could hear the worry in his voice.

Me: Hey dad, it's me.

Dad: Steve?! Are you ok?!

He called my mom over who instantly hopped on the phone, nearly in tears. I almost burst into tears myself. *But this wasn't the time or the place. I didn't want them to worry. I didn't want them to know what I was living through.* I wanted them to know two things,

1) I was alive, and
2) I would likely be home by Wednesday.

Me: Yea the conditions are ok. It's not great but we're fine. Immigration said I should be home by Wednesday at the latest. Yes, Immigration is here. Yea they feed us well. I'm ok, like I said, not the best conditions, but it's fine. Yes, I'm with the other two guys. They're on the phone with their family too. Yes, deported. 'Illegal employment' apparently. Something about my visa. Yes, I told them my visa is legal...

It was the most emotional call I had ever experienced. Just then I looked back up as the conversation continued to see how Neil and Karl were doing. Neil was still standing over the desk chatting away. And there was Karl in the corner, behind one of the black sofas. Apparently, the last remaining outlet in the lobby appeared to be on the ground. The cable was too short for Karl to sit or stand so he had to lay on the ground to charge his phone and make the call. I could only see his legs protruding from behind the couch.

Poor guy can't catch a break.

I kept the conversation going for as long as I could. I wanted to do my best to reassure my parents that I was ok, and that I would be home soon. I let them know that immigration would be notifying the US embassy of my departure who would in turn notify my parents for my arrival at SFO International.

We talked about Randy, who they had been in touch with every single day. We talked about their emails. I let them know that Randy was a terrific guy who was doing a lot to help us. I told them about Lucinda who would be flying to

Hawaii. I re-worded the story a bit to make them feel more at ease, but they were happy to hear that she would be going to a safe destination.

Hearing their voices made me feel, I don't know how to put it into words. Hearing them gave me the confidence to continue fighting. It gave me purpose. I was almost there, I just had to power through the rest of this.

In time, the conversations had to come to a close. Frank was clearly tired and probably wanted to retire home to be with his family. I did my best to reassure my parents once more that I would be ok and that I would be seeing them soon. I told them not to worry and to keep in touch with Randy. I let them know that I had to get going and we said our goodbyes:

Mom, Dad: I love you, take care.

Me: I'll be fine. I'll see you soon. I love you too.

Chapter 20:

Noise

A Torture Method Called "White Room"- Where Prisoners Are Isolated in Whe Rooms, Wear White Clothes, And Eat White Food From White Plates it

As seen with sensory deprivation, psychological torture can materialize through a range of unsuspecting mediums. Personally, the unrelenting barrage of noise was the most persistent, and arguable worse form of torture. Western audiences are generally familiar with auditory damage arising from intense sounds, but less familiar with the non-auditory health complications.

Environmental Noise Annoyance and Mental Health in Adults: Findings from the Cross-Sectional German Health Update (GEDA) Study 2012. Int J Environ Res Public Health. 2016 Oct; 13(10): 954.

"Environmental noise is an omnipresent environmental burden that threatens individual and public health. The World Health Organization estimates that each year more than one million Healthy Life Years are lost in the European Union member states and other Western European countries solely because of traffic noise. Evidence suggests physical health risks (i.e., increased risks of cardiovascular diseases) when exposed to high levels of traffic noise...

Besides hearing damage caused by loud sounds, noise can evoke extra-auditory effects, such as stress reactions: For example, noise can interfere with communication, recreation, or concentration. According to Lazarus' transtheoretical stress model, stress develops when individuals perceive that their environment and associated requirements overwhelm their resources and threaten their wellbeing. If noise-induced annoyance persists (perceived as little or uncontrollable), it might cause not only stress but also fatigue associated with ineffective attempts to cope with noise. This, in turn, could impact mental health.”[95]

Sensory deprivation is a stunning example of how unpredictable torture can be.

Everyday things that you wouldn't think about twice can be used to make your life a literal living nightmare. Surprisingly, the worst form of torture I experienced throughout my time in detention was, sound.

It's surprising to hear as most people wouldn't even consider it at all, especially given the severity of the other conditions. But like other forms of psychological torture, noise is incredibly difficult to put into words. How do you explain an uncontrollable sound that doesn't relent? For example, the lieutenant constantly screaming, the nighttime snoring or Tank randomly slapping things as hard as he could.

It's an incredibly difficult experience to convey through words.

You might understandably be thinking; well how bad can noise be? We've all heard an annoying sound or two. Who hasn't? Think back to the last annoying sound that you heard? Do you remember what it was? How long did it take before it started to bother you? Was there anything you could do to control the sound's effect on you? Could you distance yourself from it or do anything to stop or control it?

But what if you couldn't control those variables?

What if you were forced to hear that sound all day, and listen to it unabated? Maybe it started to annoy you after a few seconds. Could you handle listening to it for a few minutes? What about an hour? What do you think might happen psychologically after an entire day of relentless exposure?

So why was noise the worst form of torture I endured during my stay?

Primarily, it's the one thing that never stops. You also have no way of controlling it either. With sleep deprivation, there were minor things I could do

[95] J;, H. (n.d.). Environmental noise annoyance and mental health In Adults: Findings from the Cross-sectional German Health UPDATE (GEDA) Study 2012. Retrieved February 28, 2021, from https://pubmed.ncbi.nlm.nih.gov/27681736/

to give myself the illusion of control. I could toss from one side to the next or cover my eyes with the blanket to minimize the light.

Noise on the other hand, controls you. There's nothing you can do to stop it, and it's always a different, completely random source. In other words, it's unpredictable.

Under normal circumstances, there are things you can do to remove yourself from unwanted external stimuli. If the tv is on too loud, you can ask someone to turn it down or simply leave the room. But when you're locked in a cell with these unrelenting sounds, they infect your brain like a disease.

Soldier and Raheem would literally lie down in a corner on evenings with a blanket covering their ears and just stare into the wall because they couldn't handle the noise.

What was the source?

The Chinese inmates. As this entire book explains, there are very real cultural differences that exist between China and the rest of the world. It's worth emphasizing that this isn't a subjective opinion of mine. The Chinese are the first to readily admit to these fundamental cultural differences as well.

For example?

Personal space. It's one of the more obvious issues that becomes visibly apparent from the second you touch down on Chinese soil. There are a whole host of reasons for this and the Chinese will use everything from education to culture to try and explain it.

Regardless of where you think it stems from, the issue remains that personal space is simply not something the Chinese are raised to think about. To some degree that may be changing with younger generations, but it is still a largely non-existent concept among economically disadvantaged classes or the older generation. Fortunately for me, this was literally the demographic that I was locked in a cage with.

Personal space is a surprisingly powerful concept if you take time to think about it. A lot of important ideas stem from cultures that embrace the idea of personal space. For example?

How loud are you speaking? How close are you standing to someone else? Are any of your actions negatively influencing people around you? In other words, you're considering someone else's needs before your own and that is a powerful societal concept. It influences the way a culture thinks and operates.

Chinese inmates, on the other hand, have no concept of this. It was like being locked in a cage with teenagers that just couldn't stop gossiping about anything and everything imaginable. But it wasn't just that they wouldn't stop talking, it was the volume in which they spoke.

Their conversations were always stuck on a volume that would register to a Western audience as painfully loud and entirely unnecessary. Chinese inmates would routinely scream at someone that was standing no further than a foot or two away. They often hollered their conversations from one end of the prison cell to the other, or screamed a story at no one in particular as they paced around, etc. The conversations happened around you, through you and over you 24/7.

It never ended.

Soldier, Muhammad, Raheem and I would literally look at each other in shock. What is wrong with these people? What did their parents teach them growing up? Don't they have any manners or respect? These were some of the common questions we would ask each other every single day.

But again, the Chinese inmates didn't even notice. They weren't raised to consider these things. The idea of personal space and inside voices is a completely alien concept to them. The rest of us just had to deal with it. The noise was relentless and unbearable.

This begs an interesting question, can noise be employed a form of torture? Does noise cause any non-auditory damage to our health? Let's explore those issue by starting with a simple and important definition,

> *"Noise: A sound, especially one that is loud or unpleasant or that causes disturbance."*[96]

According to the research, *unpleasant* and *disturbance* are really the key words here. Although the research suggests that certain sounds are universally *unpleasant*, there is a lot of subjectivity at play here as well; music being the obvious example.

What then, makes a sound unpleasant or annoying?

---

[96] Oxford Dictionaries. 2018. Noise. *en.oxforddictionaries.com*. Retrieved: April 14th, 2018, from https://en.oxforddictionaries.com/definition/noise.

Surprisingly, the answer lies inside of your Amygdalae. Amygdalae are tiny almond shaped clusters in your brain responsible for controlling your decision making, memory and emotional response. What type of emotion? Your Amygdalae principally control your emotional response to fear, aggression and anxiety. So, what is the connection between your auditory cortex and your Amygdalae:

> *"Researchers from Newcastle University say that being annoyed by certain sounds comes from high levels of activity between certain brain regions that process emotion (the amygdala) and the auditory cortex, a region that processes sound.*
>
> *'It appears there is something very primitive kicking in. It's a possible distress signal from the amygdala to the auditory cortex,' said Dr. Sukhbinder Kumar, the paper's author from Newcastle University.*
>
> *Researchers studied the effects of the sounds on the brain and found that activity in the amygdala and the auditory cortex had a direct relation to the unpleasantness of a sound, meaning nasty sounds increased activity in these regions."*[97]

Surprisingly, those unpleasant sounds literally trigger a distress signal in the same part of your brain that controls fear, anxiety and aggression. You might as well have just stumbled across a violent and aggressive predator. But hey, it's just a sound! Who cares? We've all heard the unpleasant honk of a car, loud clamoring from a construction site or a song we genuinely dislike Just part of city life, right?

Unfortunately, it's a bit more complex than that. Those unrelenting minor annoyances add up over time causing a lot of non-auditory damage to your body. How might that happen? Well, those unpleasant sounds induce a harmful, involuntary stress response:

> *"Why is excessive noise hazardous to your physical health? The reason is that noise causes a stress response. You hear a loud sound, and a stress cascade begins—adrenaline is released, blood vessels constrict, muscles tense, and blood pressure rises. We are not fully in control of this stress response: 'Even though noise may have no relationship to danger, the body will respond automatically to noise as a warning signal.'*

---

[97] Moore. 2012, October 10. Science Explains Why Some Noises Are So Annoying. *www.medicaldaily.com*. Retrieved: January 1st, 2019, from https://www.medicaldaily.com/science-explains-why-some-noises-are-so-annoying-24300.

Noise is associated with increased aggression, decreased helpful behavior, reduced motivation and task performance, and even impaired cognitive development in children."[98]

Yikes! So how did noise negatively impact me in a prison cell? Unfortunately, there isn't a lot of research focused around inmates who are forced to endure an unrelenting barrage of unpleasant sounds. Luckily, there is a lot of research focused around something very similar; noise pollution,

"Noise pollution: refers to sounds in the environment that are caused by humans and that threaten the health or welfare of human or animal inhabitants."[99]

So, what might have sparked an entire field of research to obsess over seemingly inconsequential and trivial city sounds? The answer lies in the sheer volume of health complications that arise from those involuntary distress signals originating in the Amygdalae. In other words, those heightened stress levels from noise pollution, cause a horrific cascade of non-auditory damage on your body:

"Noise is pervasive in everyday life and can cause both auditory and non-auditory health effects.

Occupational noise is the most frequently studied type of noise exposure. Research focus has broadened to social noise (eg, heard in bars or through personal music players) and environmental noise (eg, noise from road, rail, and air traffic, and industrial construction). These noise exposures have been linked to a range of non-auditory health effects including annoyance, sleep disturbance, cardiovascular disease, and impairment of cognitive performance in children.

In this Review, we emphasise that non-auditory health effects of environmental noise are manifold, serious and, because of the widespread exposure, very prevalent. These factors stress the need to regulate and reduce environmental noise exposure (ideally at the source) and to

[98] Selig, Meg. September 25th, 2013. What Did You Say?! How Noise Pollution Is Harming You. *www.psychologytoday.com*. Retrieved: January 1st, 2019, from https://www.psychologytoday.com/us/blog/changepower/201309/what-did-you-say-how-noise-pollution-is-harming-you.

[99] Noise Help. 2010-2018. What Is Noise Pollution? *Noisehelp.com*. Retrieved: April 14th, 2018, from http://www.noisehelp.com/what-is-noise-pollution.html.

enforce exposure limits to mitigate negative health consequences of chronic exposure to environmental noise."[100]

Surprisingly, those harmless everyday sounds have a fascinating way of causing very real physical damage. How does that heightened stress response negatively harm your body? For one, it wreaks havoc on your cardiovascular system:

"The study also found that occupational and environmental noise exposure may be associated with high blood pressure as well as elevated levels of stress hormones, called catecholamines, that are secreted by the adrenal glands.

Catecholamines act much like cortisol, another adrenal hormone. They prepare the body for "fight or flight" by increasing blood pressure and heart rate and releasing glucose (sugar) into the body to be burned for energy.

High catecholamines in the body can cause psychological stress and restrict blood flow to the heart and brain, increasing the risk of heart attack and stroke."[101]

Before landing in a prison cell, I had never stopped to consider the health effects of noise. Then again, I had never experienced an environment with such persistent barrage of noise-based stimuli. It was unrelenting and painful in a way that words simply can't capture. Generally, I thought of these sounds as more of an annoyance but had no idea that they were harming my health. Unfortunately, the damage of noise pollutions doesn't stop at your circulatory system,

"The British Medical Bulletin article also reported that noise exposure may also slow rehearsal in memory, adversely affect memory selectivity and executive functioning/task performance.

Nighttime noise can also contribute to oxidative stress (free radical damage) and chronic inflammation, which is the starting point for a wide range of illnesses.

[100] Basner, M., Babisch, W., Davis, A., Brink, M., Clark, C., Janssen, S., & Stansfeld, S. (2014, April 12). Auditory and non-auditory effects of noise on health. *ncbi.nlm.nih.gov*. Retrieved April 14, 2018, from https://www.ncbi.nlm.nih.gov/pmc/articles/PMC3988259/

[101] Awakening from Alzheimer's. August 25th, 2017. Noise Pollution Can Damage More Than Your Hearing. *awakeningfromalzheimers.com*. Retrieved April 14, 2018, from https://www.awakeningfromalzheimers.com/heres-what-noise-pollution-does-to-your-brain-and-memory/

*Not only that, but – as we've noted many times in these pages — chronic
poor sleep also contributes to cognitive decline and Alzheimer's disease."*[102]

As we're beginning to see, there are very significant reasons for the increased
emergence of research surrounding noise pollution. The harsh reality is that
those trivial environmental sounds aren't as inconsequential as we'd like to
assume. This begs an interesting question, if left unabated, what are the long-
term health risks associated with chronic exposure to noise pollution:

> *"Within the last decade, several studies have found traffic noise (road,
> aircraft, and railway noise) to be associated with increased risk of
> cardiovascular and metabolic diseases. Already in 2011, Babisch
> published the statement 'The question at present is no longer whether
> noise causes cardiovascular effects, it is rather: what is the magnitude of
> the effect in terms of the exposure-response relationship (slope) and the
> onset or possible threshold (intercept) of the increase in risk.'*
>
> *The presented evidence further strengthens the concept that transportation
> noise per se contributes to the development of cardiovascular risk of
> coronary artery disease, arterial hypertension, stroke, and heart failure.*
>
> *With regard to understanding the pathophysiological mechanisms, a
> growing body of evidence finds that noise is associated with oxidative stress,
> vascular dysfunction, autonomic imbalance, and metabolic abnormalities,
> potentiating not only the adverse impact of cardiovascular risk factors,
> such as arterial hypertension and diabetes, but also contributing
> to the progression of atherosclerosis and increased susceptibility to
> cardiovascular events."*[103]

It's worth taking a moment to emphasize that this type of noise pollution is
laughably tame compared with the environment of a CCP torture cell.

It's a fascinating thing to take a moment and put all this research into context.
The natural environment of our world seems to have been perfectly designed
for the human brain to thrive. This ingenious equilibrium provides a pleasant

[102] Awakening from Alzheimer's. August 25th, 2017. Noise Pollution Can
Damage More Than Your Hearing. *awakeningfromalzheimers.com*. Retrieved
April 14, 2018, from https://www.awakeningfromalzheimers.com/
heres-what-noise-pollution-does-to-your-brain-and-memory/.

[103] Münzel, T., Schmidt, F. P., Steven, S., Herzog, J., Daiber, A., & Sørensen, M. (2018, February
05). Environmental Noise and the Cardiovascular System. *onlinejacc.org*. Retrieved April 14,
2018, from http://www.onlinejacc.org/content/71/6/688.

experience that doesn't drive us into a state of utter chaos. When these variables are altered, even in the slightest way, the human brain involuntarily spirals out of control.

As we've seen, the human mind breaks down when it is exposed to a stimuli-free environment, sensory deprivation, or when it is overwhelmed by external stimuli, noise pollution. Sadly, this is what makes sound such an effective tool for torture. Personal accounts of those that have endured noise-based torture is simply stunning,

> "According to a footnote in a 2005 US interrogation program memo, the CIA keeps "detention conditions" at every one of its detention facilities, where detainees are subjected to "white noise/loud sounds (not to exceed 79 decibels)" during portions of interrogations. The 2005 memo also notes that the Occupational Safety and Health Administration figures "no risk of permanent hearing loss from continuous 24-hour-per-day exposure to noise of up to 82 decibels."
>
> The thing to keep in mind, though, is that "decibels need to be correlated with the amount of time a person is exposed to the sound at a particular decibel level," according to Cusick...
>
> "Sounds are the audible manifestation of waves moving through air, and those waves necessarily produce physical effects." These effects can range from the immediate sensation of having been beaten, Cusick added, to the development, or exacerbation, of hypertension and hearing loss long after the final clangs of the "acoustical beating" ring out.
>
> 'When it stops," the Salt Pit prisoner told Cusick, "it's like a beating has stopped."[104]

So how can sound be utilized to torture people? The obvious answer would be to simply adjust its intensity. How high can the volume go before its considered torture? But what about other variables beyond the intensity of the sound? Do certain genres of music constitute as a form of torture? What about a genre of music that you hate listening to? What if I played the sound of other people being tortured?

---

[104] Anderson, Brian. December 10th, 2014. Why Sound Torture Hurts. *motherboard.vice.com*. Retrieved April 15, 2018, from https://motherboard.vice.com/en_us/article/4x374p/why-sound-torture-works.

What about a loop of harsh sounds that have been scientifically proven to cause universal discomfort?

Then there's the consideration of time as a variable. How long do you have to be subjected to unpleasant sounds for it to be considered torture? A few minutes? Hours? What if I hit the play button and leave you there for days on end? Unfortunately, the research on sound torture is limited and there are a number of conflicting views. Here's one example that provides a bit of clarity,

> "It is not clear when sound was used specifically against individuals, however, it was reported that 'uncooperative Iraqis' were being exposed to music such as Metallica and even Barney the purple dinosaur from a US children's television show...According to one proponent, 'These people haven't heard heavy metal before. They can't take it.
>
> If you play it for 24 h, your brain and body functions start to slide, your train of thought slows down and your will is broken'. Another reported that detainees subjected to strobe lights and loud rock and rap music for up to 14 h a day became, '...very wobbly. They came back to their cells and were just completely out of it'.
>
> The captive has no control over any sensory attack; he or she cannot predict or control its output; cannot withdraw or evade from it or habituate to it, the person cannot screen the incoming stimuli and this can overwhelm their psychological defense mechanisms. Although habituation to noise can occur in healthy subjects, sounds of sufficient intensity, significance, duration or stimuli that imply conflict do not completely habituate.
>
> Experimental studies with subjects exposed to intense auditory and visual stimuli showed heightened and sustained arousal, discomfort, mood changes, illusions and hallucinations and body image distortions, irritability, distraction, disorientation and a withdrawal from reality. Early work in this area reported that sensory overload could produce symptoms similar to various pathologies and produced thinking and behaviour, particularly speech content, associated with schizophrenia."[105]

I have no doubt that the CCP is well aware of this research and the impact that Chinese inmates have on foreign detainees. It's just another tool they use to overwhelm you into submission. Remember, the goal of these conditions is

---

[105] Leach, John. June 1st, 2016. Psychological factors in exceptional, extreme and torturous environments. *ncbi.nlm.nih.gov*. Retrieved April 15, 2018, from https://www.ncbi.nlm.nih.gov/pmc/articles/PMC4890253/.

to break your will. Sound is merely another medium that the CCP has weaponized to torture inmates:

"Common methods of torture and abuse in the People's Republic of China:

Sleep deprivation

The victim is prevented from sleeping for several days. Measures used to achieve this include tying the victim up in a painful position, constant lighting, noise, and especially beatings, kicks and other types of punishment if the victim attempts to lie down.

Extremely loud noise played through headphones

Over a long period of time the bound victim is exposed to extremely loud music or propaganda tapes via headphones."[106]

---

[106] ISHR. Common methods of torture and abuse in the People's Republic of China. *ishr.org.* Retrieved: April 15th, 2018, from http://www.ishr.org/countries/peoples-republic-of-china/ methods-of-torture-in-the-peoples-republic-of-china/.

Chapter 21:

God & China

China Could Become the World's Largest Christian Country

"China (Includes Tibet, Hong Kong, And Macau) 2017 Report on International Religious Freedom (US Department of State):

Christian churches stated the government increased monitoring even before the new regulations came into effect, causing many churches to cease their normal activities. Authorities continued to arrest and harass Christians in Zhejiang Province, including by requiring Christian churches to install surveillance cameras to enable daily police monitoring of their activities. An ongoing campaign of cross removals and church demolitions continued during the year, reportedly on a more limited basis than in previous years...

According to July articles by ChinaAid and in Express, TSPM Nanle County Church Pastor Zhang Shaojie's daughter said authorities beat him nearly to death after he appealed his 12-year sentence following four years of imprisonment. Zhang's relatives said prison guards had tortured him, using methods including sleep deprivation as well as slowly starving him by giving him very little to eat. Zhang is a pastor in Xinxiang, Henan Province, in prison for "swindling" and "assembling a crowd to disrupt public order" for leading a group of Christians to Beijing to file a petition concerning his church's land dispute with local officials."

Chinese Government's official remarks regarding the US Department of State's 2017 Annual International Religious

Freedom Report. Chinese Foreign Ministry Spokesperson Hua Chunying's remarks, May 31, 2018:

"Q: The US Department of State recently released its 2017 Annual International Religious Freedom Report. What is your comment?

A: The so-called report by the US is fraught with political biases against China and slanders China's religious policy. The nonsense is not even worth refuting.

The Chinese government protects its citizens' freedom of religious belief in accordance with the law. The Chinese people of all ethnic groups are entitled to full religious freedom in accordance with the law. This fact is there for all to see. We urge the US to look squarely at and respect the fact, discard biases, and stop issuing such report and using the religious issue to interfere in China's internal affairs."

China has rapidly evolved into a formidable global force both militarily and economically.

We're talking about a country that has undergone the fastest economic transformation that arguably became the envy of the world. Its annualized GDP growth was so significant that it managed to keep much of the world's economy afloat during a painful global recession.

Additionally, China's military spending has significantly increased on an annualized basis. The CCP is working furiously to assert itself as a dominant military force in the South China Sea and throughout the rest of Asia. Furthermore, China has far and away the largest population, in addition to the largest standing army, with some estimates approaching nearly 2 billion people.

As we've seen, the Chinese Communist Party has worked tirelessly to assert control over its domain and has no qualms about clamping down on those who dare dissent. Make no mistake that the CCP will continue to kick, beat, torture, execute and fight in order to maintain this authoritarian system of control it has worked tirelessly to establish.

And yet, despite all its impressive economic growth and military might, there is one thing that keeps the Chinese government awake every single night. It's the one thing that terrifies the CCP to its core because it is the only thing powerful enough to unravel the authoritarian system they've spent decades perfecting.

No, it's not the US military. It's not human rights organizations or an independent foreign media that refuses to propagate CCP propaganda.

So, what might that one thing be?

God.

I didn't really understand this before I left for China. For most of my adult life, I was a die-hard atheist. I left the Church in my early teens as I saw it as an ancient relic that didn't serve a purpose in the modern world.

And why should it? I was a man of science with a prestigious degree in chemistry. I had a smartphone and smart friends. I was well-educated and looked down on those in university that were foolish enough to believe in something as outdated as a religion.

I saw religion, Christianity in specific as the antithesis of education or progress. I viewed followers of Christianity as an ignorant bunch of has-beens clinging to an outdated belief system. I debated Christians on campus with my "enlightened" friends. I ridiculed them for having a belief in that silly little book.

I was too intelligent, educated, traveled and cultured for that nonsense.

I used China as the shining example of a competent and religious-free country achieving incredible economic success. Its people were thriving, and they had no need for simple-minded religion. They are people of science building a progressive future, I used to say. Here we are in the US, clinging to the past, and being left in the dust!

I had absolutely no idea what I was talking about. Unbeknownst to me, I had adopted the exact same mindset on religion as the CCP.

You see, one of the things I failed to realize was that China does indeed have a religion. It's just that they don't use that word religion, even though it's fundamental to the CCP's authoritarian system. Everything I used to hate about religion in the US (conformity, submission, indoctrination, etc.) are readily present in China, but even more so than you'll find anywhere in the "religious" West.

So, what is the Chinese religion?

Communism.

It's everything I used to dislike about Christianity, except it's a blind obsession and submission to a government.

You see in China's religion, there is no God. Instead, there is a chairman, who is essentially revered with the same authority. The chairman is not to be questioned or challenged under any circumstances. The difference between Christianity and communism one might ask? Dissent in China's religion is not met with some abstract threat of hell. No, dissent in communism yields very real physical abuse, incarceration, torture and execution.

Communism has a clergy too, but again, it's not called that. In China, it's called the Chinese Communist Party. The Cardinals and Archbishops have been replaced by the Politburo and the Standing Committee. The Bishops and the Priests have been replaced by the Central Committee and People's Congress. And so, on and so forth.

From the time you start school in China you are indoctrinated into a hard-core, 24/7, system of forced communist submission. It makes the most devout religious followers around the world look tame by comparison. Under no circumstances is any form of dissent tolerated.

If you're born in China, this is what every single day of your life is like for your first 18 years.

Referring to communism as a religion is a severe understatement. It's a cult where their warped ideals can only be enforced through an endless system of violence, threats, and death.

Anything that remotely deviates from this hardcore indoctrination is deemed a threat by Chinese authorities. What might those threats include? Any religious belief that threatens their religion of communism.

If you're capable of understanding this, you'll start to understand why the CCP detains, tortures and executes countless practitioners of Falun Gong, Christianity, Tibetan Buddhism and Islam.

These systems fundamentally undermine communist rule.

If any of these religious teachings reach critical mass in China, it's game over for the Chinese Communist Party. As a result, the Chinese government will literally go to war against the emergence of any competing religious beliefs,

Tibet (Buddhism):

"The United Nations is set to receive evidence that Chinese People's Armed Police troops have repeatedly opened fire on unarmed Tibetan protesters calling for religious freedom over the past seven years. Evidence of deadly attacks by the Chinese paramilitary on Buddhist demonstrators across the Tibetan Plateau – provided by witnesses, whistleblowers, and a secret government document smuggled out of Tibet – will be presented to the UN's Committee against Torture later this year.

"The usage of live ammunition against peaceful Tibetan protestors does exist and it is also disproportionate," Prime Minister Lobsang Sangay, the head of Tibet's government-in-exile, told The Diplomat. "This is clearly in violation of international law," said the prime minister, a former research fellow at prestigious Harvard Law School who wrote his graduate thesis on Buddhism and Human Rights.

Tsering Tsomo, executive director of the Tibetan Center for Human Rights and Democracy, described the serial shootings of Tibetan protesters as "crimes against humanity." She said the rights center has amassed powerful evidence that Chinese armed police consistently use overwhelming force to crush pacifist dissent in the former Buddhist kingdom.

In one assault on August 12 of last year, witnesses reported that troops fired into an assembly of protesters who were calling for the release of a detained religious and cultural leader in the village of Kardze; four of the 10 demonstrators who were shot were also arrested. Denied medical treatment for their bullet wounds, each of these captured protesters died over the course of the next five days, Tsomo said.

The Tibetan Center for Human Rights that Tsomo heads is based in Dharamsala, the ever-expanding sanctuary provided by India's government to host the Dalai Lama and a continuous stream of Tibetans who have fled into exile since the People's Liberation Army marched into their Himalayan homeland in the 1950s."[107]

Xinjiang Province (Islam):

"China is using predictive "big data" technology to police suspects in the restive western province of Xinjiang, according to a report by the Human

---

[107] Holden, Kevin. April 14th, 2015. China's Crackdowns in Tibet. *thediplomat.com*. Retrieved April 16, 2018, from https://thediplomat.com/2015/04/chinas-crackdowns-in-tibet/.

Rights Watch group, gathering personal data on everything from banking to health to prayer habits. "People in Xinjiang can't resist or challenge the increasingly intrusive scrutiny of their daily lives because most don't even know about this 'black box' programme or how it works," Ms Wang said.

Hundreds have died in Xinjiang in the past few years, mostly in unrest between the Turkic-speaking Muslim Uighur people, who call the region home, and the ethnic majority Han Chinese. Beijing blames the unrest on Islamist militants. Late last year there were reports that about 120,000 ethnic Uighurs were being held in political re-education camps in Kashgar prefecture.

The data is collected as part of a policing system known as the Integrated Joint Operations Platform, which has been operating since August 2016. It gathers information using multiple sensors, including CCTV cameras with facial recognition or infrared capabilities, Human Rights Watch reported.

One interviewee told the watchdog he had seen data gathered including basic information about name, gender, ID numbers and familial relations, as well as whether the person is trusted or not, whether they have been detained or subject to political education, for every Uighur in a particular area."[108]

Christianity:

"Thousands of Christian villagers in China have been told to take down displays of Jesus, crosses, and gospel passages from their homes as part of a government propaganda effort to 'transform believers in religion into believers in the party.'

Thousands of Christian villagers in China have been told to take down displays of Jesus, crosses, and gospel passages from their homes as part of a government propaganda effort to "transform believers in religion into believers in the party." The South China Morning Post (SCMP) reports that Communist Party of China (CPC) officials visited believers' homes in Yugan county of Jiangxi province—where about 10 percent of the population is Christian. They urged residents to replace personal religious

---

[108] Coonan, Clifford. February 27th, 2018. China using big data in Xinjiang crackdown, say rights groups. *irishtimes.com*. Retrieved April 16, 2018, from https://www.irishtimes.com/news/world/asia-pacific/china-using-big-data-in-xinjiang-crackdown-say-rights-groups-1.3407849.

displays with posters of President Xi Jinping; more than 600 removed Christian symbols from their living rooms, and 453 hung portraits of the Communist leader, according to SCMP.

"Many poor households have plunged into poverty because of illness in the family. Some resorted to believing in Jesus to cure their illnesses," the head of the government campaign told SCMP. "But we tried to tell them that getting ill is a physical thing, and that the people who can really help them are the Communist Party and General Secretary Xi."

Though the party denies the claim, some Christians in Yugan county say they were told they would not be eligible for government assistance unless their posters were removed. Before Christians were asked to take down religious displays from their homes, the Yugan church removed its cross, as dozens of churches across Zhejiang and other Christian areas have done in recent years in order to comply with government regulations."[109]

Falun Gong:

"The popularity of these beliefs – official sources estimated there were 70 million practitioners in China by 1999 – is what caused the Communist Party to see Falun Gong as an ideological challenge, ultimately leading to a massive and ongoing campaign to eliminate it.

According to the NGO Freedom House, since 1999, hundreds of thousands of Falun Gong practitioners across China have been subjected to arbitrary imprisonment and torture, solely for the peaceful expression of their beliefs. Thousands have died as a result of abuse in custody, and there is credible evidence that large numbers of Falun Gong detainees have been killed so their organs could be sold for profit.

The Chinese government uses propaganda and misinformation to undercut sympathy for Falun Gong. One method is calling Falun Gong an "evil cult" – a label that evokes visceral negative responses. The Chinese government claims, with no credible evidence, that practicing Falun Gong leads to madness, murder, and suicide.

---

[109] Shellnutt, K., Neff, D., Smietana, B., Neuhaus, R. J., & Moore, B. (November 17th, 2017). China Tells Christians to Replace Images of Jesus with Communist President. *christianitytoday.com*. Retrieved April 16, 2018, from http://www.christianitytoday.com/news/2017/november/china-christians-jesus-communist-president-xi-jinping-yugan.html.

Its media outlets report that practitioners are incapable of rational thought, thereby providing justification for the arbitrary imprisonment and forcible ideological reprogramming of innocent, law-abiding people. Sometimes they refer to Falun Gong practitioners as literal vermin – as "rats" that need to be smashed."[110]

A communist government cannot maintain power without first filling mass graves full of its own population. Unfortunately, this concept is just about impossible to convey to Western audiences because there is no point of reference. It's a concept that I wasn't capable of understanding until I was detained in a communist prison cell. As you slowly start to visualize your own death approaching, you begin to understand and view the world in a fundamentally different way.

It's a very humbling experience. Your degrees, vacations, passports, professional network, and everything else become meaningless.

I began to see how insignificant I was. I started to see a world that was fully capable of continuing without me in it. Whether you're alive or not, the same polluted air will fill Beijing's sky tomorrow. Commuters will still hop on overcrowded public transportation systems and get to work. Domestic and international detainees will still be forced in and out of this prison cell.

Life continues once you die.

But it also forces you to start searching for meaning.

Is there a purpose to any of this? Have you left anything meaningful behind in this world? Anything permanent? How long will it take until people forget that you were here? Was there something you wanted to accomplish but didn't? Was there an opportunity you missed? Do you have any regrets?

For me at least, it made me realize how desperately I wanted to experience certain things. This is going to sound stupid but, I wanted a dog. I've always wanted a dog. I never had one. I wanted to start a family. I wanted to have a wife. I wanted to get married. I wanted to write a book.

I started thinking of all the opportunities I had missed. All the things I wanted to try but never made time for. All the places I wanted to see that I had never been.

---

[110] Lin, Anastasia. June 28th, 2017. We must hold Beijing to account for its treatment of Falun Gong practitioners. *theglobeandmail.com*. Retrieved April 16, 2018, from https://www.theglobeandmail.com/opinion/we-must-hold-beijing-to-account/article35487649/

You start to realize how much you had given up and how much you had sacrificed over the years. You start to beg. How much more do I have to suffer until I can pursue these things? What will it take for me to get out of this nightmare?

In that moment, God becomes painfully real, even to an educated and hardcore atheist-scientist like myself. He's everywhere. He's watching you. He's observing you. He's looking out for you. He's the only reason I survived.

Had you said this to me before I was detained in that prison cell, I wouldn't have even bothered listening to you. I would have given you a pleasant smile and kindly walked away.

No, I'm not going to sit here and beg for you to go to church, although I suggest it. I'm not going to sit here and say that reading the Bible is going to solve your problems. I also won't suggest you get detained in a foreign country to try and find God.

If you aren't desperately searching for meaning, purpose, or direction, the idea of a God isn't going to make any sense. If you already have all the answers, reading the Bible will seem like a waste of time. At this very moment in your life, God might not be the ideal solution. I also don't believe that God can, nor should he, be forced on people who are unwilling to believe. I suppose it's different for every person. For me, I had to be pushed to the brink of death, staring over a bottomless pit to finally see the truth.

It wasn't until I could see the hopelessness of my current condition that God became painfully clear. For the first time in my life, God was as clear and tangible as anything else I have ever experienced. But that's what it took for me. I can't say with any degree of certainty that it's the same for anyone else.

I spoke to God every single day there. I talked to him about my fears. I talked to him about my hopes. I talked to him about survival. I talked to him about my daily struggles. For whatever reason, he walked me into that prison cell.

That prison cell was my opportunity at being reborn. Having God there with me gave me the courage and the strength to survive.

But it wasn't just me that God was looking out for. I was equally humbled and inspired by Raheem's devotion to God.

Raheem, a devout Muslim, prayed three to five times a day in our prison cell. The Chinese prisoners didn't get it. Raheem had been promised by Chinese authorities that he would have access to a private room for daily prayer. They promised him that he would be given access to a Quran as well.

As usual, the Chinese authorities had simply lied to his face. Raheem was forced to pray by himself in a corner of the room, on the wooden planks, with a roomful of Chinese prisoners mocking him. The differences among the prisoners was stark. The foreign inmates from Senegal, India, and Ghana were respectful enough to let Raheem pray in peace. We didn't stare at him. We didn't mock him. We didn't talk about him.

The Chinese don't think that way.

Every single inmate was either staring, mocking or talking about Raheem's devotion to God. They couldn't fathom a world where a man would bow down to anything but the iron fist of a government. Remember, to the Chinese, their God is a government. We foreigners were disgusted by their childish behavior. But that's what you would expect from the Chinese.

Remember Mr. Chi, they believe that they are a pure bloodline. They believe the Chinese are heaven-sent; the pure race. They believe that their government and chairman is the supreme leader of everything. Remember what they call themselves? They are the "Middle Kingdom." We foreigners, of any nation, must bow to them. How dare we bow down to God.

The notion of an Islamic or Christian God threatens the foundation of the Chinese order. It means that there is something superior to man, which means that there is something superior to the Chinese Communist Party.

That is a powerful concept that undermines their entire existence.

The beauty of God is that it unites people. Although Raheem and I have different beliefs and follow different religious texts, the core of our beliefs allow for mutual respect. We had the most beautiful conversations about traditional family values, building a family, children, marriage, religion & faith.

God managed to take two very different people, from very different parts of the world, and unite us around something universal, faith in a divine being. In the middle of one of the worst experiences of my life, God gave me a wonderful friend from Iraq. It's that universality, understanding, love and compassion that the Chinese Communist Party fears and hates,

> *"China has banned the Bible from being sold online as part of a major crackdown on Christianity. The Orwellian measures were announced*

over the weekend but have now taken effect — with the Christian holy book now no longer available on major Chinese retailer websites.

Websites that have stopped selling the Bible include Amazon China, Taobao and JD.com. However, some retailers are still offering related materials — like illustrated storybooks, or academic analyses of the Bible. It's part of China's bid to limit the country's growing religious scene, according to the New York Times.

Speaking to The Sun, a Christian Solidarity Worldwide spokesperson said: "The ban is deeply concerning and part of a wider pattern of violations of the right to freedom of religion or belief in China, which includes unregistered 'house churches.'

"We are seeing unregistered Christian groups being forced to shut down and in some cases, church buildings have been completely demolished. "At the same time, churches registered with the authorities are also being managed more tightly following the introduction of revised Regulations on Religious Affairs, which came into effect on February 1 this year."

From 2014 to 2016, the country removed 1,500 crosses from churches in one province."[111]

If there's only one thing you remember one thing from this book, make sure it's this,

China's Communist Party fears God.

---

[111] Sun, T. April 6th, 2018. China ratchets up its war on God. *nypost.com*. Retrieved April 28th, 2018, from https://nypost.com/2018/04/06/china-bans-online-sales-of-the-bible-as-nation-tightens-religious-controls/.

Chapter 22:

Day 21, Handcuffs & Deportation

A creepy video shows how China warns its citizens to behave or get punished by its nationwide social credit system

"A chilling announcement on a train from Beijing to Shanghai shows how the future of China could be dominated by people living in fear of a nationwide social credit system, which will rank all its 1.4 billion citizens based on their behavior.

The social credit system is basically an extension of a person's financial credit score, which will be mandatory nationwide in 2020.

In the video a female voice announced over the intercom in English that people who travel without a ticket or "behave disorderly" — like smoking in public places — would be "punished according to regulations, and the behavior will be recorded in individual credit information system."

People have already either been punished and rewarded based on their social credit: Earlier this year a student was denied his spot at university because his father was blacklisted for failing to pay off a 200,000-yuan ($28,700/£22,400) bank loan. Others have been banned from taking trains because of their score.

Those who lost all their points had their dogs confiscated and were required to pass a test on regulations required for pet ownership."[112]

---

[112] Ma, A. (2018, October 29). A creepy video shows how CHINA warns its citizens to behave or get punished by its nationwide social credit system. Retrieved February 28, 2021, from https://www.businessinsider.com/video-china-train-warns-citizens-to-behave-for-social-credit-system-2018-10

Chinese Government's official response to the United States issuing an elevated travel advisory (exercise increased caution due to 'arbitrary enforcement of local laws as well as special restrictions on dual U.S.-Chinese nationals') for China. Chinese Foreign Ministry Spokesperson Lu Kang's remarks, January 4, 2019:

"Q: The United States yesterday issued a travel advisory for China, warning the US citizens about the risk of exit bans and some causes of detentions here in China. What is your response to the decision to release that advisory?

A: We have noted the relevant reports. China always welcomes foreigners, including Americans, and ensures their safety and legitimate rights and interests, including their freedom to enter and exit the border. Meanwhile, foreign citizens in China should also respect and abide by Chinese laws.

Here I need to point out that for the small number of foreign citizens who have committed crimes in China, relevant Chinese departments will handle their cases in accordance with the law while ensuring all their legitimate rights and interests.

To be frank, the issuance of such a travel advisory by the US side does not hold water. From January to November 2018, 2.3 million visits to China were made by Americans, which means 70 per 10,000 American people made the trip, a ratio far higher than that of the Chinese visiting the US. So, this figure is a testament to China's safety. On the contrary, the US has been citing various reasons and excuses to block the entry of Chinese citizens to the US and conduct needless checks. This is a problem the US needs to pay attention to and address. We hope that the US side could do more to promote exchanges and mutual trust between the two peoples, instead of playing the opposite role."

I was thinking about how much longer I could survive these conditions.

How long can a human physically endure this environment? I knew a lot of the health problems I was dealing with were involuntary responses beyond my ability to control. There's only so much of this a human being can handle.

Would I eventually go crazy, strip down naked and try peeing on people like the guy in Karl's cell?

Like God, death too, becomes painfully real, and a lot had transpired over the past seven days.

After relentlessly pestering Muhammad about his skin color, Tank and him almost got into a fight. It was the closest our cell came to an all-out brawl. I had to use every trick in the book to translate them out of killing each other. Had I not been there, I'm willing to bet there would have been bloodshed. I'm not sure how that would have ended in a prison cell like this?

A dead body or three?

I grew painfully tired of translating everything for everyone all the time. I was the only linguistic intermediary and I had to be on constant alert to control situations that could easily spiral out of control. Whether it was the guards asking about someone on hunger strike, Chinese inmates asking to learn English, or foreigners trying to ask about what a Chinese inmate had just said, I was just mentally drained.

Our cell had also received a new inmate who had been locked up for getting into a knife fight. He was around 18 or 19 years old and looked like a Chinese version of Elvis Presley. Unfortunately, he had also been stabbed in the altercation and had a wound that was festering on the side of his jaw. The "medical" staff refused to tend his wound for days on end. He finally broke down one day when the "medical" staff, once again, refused to assist. He started punching himself in the face until blood was pouring down his face.

That's what it took for the guards and the "medical" staff to finally offer him help.

Ultimately, I became sick, with flu-like symptoms. This horrendous environment had finally caught up with me. I was surprised that my body was resilient enough, given the conditions, to stay healthy for as long as it had. Seeing the way, the "medical" staff abused and ignored inmates terrified me. I knew that no one in this facility had any idea what they were doing nor, did they care about our health or well-being.

I was already on my own, and if I got sick, I would be in a bad place, and that's precisely when it happened. Runny nose. Sneezing. Sore-throat. Low-energy. This wasn't the time or place. I could feel my body and mind withering away given the conditions. I did my best to stay hydrated, but the toxic Beijing tap water would randomly shut off in our cell leaving me sick and waterless.

That was fun.

Luckily, and for some entirely unknown reason, I managed to make a full recovery. In what I can only describe as a miracle, given the hellish conditions, the symptoms subsided after a couple of days.

I also had another near-altercation with a new Chinese inmate. This guy was an absolute a$shole. Our cell enjoyed a brief period of peace after the guards had removed Tank. We had luckily stumbled upon the right mix of inmates which allowed the foreign and Chinese inmates to coexist in peace. That short-lived utopia lasted up until this giant piece of sh!t was thrown into our prison cell.

This new Chinese inmate was a low-IQ, angry, and uneducated fu&k. One of the first things he did after arriving was to yell at Soldier. Why? Because Soldier was resting in the blanket pile after having worked shift four. *"I don't want black people touching our blankets."*

Doesn't get much more racist than that does it?

This fuc*er. I instantly stood up on the wooden planks, towered over him and unloaded on him in Chinese. I was tired, weak and burned out. But his hatred and overall stupidity gave me all the energy I needed to unload. He wasn't small, but he wasn't built like the Tank. This was a fight I would be more than happy to take, and this was a guy that deserved a swift punch to the throat. If this would be how I would go down than fu*k it.

Gotta stand up for something in life.

The inmate instantly shut up. I'm not sure if it was my size, the fact that I was towering over him, his surprise that I could scream at his stupid face in Chinese, or the likelihood that I looked like a crazy person at this point in time, but my message had been delivered.

That racist sh!t won't fly in my prison cell. My prison cell.

I didn't realize it at the time, but I had already taken ownership over my new domain. The longer you stay in a prison environment, the more seniority you build. Ever so slowly, I was establishing myself as that guy. If the Godfather could do it, chained up and awkwardly hobbling around, then so could I.

Surviving that initial encounter with Tank, kind of numbed me to the environment. The chaos was becoming normal. I was much more patient in terms of picking the battles I fought. With that said, there was one thing you didn't have a choice with, foreigners had to stick together and watch each other's backs. Call it an inconvenient truth, but prison cells sort themselves out racially. It is what it is.

After my rant, I started explaining what had been said. Soldier, understandably, looked like he was ready to kill someone. Muhammad looked pissed and was desperately trying to figure out which words had been used. Raheem, who was usually patient and calm, was furiously pacing around and looked like he was ready to draw blood. Even some of the Chinese inmates shot this dude angry looks because he had been stupid enough to disturb what had been a peaceful environment.

This fu&ker just stuck his hand in a wasp nest and disrupted the harmony that we had collectively worked so hard to achieve. If you asked me today, I couldn't even tell you what I screamed at him. It was an entirely involuntary response. The anger just spilled out. I didn't stop to even think about it, much like we don't stop to think about breathing.

Who had I become? I realized I wasn't the same guy that entered this prison cell on day one. I guess I had become whatever you had to be to survive this sh!thole. I just know I shouted and pointed angrily until something got through his thick fu*king skull. At some point he understood what was going on and sat down in silence. Message delivered.

But it wasn't all negative. There were moments of positivity as well.

A handful of inmates that had cash locked away in the holding area were unexpectedly allowed to go to a local market across the street to buy a few snacks like instant noodles, Chinese cookies, and a couple bottles of Coke. They brought everything back to the cell to share. It was a very much needed and welcome surprise.

For one reason or another Tank was randomly removed from our prison cell by the guards. His sentence wasn't up, but he was simply taken out without explanation. Although it was incredibly unprecedented, it was a huge relief.

After meeting with immigration, I was desperately praying that I wouldn't be stuck here for another month. *But who knew?*

Sure, there was a slight bit of hope that we might be released early or hell, on time. Thursday came and went without a word. Then Friday. Still nothing. Despite my best effort to not build up a false sense of hope, I was still thoroughly disappointed that we hadn't yet been released. At this point I was mentally preparing myself for another month or two of detention.

It was a very realistic possibility given Soldiers situation.

Day by day, the absence of updates slowly crushed me. Saturday too, came and went without any news. Once again, I firmly believed that my detention would continue indefinitely. Hours dragged by in what could only be described as distorted time. Every day was tirelessly repetitive, just...pacing... and bucket food...and sitting. You became a thing that was simply there to mop up resources and not die. Despite the fact that other inmates had stopped eating, I still managed to power down food.

It was hell.

Ironically, that's when we were collectively injected with a bit of divine intervention. I suppose God only pushes us as far as we can handle. All of us were at the bottom of an incredibly dark place by day twenty.

We weren't even really talking to each other anymore. There wasn't much for anyone to say at this point.

It was late in the morning, probably around 10 or 11 am when the guards arrived at our door and swung open the heavy metal gate. Roll call had finished at this point and we had already eaten breakfast. The guard stood at the door as we all looked up trying to figure out what exactly was going on. He peered into our cell, and immediately pointed at Soldier motioning for him to grab his stuff and come stand outside. Soldier froze and just stared at the guard for a moment in disbelief. He thought his brain was playing a trick on him. He literally couldn't process that the guards were releasing him.

Yup. Soldier was FINALLY being released.

Muhammad and I literally had to motion for Soldier to start moving as we were genuinely concerned that the guards might change their mind. He literally couldn't believe it. We were all overcome with emotion and I had to fight back tears as we watched Soldier collecting his blood-stained blankets.

On one hand, I was distraught at the thought of him leaving our cell. Soldier was like a brother to me and we looked out for each other here. We worked in tandem to survive the worst that this environment had thrown at us. Now it was time for me to continue this fight without Soldier; someone I had grown to respect, rely on and trust.

On the other hand, I've never been happier for someone in my life. By now, Soldier had spent over 50 days in this hell hole. How he was still alive, and fighting was nothing short of a miracle. Before Muhammad and I had arrived,

Soldier had already spent weeks in this sh!thole. At times as the only foreigner locked in here as well.

If anyone in here deserved to be released, it was him. He was finally free and he could finally go home.

For the rest of us who were still locked-up, Soldier's release offered a faint glimmer of hope. Ultimately, foreign inmates do get released from here. Sure, I had heard about it, but this was my first time actually seeing it.

Maybe we'll all make it out of here.

We said our goodbyes as Soldier grabbed his stuff. He made his way to the door and the guards instructed him to stand alongside the exterior wall as they proceeded to shut the doors. We caught one final glimpse of Soldier as he stood staring back inside, nodding goodbye. The doors shut, and we heard the guards march Soldier out through the main hallway gate. That was that.

Soldier was gone. He was finally free.

Something about his release gave the rest of us the strength to keep going. *It is possible.* That experience gave me the power to keep fighting. I prayed that I would be out of this place by Wednesday as immigration had promised. But the days continued to roll by without any news.

Monday came and went and once again, nothing. Then Tuesday, still not a word.

Once again, I was starting to doubt immigrations promises of a Wednesday departure. I was starting to feel like I too would end up somewhere around Soldier's 50-day release date.

I went to bed that night hoping and praying that immigration would keep their word.

It was around 3:00 am on Wednesday morning when my eyes shot open. Surprisingly, I had been dreaming, which was incredibly rare in here. Sleep had been my only escape in detention. It was the one place the guards couldn't monitor or control me. That night I had been fortunate enough to momentarily dream my way out of this nightmare. For a brief second, I was actually confused by my surroundings.

Why am I in a prison cell? Fu&k, that's right. I'm still here.

I looked up out of my blanket and stared at the wall in front of me as my brain clicked itself out of sleep mode. I looked up at the clock, peered over to see who was on watch and then receded back into my blanket.

This nightmare never fu&king ends.

I rolled over and forced myself back to sleep. I shut my eyes and tried to make the most of the few remaining hours I had before our 6:30 am wake-up.

But I couldn't get back to sleep.

At this point, however, I was used to being out of a consistent sleep rhythm. I just kept my eyes shut and forced it for as long as possible. I didn't really care that I was sleeping on a wooden slab. I didn't really care that the guy that stabbed people and the guy I screamed at were on watch right now.

I guess at some point you adapt to this sh!tty existence.

I laid there for as long as possible with my eyes shut and I slowly started to drift back off. I'm not sure how long I laid there like that but at some point, I heard keys at our cell door.

Fu&k, is it breakfast time already? Was I dreaming again?

I heard the door fly open.

Well this is odd. The alarm hasn't gone off. It clearly isn't breakfast time. It must still be earlier than 6:30 am? The guards never swing by before the morning song. Medical staff? Is someone hurt?

Guard: American. Come!

I looked up, confused at first. Slowly, my brain put two and two together. The guy who stabbed people was pointing at me.

Knife fight guy: Released American. You're being released.

Fu&k me. He's calling for me. I'M BEING RELEASED?!?!!? What the fuc&&&?!?!?!

I sat up, as did some other inmates who were confused at the timing, trying to figure out what was going on at such an early hour. I looked over and saw two guards standing by the cell door, staring at me.

They were standing there waiting for me. This isn't a prank. Nope, this is real.

301

My brain ordered my body to inject a heavy dose of adrenaline and I shot straight out of bed. Even though I had seen the "release process" a million times before, I never really visualized it happening to me. I grabbed the two required blankets out of the pile, threw on my sandals and darted for the door.

Just as I was about to exit, I stopped and froze.

I looked back and saw Muhammad staring at me from his sleeping area. I turned right back around and walked back over to him. Once again, I was overcome with emotion and I could feel my eyes tearing up. I felt like I was leaving my own brother behind. I desperately wanted to grab him and pull him out of the cell with me. At the same time, we both understood what this was. There is no humanity in hell. No compassion. No love.

I knew I couldn't bring Muhammad along. I knew I would be leaving him here alone without someone to translate. I knew he would still be here while I was free. That killed me. It fundamentally killed me. It was fuc7ing horrible.

I leaned over and gave him a huge hug. This was the guy that gave me a place to sleep on my first night of detention. This was the guy that was willing to talk to me when he probably didn't feel like having a conversation. This was the guy that tried to make sure I kept eating food when I was clearly depressed.

Muhammad helped me survive this nightmare.

Me: Stay strong brother. You're out next.

Muhammad: Be free brother. God bless.

There was nothing more to be said. We both understood that.

I turned around and walked straight out of the cell.

I was still surrounded by guards, in a barred detention center and wearing a prison uniform, but I had never felt freer in my entire life.

As usual, I lined up against the hallway wall as the guards proceeded to shut the cell doors and lock everything up. I looked down to my left and saw a scruffy Karl and Neil lined up outside of their cells as well.

We were finally going home.

The guards proceeded to march them in my direction ordering Neil and Karl to halt just shy of my cell door. The three of us looked like an absolute disaster. Our beards were thick and overgrown, our hair was shaggy and unkept and

302

all of us had clearly lost a significant amount of weight by now. We hadn't said more than a word or two to each other, but you could just sense the positive energy flowing through us. After enduring the worst conditions imaginable, the three of us managed to look up at each other with smiles beaming from ear to ear.

The guards marched us out of the hall, back toward the elevators that we had arrived in on day one. We stopped off at a large bin across from the elevators where we were instructed to dump our blood-stained blankets.

From there we were marched into the elevator and exited down into the main lobby. As we arrived, we were met by a large contingent of CCP police officers who cautiously eyed the three of us. It seemed as if they were going to be our escort to the airport for deportation. The guards marched us past the officers, through a hall, and into the storage room where our personal belongings had been stashed on day one. Our bags were stored in the far-back of this dimly lit room sat atop rows of worn racks. The three of us picked out our bags lugging everything next door to the room where we had initially been stripped naked and marched through a metal detector.

The guards ordered us to change our clothes and return our prison attire to the proper bins. We stripped out of our gear and proceeded to put on our pre-detention clothes. Once I had my slacks back on, I stripped off my bright yellow and blue detention jacket and walked over to the bin. I couldn't get rid of it. It seemed counterintuitive, but I wanted to keep my prison gear as a symbol of this experience. For a second, I just stood there with my arm extended out over the bin, gripping my jacket and pants. I couldn't let go.

Would I have anything tangible to remember this experience? Oh right, my underwear.

My better judgement prevailed, and I dumped my gear into the bin. I shot the jacket one last look as I turned around, walking back over to my pile of clothes on the ground.

I started putting on my shirt, tie and jacket realizing how strangely foreign they felt on my body. They were clothes that I had worn for years, but I didn't feel like myself in them.

Why?

As I got dressed, I started to realize it wasn't just the feel of my clothes that felt foreign. I was being released back into the same world that I had just been

303

physically dragged out of, but I wasn't me. It wasn't my clothes, phone, back-pack or shoes that were different either. No, they were all very much the same.

I was a different person now.

I couldn't put my finger on it but the Steve that landed here on day one was gone. Even though it had only been three weeks, I felt as if three years had passed since I last saw this room. Spiritually, mentally, physically, I had become something different.

Who was I now? Was this temporary? Would I eventually feel like me again? It was as if I had transitioned back into my old body but with a completely revamped mind. What was this? Rebirth?

I hadn't seen myself in a mirror in weeks. I looked down and stared at my body once my normal clothes were on again. Everything was in its proper place...*this was me. Right?*

This was my lipstick on a pig moment. My body was dressed up well in nice clothes, but I felt physically and mentally broken. We collected the last of our things and marched back toward the central lobby. The CCP escort-swarm ordered us to sign release documents in Chinese.

Who the fu&k knows what we're signing.

These documents, however, appeared to confirm our departure from the prison compound. Once everything was signed, the officers proceeded to handcuff us one by one.

Great.

I'd never been handcuffed before and having your hands chained behind your back is not a pleasant experience. We were transitioning back into CCP police custody as the guards who had released us retired back to the central pro-cessing desk. Neil, Karl and I were marched outside, escorted by two officers each and greeted by a noticeably cold and dark Beijing morning. It was some-where around 4:15 or 4:30 am and there was another large transport vehicle parked outside.

Luckily, this one didn't come with a cage.

The three of us were instructed to sit in separate rows inside of the van. I was placed directly behind the driver's seat. Karl was seated behind me with Neil thrown all the way in the back.

Eight CCP officers accompanied the three of us into the van. It seemed as if they had two police officers to monitor each deportee and two police officers up front to handle driving and navigation. Not a single police officer, understandably, was happy about being up at 4:00 am to drive foreigner detainees around Beijing.

The lead police officer looked back at us before starting the van and asked which of one of us could speak Chinese. I nodded my head and he proceeded to say something in Mandarin that I didn't fully comprehend. I understood that he was ordering us not to do something but there was a word in his sentence that I hadn't heard in Chinese before.

He realized that I wasn't understanding something in his sentence and told the other officer to translate it into his phone for me to read. The officer complied, translating it into English. Hey not bad! For the first time after weeks of detention, someone was finally translating something for me! He pecked buttons on the screen and pushed the screen up in my face to read,

"Do not communicate with each other during the ride or we will be forced to use coercive measures."

I didn't recognize the word *coercive* in Chinese! Nonetheless, his message had been sent the message loud and clear. He looked at me and nodded toward Karl and Neil instructing me to explain. I looked back and told them that they were not allowed to communicate with each other throughout the trip, period.

I emphasized that the word coercive had been used in the translation.

Neil understood. Karl, however, was not pleased with the threat and spoke up to convey his dissatisfaction with government authority.

Neil and I both turned around instantly shooting him angry looks. "Not now Karl. Not fu&king now." He was more concerned about us than the CCP officers now and immediately shut up.

With our collective message delivered, the driver turned the key in the ignition and the van's engine roared to life. The front headlights ripped through a pitch-black morning as the vehicle made its way through the prison's central courtyard. My brain couldn't comprehend that we were finally departing hell. Our abrupt arrival on night one instantly flashed through my mind.

I remembered seeing the massive front gates for the first time with thick barbed wire strung along the perimeter wall. I remembered having my blood drawn, all my personal belongings taken and stripping down naked to be marched through a metal detector. I remembered the heavy metal door slam behind me, separating me from Neil and Karl and the fear of being locked in a CCP prison cell full of strange inmates.

It was one hell of a welcome.

The driver honked as our vehicle approached the colossal front gates. We watched patiently as the gate guard reached across his desk to press a button, forcing the front metal gates to roar open. The driver flipped the left turn signal as our van pulled past the front kiosk, turning left onto a pitch-black road. It was hard to see anything so early in the morning, but I looked back to get one last glance at this horrid compound that nearly took my life.

Ever so slowly, it too, faded into the background and out of sight.

We made our way through this desolate zone slowly transitioning onto ever larger roads. Even though it had only been a little under a month, re-emerging into society was another seemingly alien transition. For the first time in weeks, we were seeing other, non-prison, stuff. At first it was just a single car navigating through these deserted backroads. Then it was a street vendor standing in the middle of a virtually empty intersection. Our minds were slowly re-adapting to seeing anything that wasn't four depressing walls 24/7.

As we approached Beijing's main highways, we came across other cars and flickering Christmas lights along the top of a tiny store. The flashing lights were particularly hard to process. They seemed unnatural. The sudden change of scenery was overwhelming, and my brain was struggling to re-adjust.

Traffic was moving too fast. The lights were too bright. My brain was trying to calculate distance and speed. Where are those suicide warning signs that greeted me every morning?

I started to realize that my brain had grown accustomed to sensory deprivation in the prison cell.

Gradually, we made our way onto central roads as we continued our journey north toward the center of Beijing, Guomao. We were informed that we would be making one more stop at another police station to rotate officers.

As my brain re-acclimated itself to life in the normal-world, I realized that I wasn't feeling relieved about my release any longer. Obviously, I was thrilled to be out of that horrific prison cell, but my mind was beginning to worry about a number of other possible scenarios.

What happens if we get in a car-crash?

The driver was speeding around like a race-car driver. And why wouldn't he? He's a cop in Beijing so he can do whatever the fu&k he wants. If so, I'm hand-cuffed with my arms behind my back. Could I survive a crash at these speeds with my hands cuffed behind my back? Hell, of a way to die!

Here lies Steve Schaerer, he was released from prison and died en route to deportation.

I didn't want to think about it.

What if something goes wrong at the airport? What if we miss our flights? Do I get sent back to the prison cell or have I "served" my sentence? If I do get sent back, how long would I stay this time? Would it be the same cell? Would it be a different location?

Again, I didn't want to think about it.

Around thirty or forty minutes into the drive, I overheard the lead officer striking up a conversation with the other police officer in the car.

Driver: Why were these guys arrested?

Officer: Working illegally, I believe.

Driver: Visas?

Officer: Yes, correct. Illegal employment.

Driver: Are they violent?

Officer: No, I don't believe so.

Driver: Why are they handcuffed?

Officer: I don't know.

Driver: You can unhandcuff them.

Officer: Yessir. Officers! Unhandcuff them.

The officer next to me ordered me to turn my back to him so he could reach my handcuffs. I followed his lead and he clicked the keys into place releasing the cuffs.

Thank God! At least if we get in a car wreck I won't be chained up.

My guard handed the keys off to Karl's officers and then Neil's. I wanted to look back and watch them get uncuffed, but I wanted to avoid doing anything that might prompt Karl to make another unnecessary and idiotic comment. I kept my eyes on the road, staring straight out the window as other cars raced by. Ever so slowly, daybreak emerged, and I caught my first glance of Beijing off in the distance.

As we approached the city proper, I started to identify various landmarks. For the first time in quite a while, I could actually recognize where I was. At first it was a building that I had seen before or familiar subway-stops on the outskirts of the city. As we drew closer to the center of Beijing we started passing through familiar districts, restaurants, coffee shops, and apartment complexes where my friends lived.

This is one hell of a final goodbye.

That's when the memories started flooding black.

I took some girl on a date there once! There's that bar where we celebrated John's birthday. That place makes the best 羊蝎子 *(sheep spine)* ! *Hey, that's my apartment complex. We literally drove right past my apartment building…Will I ever see any of this again? Were they going to let us pick up our stuff before we're deported? Does anyone even know that we're being deported today? Does the US embassy know? Are we even being deported? Is this another lie?*

The final 15 minutes of that ride hit me hard. It was devastating. *I had invested so much into building a life in Beijing…everything.* I put years of hard work, tears, sweat and money into developing a network here and learning Mandarin. I was preparing for the HSK 5, handwritten exam, and building a business. I had no criminal record and I was the guy who had always advocated doing everything above board and following the law, period.

It didn't matter here.

Overnight, everything I had built was being stripped from me. Why? Because of a baseless allegation without any remote semblance of due-process.

I thought about my company, my colleagues, my business partners, my clients, my apartment, my stuff, my network, my friends, my income, my life…that was all gone now.

What do I do now? Five years of my life…*poof*!

But fu&k it, at least I'm not handcuffed anymore. Small victories Steve, small victories.

To our surprise, we landed back at the same police station where they had crammed us into a holding cell on day one. Talk about déjà vu. We parked outside and waited for about five minutes until the new cops rotated into our vehicle. The entire ride from the prison compound to our favorite holding cell in Guomao took around an hour total. Once the new police officers had entered the van, we were off to our next destination; the airport.

This was going to be a very long day.

Luckily, we made our way through central Beijing early enough to avoid most of the morning rush-hour traffic. We managed to hop on the S12, the main artery in between Beijing International and downtown, without any traffic.

Karl, Neil and I sat in absolute silence piecing together how strange and dangerous this had all been. *What exactly had we just survived?* My mind was still going million miles a minute contemplating all the horrible scenarios that could still make this end horribly. I was frustrated because this entire situation could have easily been resolved in a far more civilized manner. This entire process had been a laughable waste of time, money and resources for every single party involved.

I wasn't even angry any longer.

I was fortunate. I would be able to leave today and go back to a country where human rights is allowed to be part of the national discourse. But I felt bad for people who would remain stuck in this oppressive country. I felt bad for the police officers who had to play this game and pretend like we posed a serious threat to China. I felt bad for Chinese citizens that were educated to fear and hate foreigners. I felt bad for Chinese government officials that had been brainwashed into thinking that it was acceptable to treat their countrymen, or any human being, in this manner.

What a sad, depressing and fu&ked up country.

Had I understood any of this was even possible, I would have never considered China as an option to move to. I thought about that brilliant woman at the bank I had met before I moved here, "China? You know that's a communist country, don't you?" Nope. No, I did not. She might as well have been speaking Japanese or Russian. Brilliance and wisdom masquerading as ignorance, I think, is the punchline of the human condition. I knew I was right. I was well traveled. I was well-educated. I was analytical. I was well read.

In reality, I was a complete and utter fool. I was blissfully ignorant. I was blind. I knew nothing. She warned me, straight to my face. I didn't listen. I knew better. And now, I realize that I know nothing. Listen to your elders.

The final leg of our journey, a 40-minute ride from our favorite holding cell to Beijing's T3, the second largest airport terminal in the world, seemed to fly by.

Here we go.

To my surprise, we hadn't been directed to some special side-entrance for deportees. Nope, we landed smack dab in the middle of Beijing's T3. The police transport van pulled up right outside of the main terminal in the middle of a sea of other travelers. Slowly, the police officers exited the van and motioned for us to exit as well. One at a time, we slowly emerged into Beijing's notoriously cold winter weather. It was freezing, but I didn't even care.

This was the first time I was kind of able to move freely OUTSIDE of that hellish CCP prison complex.

It was a resoundingly strange experience. There were any number of people standing no further than five or ten feet away that had no idea what the three of us had just survived. Waves of travelers came and went, just going about their business. Off in the distance I saw families taking selfies, another group offloading luggage out of their car, while a group of flight attendants passed by curiously eyeing the three of us.

Just another normal day at the airport...

And there we were, surrounded by police and immigration officers, trying to re-adapt to the feel of sunlight hitting our eyes for the first time in days. We had been plucked up out of the world by the dark hand of China's Communist regime and hidden in some unmarked prison complex locals likely didn't even know existed. Whether we emerged out of that prison cell alive or dead didn't make a tiny sliver of a difference in the bigger scheme of things. Flights would still come and go on schedule, selfies would be posted on social media and life would just bang on.

We didn't matter. Nobody knew. Nobody cared. That's the value of a human life in China.

As we looked around, we realized that off in the distance, a group of people were slowly making their way toward us. I was surprised to see a few of my colleagues from the office, and others who had been notified of our release walking in our direction.

We were stunned.

It was incredibly overwhelming to see other people we knew. Although police and immigration kept a very close watch on us, they allowed us to hug and greet our visitors who started asking all about our experience. Apparently, immigration had notified them of our impending release, giving them a bit of a warning in terms of when and where to meet us prior to deportation. Luckily, one of my friends had a key to my apartment and managed to pack up all my personal belongings. She crammed as much as humanly possible into two massive suitcases.

I was lucky beyond belief.

Karl and Neil weren't so fortunate. No one had access to their apartments, and since we weren't allowed to gather our belongings prior to deportation, they would be going home empty handed. No clothes, no personal belongings, nothing. Luckily, our visitors assumed the horrific conditions that we had endured over the past month, and they were kind enough to arrive with ample coffee and snacks in hand.

One of my friends handed me a warm chicken panini and a steaming caramel macchiato. Words are wholly unable to capture what those first few bites and sips tasted like. After 20 something days of eating piss yellow liquid "porridge" out of a bucket, this was simply indescribable.

It's the single best meal I've had in my entire life.

I thanked my friends and colleagues for taking the time to help pack my belongings and bring all my stuff to the airport. It was a kind gesture that I simply couldn't ever hope to repay. Although we were still under careful watch and surrounded by police and immigration officers, we were allowed enough freedom to stand there and converse with our group.

One of the most noticeable things that they had mentioned was that we had clearly lost a ton of weight. Despite the fact that I managed to eat throughout the vast majority of my stay, the "food" we were eating wasn't nutritious. What we were fed was meant to make us not die and not much more than that.

My friends offered to grab more food and I gladly accepted. I was hungry, and it was so nice to have a warm meal and something that didn't taste like I was gnawing on a rock. I asked the guards if I could go to the restroom and they looked around at each other deciding that I needed to be escorted there.

The lead officer selected two of the younger cops to escort me alongside an immigration officer. The police stood on either side of me with the immigration officer walking directly in front of me, leading us toward the main T3 entrance. Although I had flown in and out of Beijing's T3 countless times before, I knew that this final trip would be the most unforgettable. As I entered the terminal, I was once again blown away by the normal-ness of everything.

Countless people stood in line waiting at check-in counters while others were deciding what to buy at souvenir shops. And there I went, escorted around by CCP police and a Chinese immigration officer on my way to the bathroom.

Yup, definitely my most memorable T3 experience.

We were about halfway to the restrooms when I first started to notice that people were staring. Not just one or two, but large groups of people waiting in line at check in counters. Families, tourists, businessmen/women all wondering why the foreigner wearing a shirt and tie was being marched around by CCP police.

At least I'm not still handcuffed?

As we approached the restroom, the guards stopped and posted up outside the door. The immigration officer followed me inside keeping an eye on me from a distance as I walked over to the urinals and did my business.

As I finished up, I walked over to the sinks and started washing my hands. I looked up and realized there were mirrors above the sinks. That's when I realized that I was now clearly seeing myself for the first time since my arrest.

I finally realized why everyone was staring. I looked like an absolute mess.

I hadn't showered for a few days, so my hair was long, messy and generally all over the place. My beard had grown out pretty extensively at this point along with a pretty thick and unattractive neck beard. I had clearly lost a lot of weight and I could see the skin on my face was pale and had receded a bit from where it normally was. In a country like China where appearance matters, I noticeably stood out.

It's worth emphasizing that I was one of the few people who managed to consistently eat in detention.

My only saving grace was that I was well dressed. I had on my shirt, tie, nice jacket and slacks. Thank God for that. But you could easily see past the clothes and I didn't look normal by any stretch of the imagination. I was pale, far too thin, and my hair was unkept. I stood there at the sink for a minute trying to work with my hair but soon realized that I wasn't doing much to make myself look any better.

Water and soap isn't going to cover up malnutrition.

I dried up my hands, and slowly walked back toward the immigration officer who led me back to my CCP police escort. We walked back past the groups that had been staring, toward the main doors and back out the main entrance. We stood next to the van and once again struck up a conversation with our group. They greeted me with another panini and I immediately started devouring it.

I knew we didn't have much time left here and we would soon have to start saying our goodbyes before departing. After about 30 minutes, one of the police officers approached me and told me to get back in the van. It's hard to explain but that was arguably the most soul crushing thing he could have said at that point.

I finally felt the slightest little bit of freedom standing outside in the freezing cold. Even though I was still being escorted around, it felt really good to just stand there breathing fresh air, talking to people and eating normal food. For once, I didn't feel like I was still in detention. Being ordered to re-enter the van felt like being told to walk back into the prison cell.

It was horribly uncomfortable and I made the mistake of asking why.

It wasn't even that I was trying to be difficult, it was just a natural reaction to a painfully uncomfortable request. The officers' demand broke with the linear path we had been following toward freedom. Just as I was about to escape this nightmare country, I was being asked to voluntarily take a giant fuc&ing step backwards.

Police officer: WHAT DID YOU SAY?! I DIDN'T ASK YOU. IN THE VAN!

I was stunned at his furious response.

So was our group of Chinese nationals that were nice enough to greet us at the airport. But there was nothing any of us could do. We were at the mercy of a communist police force. The three of us immediately walked back to the van and got in. As with all the documents we had been forced to sign along this journey, it was never a request; it was always an order.

I wonder what they do to murderers here?

Once we were back inside the vehicle, we watched our group re-enter T3 to escape the cold weather. We both wondered if we would see each other again before our departure. Again, we sat in there in silence, waiting for whatever might come next in this chaotic experience.

Being back in the van was horribly and painfully uncomfortable. That's when the real fear started to set in.

What if they purposefully make me miss my flight? What if the flight is delayed? What if they arbitrarily decide to take us back? What if, what if, what if…? In a country like China that is notorious for human organ harvesting without the use of anesthetics, they can get away with anything. There is no accountability.

The closer I got to freedom, the more I felt could and would go wrong.

Maybe they were just toying with us. Who knew what they really had planned? This has to go right. I'm getting out of this fuc&ing country and never, ever coming back.

Every minute in this van felt like an hour. The silence, the desperation, the conditions, the waiting, being surrounded by CCP police in such close quarters, you might as well have just thrown us back into the prison cell.

I survived so much to get here, I can't mess up now.

I wasn't sure exactly what time my flight was, but I could gather that it was coming up soon.

Was I going to be on a plane full of other deportees? Was I going to be on a normal flight? Would I be handcuffed until I landed in the US? What happens once I land in the US? Will I be arrested in the US? Would I be allowed to legally re-enter the US? Would I face charges once I landed back in the US?

As I sat there staring at the main doors of the airport, I saw one of the immigration officers emerge from the main entrance. He was walking in the direction of our transport van with papers in hand. I didn't even have to ask, I knew what was about to happen.

This is it, I guess. Deportation time.

As he approached, two of the lead officers exited the van to speak with him. He combed through the documents as he started barking instructions at the officers, pointing in our direction. The two officers looked back toward the van, pointing in unison, to make sure they understood whatever it was he was trying to convey.

Once everything was said and done, the officers separated with some walking over to the van to open the door. One of the police pointed at me, motioning for me to exit the vehicle, and I quickly followed. I gave Neil and Karl one quick glance back and nodded.

That was our goodbye. We would be very much on our own from this point forward.

I re-emerged into Beijing's cold morning air. I did one quick glance back in the direction of Beijing, a city I would probably never see again for the rest of my life. There was that city that I had hustled and grinded through for the past five years of my life. A city I imagined showing my kids someday. A city I planned to take my family to visit and discover like I had someday.

Would the old restaurants I used to eat at still be there in ten or twenty years? Would I be able to show my future wife and kids the apartments I lived in or the offices I worked at? Would I still be able to recognize anything after that many years had passed?

That future was gone now, and for what?

I would have to find time to process all of that later. For now, I was ready to get the fu&k out of this backwards country. I followed behind the immigration officer assigned to me and I was once again surrounded by my Middle Kingdom police swarm. We made our way back inside where I met up with my group who was still holding on to my luggage. At this point, I could only guess at what might come next.

The officers allowed me to reconnect with my group who accompanied me to the airline check-in counter. That was the first time I found out that I was being deported on what was a standard commercial United Airline flight. We marched our way over to UA's check-in counter where I was escorted directly to the front desk, bypassing the entire line of non-deportees. One of the members in my group handed the officers my luggage and the police took everything up to the check-in counter.

315

The immigration officer informed the UA attendant in Chinese that I was being deported back to the US. They spoke for a while as paperwork was handed back and forth with corresponding information being punched into a computer terminal. As they spoke, I took a second to look around.

Every person in line at the check-in counter was staring at me.

I started processing that this was just a normal nonstop flight from Beijing to San Francisco. The people on my flight were your average Chinese tourists visiting the US for the first time. There were families with their kids, businessmen and women traveling for work, and…me; the deportee. The crazy looking guy surrounded by a CCP police force being checked-in to their flight.

What the fu&k did he do? Why the fu*k is he on our flight? Why is he under armed escort? Will security board the plane and keep an eye on him? You could instantly see the worried looks on their faces. I couldn't blame them.

These were the completely rational and appropriate concerns. I could see people whispering to each other and pointing in my direction, while some laughed and cracked jokes. There was nothing I could do. I slowly turned my gaze back to the check-in attendant waiting to be cleared by immigration.

Once the appropriate paperwork was complete, I was treated like any other passenger checking in their luggage. The UA employee asked for my luggage, which I handed over. She thanked me and handed my boarding ticket over to immigration.

One upside to deportation, you get to skip all the lines!

The officer informed me that we now had to go through security and that I would be escorted to my gate where I was supposed to board my flight. As we turned around and left the check-in counter, I glanced back over at the long line of people still awkwardly staring at me.

Do I wave or smile? Someone needs to write a deportation 101 handbook…I'm not sure what the protocol is here.

I was allowed to approach my group one last time and say my final goodbyes. We promised to stay in touch and I told them that I would notify them once I arrived in the US. I looked around for Neil and Karl, but they were likely at their respective airlines at this point. I thanked everyone for their help and willingness to see me off under these insane circumstances. They stayed put by the UA check-in counter and watched as I was being carted off by security to the security check.

The lines at security were overflowing and once again, I started to grow concerned. I knew my flight time was rapidly approaching and I didn't know what would happen if I missed my flight because of backed up security lines.

Would I be taken back to prison? Would I be stranded here at the airport? Would I be locked down in an airport prison cell until the next flight?

There's no rulebook for this sh!t and the guards don't want to speak to you. Luckily, I was escorted to the far end of the security checkpoint, once again bypassing all of the lengthy lines. My immigration officer struck up a conversation with the director of what seemed to be China's TSA. I don't know what was communicated, but they unhooked a rope and motioned for me and the police officers to come through.

As before, most of the travelers stuck in security watched curiously as I was escorted through the side with my police swarm.

I guess this is what it feels like to be famous? Everyone just stares at you constantly? Do I smile and wave?

I was seated in a chair and told to wait until the immigration officer finalized my paperwork with Chinese TSA. I sat there patiently, watching a flood of bodies scan their way through Beijing's security checkpoint. One by one, they curiously stared right back at me. About ten minutes had passed when a Chinese officer returned with a Chinese TSA agent that proceeded to pat me down.

As I was cleared, they allowed me to walk through and that was surprisingly the end of the process.

I guess there is one upside to deportation...no lines.

As I put my jacket back on, we continued to make our way through Beijing's endless T3 toward the flight gates. Beyond the security checkpoint there were several high-end luxury shops with crowds of people coming and going in every conceivable direction. Just past the shops, I could see the first row of gates off in the distance.

As I walked past gate after gate, seas of people looked up and stared at the skin and bones, malnourished foreigner and his CCP escort swarm.

Fu&k it, I'm gonna smile. But no waving. I grinned at a large cluster of Chinese tourists who immediately looked away in sheer terror. Surprisingly, one female in the center actually smiled back? Maybe she had a thing for recently released foreign inmates? *Do I have street cred now? Even more surprisingly, she actually waved goodbye as I was escorted out of sight. I guess a police swarm has its upsides?*

Groups of unsuspecting travelers darted out of our way, shooting confused looks at the immigration officer who continued ploughed through the crowds.

We drew a lot of unwanted attention on that walk.

Eventually, we approached my gate which was situated near the end of the hall. One by one, a sea of faces looked up at the malnourished foreigner with an overgrown beard being escorted by a CCP police swarm into their gate. The immigration officer sat me down in the last and empty row of seats and proceeded to sit just opposite of me. Following his lead, one police officer sat down to my immediate left with another sat on my right side.

I was being treated as if I had murdered someone.

We arrived at my flight gate with about ten minutes to spare as my immigration officer continued ruffling through more paperwork. I sat there in silence as a sea of people began lining up to start boarding the plane. I watched on as a terrified gate of onlookers were staring at me and trying to figure out if I would be hopping on their flight too.

The gate area was slowly emptying as concerned individuals glanced over at me one last time before they were scanned and waved to proceed to the plane.

When would I be allowed to board? Again, I started to grow even more concerned. Would they just say that I was brought to the airport but accidentally missed my flight? Was this all for show? Fu&k, not when I'm this close.

No, these guys had to know what they were doing. Maybe they just had deportees board last? At this point 95 percent of the gate had already boarded the plane and the check-in crew started to make final calls for my flight.

At that very moment, as if it were a well-practiced routine, the immigration officer looked up at me and handed me a sheet of paper along with my passport and personal documents.

Immigration: Steven Schaerer you are being charged by the Chinese government with illegal employment in China and you will be deported as punishment. Additionally, you are being given a three-year ban on re-entering China. Keep this document for your records.

I took the paper. I wanted to scream at him about how I would never come back to this sh!thole. But, at this point, I knew better. I wasn't Karl.

My victory was deportation. My victory was being back in a country that valued human rights, freedom and liberty. That's how I would win this game.

I took the paper and followed his lead as he motioned for me to stand up. The police stood up as well and marched me over to the main check-in counter. The crew stared at us as we approached. The immigration officer had a word with the check-in associate and handed her my boarding ticket. She handed the stub back over to me and welcomed me on my flight with an awkward smile.

The immigration officer stood there with the police officers. This was the end of my escort. I was finally free...kind of.

Immigration: We will monitor you to ensure that you board your flight and exit the country.

I walked forward, where I was stopped by another counter and the staff asked to inspect my backpack. I took one last look back as they were going through my stuff, and saw the three officers standing, staring, and watching my every move. I quickly turned around, hoping the inspection would finish as soon as possible.

I still felt horribly uncomfortable. Had they put something in my backpack like drugs? Was this all for show? Would they do something to keep me imprisoned longer? Who knew at this point?

The staff member zipped up my bag and handed it back to me.

UA Staff: You're all good to go sir.

I grabbed my bag and didn't look back. I just walked straight ahead. I wanted to run, but I was more focused on disappearing entirely off their radar. I walked forward and turned left into the boarding hall that led me to the plane's entrance. There wasn't a line any longer and I would certainly be the last person boarding.

I approached the door and slowly stepped into the plane, handing my boarding ticket to the flight attendant. She curiously looked me up and down and waved me on toward my seat. Once again, I emerged in front of a full plane of passengers who did their best to disguise the obvious discomfort on their faces.

There he is again, I could sense them thinking. Where is his police escort? What did he do? He must be dangerous.

I made my way to the back of the plane, past row after row of genuinely concerned looks being cast in my direction. Eventually, I made my way to the back of the plane, found my row number and plopped down. I was tired. People were looking back and staring at me. I didn't care anymore. My only concern now was exiting Chinese airspace.

Anywhere but here I thought. Anywhere but fuc&ing here.

I asked a flight attendant for some water and snacks. I explained, briefly, what had happened, and surprisingly, she totally understood. Apparently, she had seen other deportees come through before. She was incredibly kind and did everything possible to accommodate me.

Shortly thereafter the plane rolled its way onto the tarmac. The plane's engines screamed to life once the pilots were given the go ahead for take-off. The plane began to pick up speed as it raced through the runway. As we hit critical speed, the plane slowly lifted up off-the ground propelling us into the air. I sat there peering through the window, watching as Beijing slowly faded into the background.

My mind was exhausted, and I desperately needed sleep. But I couldn't peel my eyes off the map on the screen. Ever so slowly, we were looping our way north, still over Chinese land and making our way toward Russia's border. My mind couldn't rest until we exited Chinese air space and safely made our way over Russian territory.

Putin's Russia had surprisingly become my safe space.

As I finally breathed a sigh of relief, a concerned passenger seated next to me looked over asking if I was ok. She appeared to be in her mid-50's and dressed in professional business attire.

Me: Where are you from?

Passenger: New Delhi, India. What about you?

Me: California, the US.

Passenger: What happened to you, you look terrible.

Me: They detained me in a prison cell for three weeks and charged me with illegal employment. All of my documents were legal. They just didn't care. The conditions were pretty horrible.

Passenger: Those fu&king communists! These assholes do the same sh!t to India, they have no respect for other countries! That's why I always hate coming here, these fu&king communists...

She was angrier than I was. She went on a tirade that I would never forget. Thank God for India and sensible people.

Ultimately, we escaped Chinese airspace and for the first time, I could breathe a genuine sigh of relief. Eventually, the flightpath took us past the Alaskan Coastline, and I could feel a sense of calm come over my mind.

American airspace.

I was finally free of that crazy country with its backwards, violent, tyrannical, authoritarian, Orwellian, corrupt and communist government.

I swore to myself that I would never ever step foot on Chinese, or any communist country's soil, ever again. I was finally free.

I survived.

I'm alive.

I survived.

Thank God for the United States of America.

Warning Signs of Communist Tyranny

1. **Censorship:**

Any censorship, by any entity (private or public), for any reason at any time.

"The Chinese government has long kept tight reins on both traditional and new media to avoid potential subversion of its authority. Its tactics often entail strict media controls using monitoring systems and firewalls, shuttering publications or websites, and jailing dissident journalists, bloggers, and activists.

China's constitution affords its citizens freedom of speech and press, but the opacity of Chinese media regulations allows authorities to crack down on news stories by claiming that they expose state secrets and endanger the country. The definition of state secrets in China remains vague, facilitating censorship of any information that authorities deem harmful [PDF] to their political or economic interests.

In 2016, Freedom House ranked China last for the second consecutive year out of sixty-five countries that represent 88 percent of the world's internet users. The France-based watchdog group Reporters Without Borders ranked China 176 out of 180 countries in its 2016 worldwide index of press freedom.

Certain websites that the government deems potentially dangerous—like Wikipedia, Facebook, Twitter, YouTube, and some Google services—are fully blocked or temporarily "blacked out" during periods of controversy, such as the June 4 anniversary of the Tiananmen Square massacre or Hong Kong's Umbrella Movement protests in the fall of 2014."[113]

America 2021:

"When my family and I legally immigrated to the United States after the 1979 Iranian revolution, we fled a government that controls the media and what its people hear, while also censoring and persecuting its people based on their religion, as well opposing ideology and views.

Today, platforms like Facebook, YouTube and Twitter remain banned to people in Iran, mainland China, North Korea and Syria. As we've seen with the removal of Parler from the Amazon cloud, Apple and Google, these tech titans are creating a shockingly parallel line of banning speech in the United States, very much like these oppressive nations.

But regardless of what happens, banning accounts of conservative voices on social media platforms, with 330 million actively monthly users on Twitter and 2.7 billion on Facebook alone, demands Congress' immediate action. As Florida Sen. Marco Rubio aptly said, "We are now living in a country where four or five companies, unelected, unaccountable, have the monopoly power to decide, we're gonna wipe people out, we're going to erase them, from any digital platform."[114]

"Sunday (tomorrow) at midnight Amazon will be shutting off all of our servers in an attempt to completely remove free speech off the internet. There is the possibility Parler will be unavailable on the internet for up to a week as we rebuild from scratch. We prepared for events like this by never relying on Amazons proprietary infrastructure and building bare metal products.

We will try our best to move to a new provider right now as we have many competing for our business, however Amazon, Google and Apple purposefully did this as a coordinated effort knowing our options would be

[113] Media censorship in China. (n.d.). Retrieved February 28, 2021, from https://www.cfr.org/backgrounder/media-censorship-china

[114] 1. Makki, A. (2021, January 18). In censoring conservatives, big tech is acting like Iran or North Korea: Column. Retrieved February 28, 2021, from https://www.tampabay.com/opinion/2021/01/18/in-censoring-conservatives-big-tech-is-acting-like-iran-or-north-korea-column

limited and knowing this would inflict the most damage right as President Trump was banned from the tech companies."[115]

2. Social Credit Score and Citizen Monitoring:

Any attempt by the government or private institutions to rank, monitor, or categorize private citizens, organizations, or businesses for any reason.

"China's social credit system, by its wide definition, is a set of databases and initiatives that monitor and assess the trustworthiness of individuals, companies and government entities. Each entry is given a social credit score, with reward for those who have a high rating and punishments for those with low scores.

Most of the data is gathered from traditional sources such as financial, criminal and governmental records, as well as existing data from registry offices along with third-party sources such as online credit platforms. The Chinese government is also experimenting with collecting data via video surveillance and real-time data transfers, such as monitoring emission data from factories, although these are not considered primary sources.

And while it is similar to the credit ratings provided for individuals and corporations in other countries, the Chinese version is also capable of expanding from personal credit to other aspects of life to include bill payments and criminal convictions.

Business entities, including foreign businesses in China, are subject to a corporate credit system, tracking information such as tax payments, bank loan repayments and employment disputes."[116]

America 2021:

"With more services than ever collecting your data, it's easy to start asking why anyone should care about most of it. This is why. Because people start having ideas like this.

[115] Administrator, A. (2021, January 10)."This was a coordinated Attack": PARLER ceo speaks out after Amazon boots From AWS, vows to Rebuild 'from scratch'. Retrieved March 02, 2021, from https://www.theburningplatform.com/2021/01/10/this-was-a-coordinated-attack-parler-ceo-speaks-out-after-amazon-boots-from-aws-vows-to-rebuild-from-scratch/

[116] What is China's social credit system and Why is it controversial? (2020, December 15). Retrieved February 28, 2021, from https://www.scmp.com/economy/china-economy/article/3096090/what-chinas-social-credit-system-and-why-it-controversial

In a new blog post for the International Monetary Fund, four researchers presented their findings from a working paper that examines the current relationship between finance and tech as well as its potential future. Gazing into their crystal ball, the researchers see the possibility of using the data from your browsing, search, and purchase history to create a more accurate mechanism for determining the credit rating of an individual or business. They believe that this approach could result in greater lending to borrowers who would potentially be denied by traditional financial institutions.

"Banks tend to cushion credit terms for their long-term customers during downturns," the paper's authors write. This is because they have a history and relationship with the customer. Now, imagine the kind of intimate history that Facebook could have with a borrower and suddenly its digital cash initiative starts to make more sense."[117]

"Five years ago this week, Edward Snowden handed over a vast cache of close to ten thousand highly classified documents to reporters, revealing the scope and scale of the US government's mass surveillance effort -- and of its many global intelligence-gathering partners.

First, the world learned that the National Security Agency (NSA) had been collecting the daily phone records of millions of Americans. Then, Silicon Valley was accused of willful participation in the PRISM data collection program. And the disclosures kept coming.

Reporters have published the most explosive stories that focus on government abuse and unethical intrusions -- said to be only a fraction of the total number of documents taken from NSA's Hawaii complex, where Snowden worked. He upended years of government work in the space of just a few days."[118]

"Bill Binney believes that 9/11 was preventable. A month after it happened, he resigned in protest from the US National Security Agency (NSA).

---

[117] Jones, R. (2020, December 21). Your credit score should be based on your web history, imf says. Retrieved February 28, 2021, from https://gizmodo.com/your-credit-score-should-be-based-on-your-web-history-1845912592

[118] Whittaker, Z. (2018, June 06). Five years AFTER SNOWDEN: What changed? Retrieved March 02, 2021, from https://www.zdnet.com/article/edward-snowden-five-years-on-tech-giants-change/

He belongs to an intimate group of four whistleblowers, each of whom left the NSA after raising concerns about failures in the agency's intelligence-gathering capabilities.

Binney's track record is impeccable. He spent four years in the Army Security Agency during the Vietnam War before transferring to the NSA in 1970.

He rose to become technical director of World Geopolitical & Military Analysis at the Signals Intelligence Automation Research Center (SARC), a 6,000-strong research centre he co-founded at NSA's headquarters in Maryland, US.

In a wide-ranging interview with Computer Weekly, Binney raises serious concerns over the NSA's current surveillance programmes. He alleges:

+ *The NSA buried key intelligence that could have prevented 9/11;*
+ *The agency's bulk data collection from internet and telephone communications is unconstitutional and illegal in the US;*
+ *The NSA is ineffective at preventing terrorism because analysts are too swamped with information under its bulk collection programme;*
+ *Electronic intelligence gathering is being used for covert law enforcement, political control and industrial espionage, both in and beyond the US."*[119]

3. **Human Rights and Religious Suppression or Censorship:**

Any attempt to eradicate or restrict human rights advocacy or organizations or any attempt to eradicate or restrict religious freedom in any capacity.

"China's hardline response to protests in Hong Kong this summer are part of a wider policy shift under President Xi Jinping that includes increasing persecution of religious and ethnic minorities. The Chinese Communist Party and Xi appear to have decided to consolidate power by reverting to a harder line on human rights than was witnessed in the years since China opened to the rest of the world after the era of Mao Zedong.

Beijing's repression of more than 13 million Muslims in Xinjiang and its increased surveillance of Christians and Tibetan Buddhists is getting worse. China has not respected freedom of religion and belief since the

[119] O'Cleirigh, F. (2015, April 25). Bill Binney, the 'ORIGINAL' NSA WHISTLEBLOWER, on Snowden, 9/11 and illegal surveillance. Retrieved March 02, 2021, from https://www.computerweekly.com/feature/Interview-the-original-NSA-whistleblower

1949 communist takeover. But just as the suppression of dissent in Hong Kong represents a turning away from the promise and practice of relative freedom over the last few years, mass arbitrary detention, torture, and prohibitions on Islam in Xinjiang are appalling even by China's standards."[120]

"As the tenth anniversary of the crackdown on student protestors in Tiananmen Square approaches, Beijing's nervousness is obvious. The government has quelled activity that appears to challenge the supremacy of the Chinese Communist Party (CCP), notably the attempts of a small group of activists to establish an opposition party. In response, the United States has redoubled its efforts to censure China in the international community. These initiatives, such as the unsuccessful sponsorship of a China resolution at the annual meeting of the United Nations Human Rights Commission (UNHRC), have symbolic value but little effect on Beijing's human rights performance.

Since the Chinese government's suppression of the Tiananmen Square movement, the United States and China have, with few exceptions, held opposing positions on human rights issues. The American policy community has been locked into a zero-sum debate on China, which is broadly (but inadequately) defined as engagement versus isolation and carrots versus sticks.

China's seeming intransigence is rooted in more than the regime's determination to maintain political control. Washington and Beijing disagree on issues of both priority and proportion in human rights. American concerns about Chinese human rights include religious and reproductive rights, but the overwhelming focus remains on the right to political expression and activity.""[121]

America 2021:

"Christian content is often censored and removed from TikTok, according to several creators on the platform.

---

[120] Diplomat, F. (2019, August 30). Confronting China's suppression of religion. Retrieved February 28, 2021, from https://thediplomat.com/2019/08/confronting-chinas-suppression-of-religion/

[121] Dalpino, C. (2016, July 28). Human rights in China. Retrieved February 28, 2021, from https://www.brookings.edu/research/human-rights-in-china/

The China-based social media app hosts short, snippy videos ranging from inspirational mini-speeches to musical and dance performances and is popular with teenagers and young adults. The platform reports over 800 million active users, with 30 million active users in the U.S.

Researchers have grown concerned over the app's reach and the possibility of it bringing Chinese-style censorship to mainstream U.S. audiences. In September, the app purportedly removed content posted by pro-democracy activists in Hong Kong. More recently, pro-life accounts on the app were disabled and later reinstated.

Despite these accusations, the platform seldom provides public comment about the videos it removes or its claimed independence from censors in Beijing. A month after she launched her (Christian themed) account, one of her videos went viral with 1 million views.

Followers started pouring in and strangers were asking her questions about God and the Bible, she said. Then things started to take a turn.

Two weeks ago, on a livestream Bible study with her sister, the screen went black in the middle of a Q&A session. "A little box popped up that said, 'You have been permanently banned,'" Abby said. When *Religion Unplugged* asked about this issue, TikTok declined to provide a statement."[122]

4.   **Disarming a Population or Registering Armed Citizens:**

Any attempt to regulate, monitor, disarm, or register armed citizens in any capacity.

"The greatest mass murderer of the 20th century was China's Mao Zedong. According to the authoritative "Black Book of Communism," an estimated 65 million Chinese died as a result of Mao's repeated, merciless attempts to create a new "socialist" China. Anyone who got in his way was done away with — by execution, imprisonment or forced famine. The Nationalist Chinese government established gun control in 1935.

Mao Zedong famously said on at least two occasions in speeches "Every Communist must grasp the truth: Political power grows out of the barrel of a gun." Although he was likely referring to the use of firearms in times

---

[122] Vandenboom, L. (2020, September 11). Christian TikTok videos are censored and deleted in the US, creators say. Retrieved February 28, 2021, from https://religionunplugged.com/news/2020/5/28/christian-tiktok-content-is-often-censored-and-deleted-creators-say

of war given the number of Chinese citizens and dissidents killed under his régime we presume that his "truth" applied to gaining power by killing innocent people."[123]

America 2021:

"President Joe Biden on Feb. 14 urged Congress to strengthen existing laws concerning gun ownership on the third anniversary of the mass shooting at a high school in Parkland, Florida.

"The Parkland students and so many other young people across the country who have experienced gun violence are carrying forward the history of the American journey. It is a history written by young people in each generation who challenged prevailing dogma to demand a simple truth: we can do better. And we will," Biden said in a statement.

"This Administration will not wait for the next mass shooting to heed that call. We will take action to end our epidemic of gun violence and make our schools and communities safer. Today, I am calling on Congress to enact commonsense gun law reforms, including requiring background checks on all gun sales, banning assault weapons and high-capacity magazines, and eliminating immunity for gun manufacturers who knowingly put weapons of war on our streets.""[124]

---

[123] Spartan. (2019, August 31). A brief history of gun control: A disarmed population is easier to oppress than an armed one. Retrieved February 28, 2021, from https://www.spartanfirearmstraininggroup.com/a-brief-history-of-gun-control-a-disarmed-population-is-easier-to-oppress-than-an-armed-one/

[124] Durden, T., & @zackstieber, F. (n.d.). Biden calls on Congress to strengthen gun ownership rules. Retrieved February 28, 2021, from https://www.zerohedge.com/political/biden-calls-congress-strengthen-gun-ownership-rules

About the Author

Steven Schaerer survived communist Chinese incarceration, torture, and deportation. Steven is a proud first generation American from California's Bay Area, and is the proud bi-racial son of immigrant parents from Switzerland and Mexico.

He was the first person in his family to attend university earning a degree in chemistry from Sonoma State University in Northern California. In addition to English, Steven also speaks Mandarin, Spanish, and successfully co-founded a business in Beijing in his mid-20's.

Steven is a staunch advocate for and defender of freedom, liberty, the Constitution, free-market capitalism, Human Rights and the American way of life.

CPSIA information can be obtained
at www.ICGtesting.com
Printed in the USA
LVHW032131210821
695820LV00007B/421